S0-AIA-982

After the Revolution

AFTER THE REVOLUTION

*The Smithsonian History
of Everyday Life in
the Eighteenth Century*

BARBARA CLARK
SMITH

*Pantheon Books
National Museum of American History
New York*

LIBRARY
COLBY-SAWYER COLLEGE
NEW LONDON, N.H. 03257

E
163
.S63
1985

476

FOR THE PEOPLE AT 12TH AND RANDOLPH

Copyright © 1985 by Random House, Inc.

All rights reserved under International and Pan-American Copyright
Conventions. Published in the United States by Pantheon Books, a
division of Random House, Inc., New York, and simultaneously in
Canada by Random House of Canada Limited, Toronto.

Since this page cannot accommodate all permissions acknowledgments,
they appear on pages 209–210.

Library of Congress Cataloging-in-Publication Data

Smith, Barbara Clark.
    After the Revolution.
    Includes bibliographical notes and index.
    1. United States—Social life and customs—Revolution,
1775–1783. 2. United States—Social life and customs—
1783–1865. 3. National Museum of American History (U.S.) I.
Title.
E163.S63 1985   973   85-42853
ISBN 0-394-54381-5

BOOK DESIGN BY GINA DAVIS

97897

Manufactured in the United States of America

FIRST EDITION

Acknowledgments

Many people made contributions to this book. Curators, archivists, and librarians at a variety of institutions helped me track down Coltons, Springers, Saunderses, Allens, and others. I am particularly grateful to Mabel Swanson, curator at the Longmeadow Historical Society; the archivists at the Virginia State Library, most especially Lyndon Hart; the staff at the Delaware Hall of Records; librarians at the Moorland-Springarn Research Center at Howard University; and librarians at the Library of Congress and at the National Museum of American History. I would also like to thank Helen Haverty King and Alvin P. Reynolds, Jr., both of Isle of Wight County, Virginia, for their kind assistance.

The book has benefitted immeasurably from the thoughtful criticism of many scholars. Michael Zuckerman discussed the project with me from the outset and offered careful comments on the manuscript version of several chapters; he is responsible for many improvements in both style and content. I am deeply indebted to Christopher Clark, who spent long hours discussing the eighteenth century, reading chapter drafts, and encouraging me to broaden my thinking and refine my arguments at many points. I wish also to thank Gary B. Nash, who devoted time and effort to improving my understanding of Richard Allen and the free black community of eighteenth-century Philadelphia, and who generously made his own research findings available to me. Many friends and colleagues have read and offered comments on early versions of various chapters. My thanks to Daniel Bluestone, Spencer Crew, James Horton, David Jaffee, Steven Lubar, Jack Michel, William Pretzer, Rodris Roth, Robert Selim, Terry Sharrer, and Susan Smulyan for their interest and help.

Finally, the staff of the National Museum of American History's "Life in America" project, Fath Davis Ruffins, project manager, have all worked on a parallel course over the past few years, worrying about such matters as Anne Saunders's death, Samuel Colton's patriotism, and Elizabeth Springer's children. Few authors have the benefit and the enjoyment of co-workers who share their fascination with such details of the past. I especially want to thank Lynn Fliakas Chase,

Camilla S. Clough, and William H. Yeingst for their unfailing interest as well as for sharing with me the results of their own work on graphics, photographs, and captions. Beatrix Roesler also helped enormously with the graphics pictured in this book, and many other colleagues at the National Museum of American History have given their encouragement. I owe a special debt of gratitude to Gary Kulik for his support throughout this project. Last, but not least, many sincere thanks to Wendy Wolf.

Contents

Preface

Like the exhibit from which it grew, this book takes as its starting point three "period rooms" from houses built in the eighteenth century and now in the collections of the Smithsonian Institution's National Museum of American History. They include a paneled room from a Connecticut River valley mansion built in the 1750s; the ground floor from a 1½-story log house built along Mill Creek, northern Delaware, in the mid-1790s; and a room from a small manor house built in the same decade in Isle of Wight County, southeastern Virginia.

Though it begins with these rooms, the book is about the experiences of some of the people who lived in them in the closing decades of the eighteenth century. The characters in these pages include Samuel Colton, a well-to-do merchant; Elizabeth and Thomas Springer, who ran a family farm; and the household—black and white—of a Virginia planter named Henry Saunders. To their stories is added a fourth—the history of a man represented in the exhibit not by a house or a room but by the surviving furnishings of his church: Richard Allen, slave and then freedman of Delaware and Philadelphia.

Curators at the Smithsonian are not certain who actually lived in the Connecticut River valley room now on exhibit. Acquired in 1923, the fully paneled pine walls were initially thought to have come from the house of Springfield joiner Reuben Bliss, a house built in the middle of the eighteenth century and demolished in 1922. Relying on the information supplied by the room's donor and the dealer who sold it to her, the museum exhibited the room as the "Bliss parlor" for many years. Recently, however, armed with maps, photographs, and other Springfield records, an architectural historian has neatly unsettled that identification. Given its dimensions and the placement of its fireplace, windows, and doors, the room simply would not have fit in the Bliss house. Yet the style of the woodwork and the corner cupboard in the Smithsonian room confirm that it dates from the mid-1700s and point to its origin in the Springfield area. The best candidate, it now appears, is the Merchant Samuel Colton house, constructed in Longmeadow, Massachusetts between 1753 and 1755 and demolished in 1916.[1]

This decoratively carved serpentine-front desk, made in eastern Massachusetts about 1760, epitomizes the high-style antique.

The museum's mistake about the origins of the room points up a key issue in considering the way museums teach us history. The error did not reflect carelessness on the part of the Smithsonian's curators in the 1920s so much as the particular priorities of their time. In the early twentieth century, what mattered most to collectors of period spaces was not who actually lived there, but what the rooms (and objects in them) represented or could be made to represent. To many people in the 1910s and 1920s, these early artifacts seemed to represent a high point in the development of American style and taste. During these decades, influenced in part by the isolationism that followed World War I, wealthy American collectors began to turn from European to American antiques. Previously passed over as inferior to Old World furnishings in design and workmanship, American decorative arts (furniture, textiles, ceramics, glass, and metalwares) came to be perceived as having an elegance of their own. Private collectors began searching for old houses and buying old architectural elements— paneling, moldings, and fireplace mantels—both because these artifacts struck collectors as beautiful in themselves and because they could serve as attractive backdrops for antique American furnishings.[2]

Where collectors led, museums followed. The donor of the Smithsonian's Connecticut River valley room, Mrs. Gertrude D. Ritter, also gave furnishings from the colonial period that seemed appropriate to the room. Through her generosity, the Smithsonian joined other museums that had begun to collect period rooms for their artistic as well as their historic significance. If curators did not investigate the actual background of the room too closely, that was probably because the lives of the people who lived in the room seemed secondary to the room's aesthetic value as a piece of American art and as a proper historic setting for antiques.[3]

The new popularity of early American decorative arts was only one expression of the resurgence of interest in early American life known as the "Colonial Revival." For many, that interest was linked to a mounting dissatisfaction with the changes brought by nineteenth-century industrial society and doubts about the certainty of social progress. Beginning in the late 1800s, while some extolled American growth in industry, national wealth, and international power, others began to question the easy assumption that industrial development necessarily spelled improvement. Was it "progress" for a few to amass great riches while many more sweated long hours in workshops for very little pay? Did the manifest poverty of urban slums represent "improvement"? Some Americans thought not. Critics lamented the plight of the poor and the degradation of work: industrialization, it seemed to some, stripped work of its creativity, for it replaced hand craftsmanship with the limited skills and deadening, stultifying tasks of the assembly line; meaningful work with routinized factory labor; individual design with mass production. Looking at these changes, a fair number of Americans thought that the preindustrial past compared favorably with their industrialized present.[4]

In response to the problems of industrialization, some proposed alternatives to or reforms of a capitalist organization of society. Others cared less about the quality of workers' lives than about the quality of workers' products. Collectors of antiques, few of whom suffered hardships as a result of industrial development, were less likely to promote social change than to promote aesthetic appreciation for preindustrial goods. Late in the nineteenth century, among those whom social critic Thorstein Veblen dubbed "the leisure class," there occurred a curious reversal of values held earlier in the century: machine-made products, long supposed superior, now appeared less desirable than handmade goods. Part of the appeal of American antiques, then, lay in the way they came to represent the newly supposed superiority of the preindustrial world.[5]

One other development encouraged some Americans' nostalgia for the preindustrial past. In the nineteenth century, Germans, Irish, and other immigrants to the United States had all faced hostility and prejudice from the descendants of earlier arrivals. Starting about 1890, however, new immigrants—the majority now from southern and central Europe—faced discrimination and prejudice on a heightened scale. As they watched Italians, Poles, Russian Jews, Greeks, and others stream into the growing cities of the Midwest and Northeast, members of the old Anglo-Saxon elite became concerned with preserving their own so-called American culture. In the teens and twenties, some people organized and lobbied to limit immigration, others to

"Americanize" those immigrants who came. At its best, the "Americanization" movement aimed at helping newcomers to fit in; at its ugliest, it embodied a smug superiority, hatred of "foreigners," and the desire to "educate" people out of their own various cultures. Indeed, the "Americanization" movement was part of a decade of conservative reaction. The twenties saw the growth of the Ku Klux Klan, the forceful suppression of radicals, reformers, and labor unions, and renewed hostility toward Catholics and blacks as well as the "dirty little dark people" who came from southern and eastern Europe. Although some people opposed racism, a wide range of Americans shared at least some concern for preserving an "American" culture. Warren Harding's campaign promise of a "return to normalcy" called up a mythic past of harmonious ease and stability, free of immigrants, industry, and class conflict.[6]

In the context of these social currents, to collect American antiques and architectural elements could be a way of appropriating as well as appreciating the past—that is, taking control of history and claiming it as one's own. Some people interested in antiques expressed that idea explicitly. In 1924, for example, when the Metropolitan Museum of Art displayed decorative arts set in period rooms in its new American Wing, the Daughters of the American Revolution magazine applauded: "Patriotic Americans who treasure the memory of our forefathers can do no better than to reproduce in their homes the furniture and decoration which have been so well preserved and arranged by the builders of the American Wing." With furniture, in other words, it was possible to distinguish oneself from newcomers (whether new immigrants from abroad or else members of the new industrial rich), asserting one's pedigree and loyalty to old American values.[7]

In museums, early American furnishings and period rooms had a further function: they exposed immigrants and the public in general to the aesthetic accomplishments of the DAR's forebears. They taught Americans outside the ranks of the old elite to adopt that elite's values and tastes—or at least to acknowledge their superiority. Prestigious institutions collected and displayed early decorative arts, authoritatively presenting fine colonial furnishings as the best of the American past. That judgment had implications for the society's present and

Museums often prized artifacts associated with famous historical figures. These French porcelain dishes were part of a service purchased by John Adams in the 1780s for formal entertaining.

future too. America, according to this view, was not to be defined in terms of the aspirations and efforts of those who came, but by those who had been here: "Americanism" was a set group of values, into which the immigrant was expected and required to fit. Cultural authority, at least, belonged in the hands of the descendants of the "Founding Fathers," the Anglo-Saxon old guard who, since the 1880s, had been busy setting themselves apart in societies like the DAR.[8]

Many of the period rooms displayed in museums, then, carried a very particular and partial interpretation of the past. First of all, focusing on "beautiful" objects meant limiting oneself to the story of the early American upper classes, the minority of Americans who had been able to afford such things. Moreover, some collectors and museum professionals had an explicit case to prove about that elite: among the most prominent American collectors was Henry Francis Du Pont, who expressed the conviction that colonial America had produced a "genteel" class of people whose refinement, taste, and culture had matched that of upper-class Europeans. Similarly, John D. Rockefeller, Jr., funded the excavation and rebuilding of eighteenth-century Williamsburg, Virginia, creating a colonial village to celebrate the taste and culture of the early Virginia elite. The message of such celebrations was implicit: twentieth-century Americans derived a valuable heritage from the colonial upper classes, a heritage that now resided in the custody of the contemporary elite.[9]

Of course, such celebrations of the past represented distortions of history. The restored colonial Williamsburg, for example, gave no evidence of the fact that half of the city's population in the eighteenth century had been black slaves, or that slave labor had made it possible for white planters to cultivate fine taste in furnishings. Elsewhere the effect of spotlighting the elite was the same. Looking at the rich and the privileged in isolation left out all the parts of history that might make enthusiasts for "Americanization" uncomfortable: the diversity of the population and its values, a long history of dissent, conflicts among Americans of different beliefs, regions, classes, and backgrounds.[10]

There were exceptions, of course—people in the 1920s who showed greater interest in the lives of colonial craftsmen than in their wealthy

George Washington imported this British silver-plated bottle stand and used it in the presidential mansion in Philadelphia.

Artisan Austin Crocker of Boston put his name prominently on the handle of this posnet, or saucepan—a practice interpreted by some as an expression of a preindustrial pride of craftsmanship.

Focusing not on political history but on such routine activities as cooking and preserving, the Hall of Everyday Life considered women's experience as a matter of course. Shown below is a ladle.

customers, or cared about the daily lives of ordinary people. Some curators of period rooms made efforts to portray as accurately as possible how eighteenth-century people had actually lived. But most people felt no need to abide by the realities of the past. Du Pont was only one of a number of collectors who bought up architectural elements from old houses, cut the rooms to the size he wanted them, then filled them with antiques the way he thought them most elegant and attractive. The willingness of men like Du Pont to rearrange architectural elements to suit their own taste matched their willingness and sense of entitlement to turn history to their own uses. Generally speaking, the early American "period room" came hand in hand with an interpretation of history that was limited, entangled with aesthetic judgments, and most often biased on behalf of the upper classes.[11]

$\mathcal{T}$hirty years after its accession by the Smithsonian, the so-called "Bliss parlor" went on display in an exhibition designed to shed all remnants of that old bias. The exhibit, called "Everyday Life in the American Past," was planned in the late 1950s and installed for the opening of the new Museum of History and Technology on the mall.

From the outset, the framers of the Hall of Everyday Life made a clear commitment to presenting period rooms and other artifacts as history rather than art. Other museums and many historic houses could use their decorative arts collections to record, preserve, and celebrate the finest achievements of early American craftsmen and the taste of those craftsmen's customers. In contrast, the Museum of History and Technology used its collection of artifacts to shed light on how people actually lived. Ordinary iron housewares, curators thought, might be as valuable as expensive silver teapots as evidence about the past. And where decorative arts museums might arrange furnishings to make them particularly attractive, the curators of "Everyday Life" sought to make their presentations accurate. They researched the "material environment" in which colonial Americans had lived, trying to reconstruct what their daily surroundings had been like. Where possible, they consulted probate inventories, lists made at the time of some eighteenth-century householders' deaths, recording what they had actually owned, to learn how people in the past had furnished their rooms.[12]

Behind this approach lay a different conception of the sort of history that mattered. Since the Smithsonian was the national museum, it seemed appropriate to present a broader view, encompassing not only "treasures" but ordinary things, including not only the rich but more ordinary people. As interpreted in the Hall of Everyday Life, the American past became the story of people of the middle class. That focus fit the kinds of artifacts that the museum had in its collections: rich people's possessions were expensive to collect; poor people's possessions rarely survived or got saved from the past. Yet, for the museum, the emphasis on the middle class was a virtue as well as a necessity, a reflection of a particular philosophy of history. "Although we propose to touch on poverty and slavery at one end of the scale and on wealth and aristocracy at the other," said a summary of the Hall, "the stress will be upon the material environment of those most responsible for the building of America—the anonymous farmers, artists, artisans, ministers, seafarers, storekeepers, ranchers, and homesteaders, who comprised the dominant American middle class."[13]

The "Bliss parlor" (as it was still known) found a central place in the exhibit: Reuben Bliss had been a joiner, a skilled craftsman who had apparently devoted substantial effort to making his house particularly fine, but who was solidly middle class. Curators added other period spaces to illustrate the lives of middle-class Americans. In 1954 the Smithsonian had acquired a room from a small plantation house built about 1796 in Isle of Wight, Virginia. Though the elaborate decoration of the room showed that he had aspired to the style of the great planters, and though he had owned slaves, the owner of this house ranked well below the powerful and wealthy planters whose lives were illustrated at Williamsburg. In an even more dramatic departure from upper-class history, the Hall included the first floor of a log house, dismantled in 1962 from a site along the banks of Mill Creek in northern Delaware. Built of simple planked logs, dovetailed at the corners, the log house epitomized the museum's interest in examining the day-to-day lives of people outside the ranks of the wealthy and powerful few.[14]

Relatively ordinary objects like this iron footscraper have found favor with some collectors as reflections of the daily life of common people.

There were changes in the Hall in the years that followed, but through the 1970s, curators took care to maintain its "unique concentration on the average man as opposed to the exceptional." The goal remained the same, according to the museum: "When the visitor leaves he will have in his own mind's eye a clear impression of what the average American . . . held as his obtainable ideal."[15]

In its attention to the daily work of farm women and to life in the home, the Hall anticipated academic historians' discovery of women's history. In its emphasis on everyday life, it anticipated later historians' interest in the customary and mundane patterns of people's lives. And by using such documents as inventories and such evidence about the past as came from surviving objects, the Hall anticipated social historians' attention to such sources as ways of learning about the lives of the illiterate and inarticulate, those who wrote few letters and diaries or whose writings have not survived. In short, the Hall represented an extraordinary step beyond a sort of history meant to glorify the elite classes of the American past.[16]

Yet the history presented in "Everyday Life" had its drawbacks too, weaknesses that it shared with the version of history presented in many fifties classrooms and textbooks, which also centered on the story of the middle class. As in earlier decades, views of history in the 1950s reflected ideas about the present. In a time of military intervention abroad and cold war at home, Americans exhibited both a sense of celebration and a sense of defensiveness about their country, its values, and its history. The fifties saw a sharp stifling of internal dissent and the enforcement of a strict political orthodoxy; it was a time when departure from mainstream ideas seemed "un-American." Accordingly, the average fifties textbook painted a picture of the past that worked to bolster and justify this reality. According to the textbooks, the nation had known little injustice, little inequality, and therefore little struggle or even disagreement. Following this interpretation, the road from past to present seemed an even and direct one. Although there had been technological innovations and overall "progress," nothing much had really changed since the Revolution, and even the gaining of independence appeared as a merely political—almost superficial—change. America, the argument ran, had always been what many took it to be in the fifties: a place of middle-class families who shared common values and enjoyed widespread economic abundance. Though at times "Everyday Life" transcended the limitations of this view, beneath its nod to diversity lay a commitment to the centrality of "the middle class." Like looking at the history of elites in a vacuum, looking at the middle class alone distorted the past: still left out of account were such things as conflict, dissent, and difference.[17]

Cracks began to appear in this so-called "consensus" view of the past in the 1960s and 1970s, as a wide range of social movements brought greater visibility to different groups of Americans and to deep-seated tensions in the society. Early in the 1960s, the National Association for the Advancement of Colored People protested that history books often excluded or stereotyped blacks, and other groups raised their voices in protest against the orthodox view that assumed "the average American" to have been white, male, and middle class and most everyone else to have been irrelevant. With the resurgence of a women's movement, the movement for Native American rights, and a generally heightened awareness of ethnicity and class, the study of "history" began to change. Historians began to record the lives and aspirations of blacks, women, American Indians, workers, immigrants, the poor, and other participants in the American past. In the face of diversity and unrest in the 1960s, historians discovered that the past, too, had contained wealth and poverty, prejudice and racism, radicalism and struggle. America had known greater diversity and conflict than the "middle class" history of the 1950s had allowed.[18]

Much more has been involved in these revisions, then, than an effort to make up for past omissions. As historians gave their attention to different Americans' experiences, they found the whole shape of the past changing in front of their eyes. It was impossible merely to add on the stories of people previously ignored, for those people's stories required a broad reinterpretation of the past as a whole. Historians could not study Jefferson's slaves, for example, without adding depth to their understanding of Jefferson, nor look at working people's experience of industrial growth without recasting their view of industrial leaders and nineteenth-century social and economic change. The result has not been to replace the study of powerful groups with the

The life of Job, "Son of Solliman," fit few of the stereotypes presented in history textbooks of the 1950s. Born the son of an African king, Job spent two years as a slave in Maryland. His knowledge of the Koran and his literacy in Arabic helped him enlist a noted Oxford linguist in his effort to gain freedom. Job returned to his father's kingdom and assumed the throne in the 1750s.

study of the powerless. Rather, revisionists have aimed at removing the elite or middle class from the vacuum in which they have been placed and restoring them to the wider context that framed their lives. The great virtue of history done "from the bottom up" is that it moves toward an understanding of the *whole* of a past society, refusing to cast one group as "representative," attending to the experiences and inter-relationships of all.[19]

These developments in historical thinking have left us with a more sophisticated image of the past. It is no longer possible to omit black slaves—roughly 20 percent of the population in the thirteen continental colonies in 1776—from a list of those who built America. Nor is it possible simply to lump such groups as "seafarers" inside "the middle class," ignoring the difference between prosperous sea captains and their often impoverished crew members.[20] We can no longer simply subsume a planter and slave owner into the category of "farmer," nor set out to represent "the average American" of 200 years ago. Like historians in the academy, curators and historians who work at museums face the challenge of building greater complexity into our interpretations of history.

In 1980, the Museum of History and Technology became the Museum of American History, a change of name that signaled, in part, the museum's intention to incorporate the insights of recent scholarship into its interpretation of the American past. "After the Revolution" represents one outgrowth of that effort, a step in the direction of greater breadth and complexity. Once again period rooms and antique furnishings appear on the second floor of the museum on the mall, now aiming at a more inclusive presentation of history, a truer vision of late eighteenth-century American life. It has required substantial research about the people who lived in the period rooms—their lives, their aspirations, and their places in their communities—in order to identify and interpret the rooms with accuracy. The museum has tracked down tax lists, wills, and other records and slowly gained closer acquaintance with the rooms' inhabitants. Visitors to "After the Revolution" will not find "the Yankee merchant" (still less, "the colonial American") there. Instead they will encounter Samuel and Lucy Colton, people who ran a store in Longmeadow, Massachusetts in the late eighteenth century. Though they shared common experiences with many others of their day, the Coltons were neither "typical" nor "average"; no easy generalization about their neighbors and other countrypeople emerges from their portrait.

Research into the families who lived in the rooms has also led curators to a new understanding of the collections of artifacts we have inherited, why they were put together, and what their limitations are. As in most collections, poor people's possessions do not appear in large numbers; those possessions were rarely made of lasting materials to begin with, and their owners generally used them, mended them, and handed them down to others for reuse. Things that did not wear out were rarely collected by antiquers anyway; a class bias remains from the aesthetic considerations that have influenced collecting and preservation. Even the owner of the museum's log house, it turns out, was a surprisingly prosperous farmer for his part of Delaware and an owner of slaves. That the people who lived in all of the museum's period rooms held slaves underscores the degree to which that institution was an integral part of eighteenth-century American life. Out of that recognition, the exhibition looks at black American life in the Chesapeake and at part of the free black community of Revolutionary Philadelphia. Out of an awareness of the gaps in the museum's collections, planners of the exhibition have borrowed objects from other museums and turned to the use of graphics, so as to include black history, urban artisans, and American Indian groups as well. What emerges from all the research, what we have reached for in "After the Revolution," is a picture of the extraordinary diversity and surprising level of conflict that marked eighteenth-century life in America.

Yet if we no longer view period rooms and their furnishings either as art or as tokens of the good taste of early Americans, we still do not fully know how to understand them as documents that can tell us about history. The museum's collections contain quilts, Windsor chairs, carpenters' tools, prints and drawings, and many other survivals from the past. How do we learn from them about the thoughts and experiences of their makers and users? How do we discover the role they played in people's lives? Although we can touch the fabric, wood, iron, or paper that compose them, we have lost an essential constituent

Few of us today would look at a cradle and think about death. But in the eighteenth century, when many families lost a child in infancy, an empty cradle might commonly evoke feelings of grief and loss as well as those of joyful expectation. As human experience has changed, people have endowed objects with different meanings.

of these artifacts: the social and cultural context in which they took on meaning. It has been possible to reconstruct that context, to find out about such matters as the geographical dispersion, customary uses, and various meanings associated with different eighteenth-century objects, only in some cases and only in part. The photographs and text that follow sometimes fit nicely together, illuminating and expanding upon one another; at many other times connections are difficult to draw, and readers will feel a gap between the objects and images on the one hand and the stories of past lives on the other. Yet even in such cases, placing these artifacts and histories in juxtaposition may prove suggestive. If they combine to tell no simple story, nonetheless I hope that together they may reveal more about life in the late eighteenth century than either would do alone.

Two hundred years ago, some of the ancestors of some Americans formed a new nation on the North American continent. Through a decade of debate with the British Parliament and the British king, through nearly another decade of warfare, eighteenth-century Americans turned thirteen British colonies into thirteen sovereign states. A few years later they formed a federal government to unite those states, creating a nation that would become one of the major international powers of the two centuries that followed. Through history book, oratory, pageant, and ode, educators and government officials have celebrated that accomplishment and schooled the American people in the virtues of our revolutionary heritage. We have learned that the nation the eighteenth century produced was "conceived in liberty," and though its practice of liberty has been flawed, nonetheless it has promised liberty to almost all. On the strength of that promise, some descendants of the Revolutionaries, some descendants of their enemies, and other Americans whose ancestors spent the eighteenth century in Europe, Africa, or Asia have embraced aspects of that revolution as their own.

At times, however, we have shown ourselves confused about what we are celebrating, uncertain whether it is the powerful nation-state or its dedication to liberty that is worthy of our loyalty and commitment. This is an inherited dilemma, for the same confusion plagued some of the Revolutionaries themselves. Particularly among the upper classes of the revolutionary generation, some coupled visions of empire with the pursuit of independence. Thus, David Cobb of Taunton, Massachusetts wrote in early 1776 of the possibility for forming "a Great and Glorious Empire" in America, a nation that, with God's blessing, might "bid defiance to the world." Urging members of the Continental Congress to declare independence from Great Britain, Cobb cast the nations of the world as parts of a single system: "Pray hasten that glorious Day when we shall no longer continue one of the Circulating Orbs of the System, but like our predecessor, the Sun, be fix'd in the center, shine with unborrow'd Lustre and kindly defuse the Rays of our Influence upon the Worlds around us." Cobb imagined that America would be beneficent in its power; that it would be powerful and imperial in nature he showed no doubts. When men such as Cobb spoke of liberty, they conceived it in terms of empire.[21]

Joseph Brant, portrayed by Charles Willson Peale in 1797, was a powerful Mohawk, influential in bringing the Six Nations of the Iroquois into the American Revolution on the side of the British.

Yet other eighteenth-century Americans were inspired less by visions of empire than by more humble ideas of "liberty." Not everyone who participated in the resistance movement against British rule, and in the Revolution that followed, foresaw or desired the creation of a powerful nation-state. Indeed, as many historians have recently reminded us, the eighteenth-century movement for liberty had purposes and principles that our present-day celebrations often pass by. There were *many* revolutions, not just one. From the outset, the patriot movement comprised a coalition—between northern merchants, southern planters, and farmers, artisans, and laborers throughout the colonies. All patriots, by definition, wanted independence, but they held various ideas about what else they wanted, and their alliance was never an easy one. Patriots cherished very different visions of the society they wanted to make at home. If some sought to become like Great Britain, "fix'd in the center" of the Atlantic economy, others rejected the model of empire, picturing a more equal and "virtuous" society than Britain's. Patriots quarreled over religious freedom, economic policy, slavery, and the extension of political rights to men of little or no property. Long after the war was over, some pressed for greater liberty, some feared they'd gone too far. Moreover, there were other revolutions too: black Americans took the opportunities offered by the white people's war to press for their own freedom, and American Indians west of the Appalachians fought *against* the patriot cause for their own independence. Far from every American joined the same movement as every other. Far from every American—even among the patriots—necessarily won his or her revolution.[22]

This book is, in part, about the complexity of the American Revolution, some of the many sides of the eighteenth century's struggle for liberty. Yet these are grand themes, and the text here relatively humble. It tells the stories of a handful of Americans who lived in the years during and after the American Revolution. It looks hardly at all at battles, government policy-makers, or famous events. Only one of its major characters, a Virginia planter named Henry Saunders, seems to have fought in the Revolution at all—and although he may have faced the British troops who raided the Virginia countryside in 1778, much of his service was probably spent in the unglamorous job of protecting stockpiled supplies and preventing slaves from escaping to British lines. Other people in these pages gave support to the patriots' military effort too: a Massachusetts merchant named Samuel Colton sold provisions to George Washington's army, and a slave named Richard Allen drove wagons of salt for the revolutionary government of Delaware. Yet none of these men was a revolutionary hero, none of them suffered at Valley Forge or debated policy in the Continental Congress at Philadelphia. And many other people in these pages—a farm wife in Delaware, a slave boy, a white Methodist preacher—did not (so far as we know) contribute to the war effort at all. With one exception, the people in this book appear here not because they were important but because of an accident: some part of the houses they lived in has survived in the collections of the National Museum of American History. While that means that the book includes particularly prosperous people—the sort of people whose houses have been saved and collected by museums—it does not mean that they were present at momentous events or central to the great developments of their time. Even Richard Allen, despite his accomplishments and fame, is not the sort of person normally included when textbooks name the "Founding Fathers." For the most part, these are the histories of unnotable, ordinary people.

Yet, despite that, it seems to me possible that the Revolution might still be their story. Revolutions, after all, do not just take place on battlefields or in legislatures; as John Adams recognized, they take place "in the hearts and minds" of the people as well. Adams thought that the American Revolution consisted in an altered sense of identity, a moment in which many British colonists in the New World came to see themselves as no longer English but "American." He thought that moment took place well before colonial representatives declared independence in 1776.[23] By the same token, the working out of that "American" identity, the shaping and discovery of its many meanings, continued well beyond the war years and the new states' peace settlement with Britain in 1783. If the generation that did the fighting made the Revolution, the generations who lived after the war gave meaning to independence. Even ordinary people have hearts and minds, and the lives of slaves and freedpeople, farmers and storekeepers, housewives and widows, slaveholders and artisans, however undistinguished, do not seem irrelevant to the new society that grew out of the Revolutionary War.

At the same time, as the title indicates, these histories look at everyday lives—the daily round of labor and rest, the local world of neighborhood visits and transactions, as well as the broader world of revolutions and marketplace transformations. If at times this book asks its readers to broaden their understanding of the boundaries of the Revolution, at other times it asks them to leave that revolution—at least momentarily—far behind. Some human experiences are not to be understood through their connection to "larger" matters. The war touched Samuel Colton, but who is to measure its importance in his life, as compared to the deaths, some twenty years earlier, of his infant child and his first, young wife? Other characters in these pages faced crises of their own: a slave named Mage was convicted of stealing; a man named Richard underwent a powerful religious conversion; and white women named Anne Tallough, Margaret Wells, and Lucy Colton all made decisions to take "the dark leep"—marriage.[24]

This plaster cast shows a detail from the gravestone of Susanna Jayne, buried in Marblehead, Massachusetts, in 1776.

Whatever their connection (if any) to a nation's struggle for independence, such events command our efforts at understanding.

Moreover, part of my purpose has been to reconstruct occasions that were simple and mundane as well as those most critical. The clearing of fields, the raising of children, visits with neighbors, purchases at a store—all were among the threads that formed the fabric of eighteenth-century lives. Many customary practices that were unremarkable 200 years ago are difficult to recapture now. Yet it is within the framework of their ordinary lives that people came to understand extraordinary (or revolutionary) events. Taken-for-granted routines shaped people's expectations about such matters as economic ambition, social and political authority, and individuals' obligations to their neighbors. So these histories reach to politics on the one hand and to daily and mundane matters on the other. Of course the two are linked, and sometimes, I hope, these histories will suggest how that was so. And while often it is hard to connect these people to one another or to the great events of their times, in small ways we can link them to the society they had inherited and the society they were busy making.

It has been difficult to learn as much as we would like about these people, to discover their sense of "America," the sort of society they wanted, their values and ideals. We have been left with frustratingly few traces of how they lived, of the details of their daily experience. Few of them wrote down their thoughts about their society's future. Some (especially the black slaves) were probably illiterate; some (especially the white women) were taught that they were not qualified to have or express opinions on such matters; if these slaves or women recorded their thoughts—or even the daily events of their lives—no one has saved those records.

As is usually the case, it has been easier to find out about the white men, the ones whose names generally appear on the land deeds, tax lists, and probate records that still survive. But even here the evidence is often scanty. We are lucky to have written evidence of Samuel Colton's experience of the Revolution and of Richard Allen's understanding of liberty. We have to read slaveholder Henry Saunders's aspirations from a few of his actions and—at a time when some of his neighbors were freeing their slaves and changing their own lives—

from his inactions as well. As the notes show, I have drawn extensively on the work of a great many other historians in order to illuminate these people's lives. Yet despite that, there are large holes in these stories, silences, and troubling questions left unanswered.

A handful of histories—with so many other Americans left out. Ordinary, unrepresentative, untypical individuals, families, and households.

If history on this scale has value, perhaps it lies in its ability to remind us of simple truths about the past: it is worth remembering, after all, that history happens to everyone, that the large trends and transformations historians speak about—the growth of the Atlantic marketplace, the spread of the idea of liberty, shifts in patterns of birth, death, and disease—all make themselves felt in the lives of individual households and communities. It is worth remembering, too, that everyone makes history, that ordinary people living ordinary lives still indelibly mark their society with the choices they make, the struggles they undertake, and the aspirations they hold dear.

NOTES

1.   Edward F. Zimmer, "A Study of the Origins of the Connecticut Valley Parlor in the National Museum of American History, or Ignorance Is Bliss" (Report for the National Museum of American History, Smithsonian Institution, September 1981), pp. 1–67.

2.   On the origins of the period room, see: Dianne H. Pilgrim, "Inherited from the Past: the American Period Room," *The American Art Journal* 10 (May 1978): 4–23; Elizabeth Stillinger, "Windows on the Past," *Portfolio: The Magazine of the Fine Arts* 5 (March/April 1983): 106–11. Also of interest are Christopher Monkhouse, "The Spinning Wheel as Artifact, Symbol, and Source of Design," in *Victorian Furniture: Essays from a Victorian Society Autumn Symposium,* ed. Kenneth L. Ames, published as *Nineteenth Century:* vol. 8, nos. 3–4, 1982, by the Victorian Society in America, pp. 153–72; Richard Saunders, "Collecting American Decorative Arts in New England, 1793–1876," *Antiques* 109, no. 5 (May 1976): 996–1003 and 110, no. 4 (October 1976): 754–63.

3.   Zimmer, "Origins of the Connecticut Valley Parlor," pp. 1–2.

4.   Elizabeth Stillinger, *The Antiquers* (New York, 1980), pp. 52–55; Wendy Kaplan, "R.T.H. Halsey: An Ideology of Collecting American Decorative Arts," *Winterthur Portfolio* 17 (Spring 1982): 47–48.

5.   Kaplan, "R.T.H. Halsey," pp. 47–49. Stillinger, *Antiquers,* pp. 45–47, 56–60. Thorstein Veblen, *The Theory of the Leisure Class: An Economic Study of Institutions* (New York, 1934), pp. 126–33. On American responses to industrialization, see also T. J. Jackson Lears, *No Place of Grace: Antimodernism and the Transformation of American Culture, 1880–1920* (New York, 1981).

6. Michael Wallace, "Visiting the Past: History Museums in the United States," *Radical History Review* 25 (1981): 63–100. On nativism, see John Higham, *Strangers in the Land: Patterns of American Nativism, 1860–1925* (New Brunswick, N.J., 1955), esp. pp. 137–39, 236–37. Frances FitzGerald, *America Revised: History Schoolbooks in the Twentieth Century* (Boston, 1979), pp. 76–79 discusses the reaction in history textbooks to the new immigration.

7. Stillinger, *Antiquers*, pp. xiv, 48–51, 195–214, and chaps. 7–9. The quotation is in Kaplan, "R.T.H. Halsey," p. 48.

8. Kaplan, "R.T.H. Halsey," pp. 48–51. Stillinger, *Antiquers*, chaps. 13, 16. Wallace, "Visiting the Past," pp. 66–68.

9. Kaplan, "R.T.H. Halsey," pp. 51–53. Stillinger, *Antiquers*, pp. 195–232, discusses period rooms, esp. pp. 222–32 on Du Pont. On Rockefeller and Colonial Williamsburg, see Wallace, "Visiting the Past," pp. 76–78.

10. Wallace, "Visiting the Past," p. 77. Colonial Williamsburg began mentioning slavery in the 1970s, ibid., pp. 86–88.

11. On other approaches to the past through period rooms and historic villages in the 1920s, see Wallace, "Visiting the Past," pp. 69–76; Pilgrim, "Inherited from the Past," pp. 4–23; Stillinger, "Windows on the Past," pp. 106–11; Stillinger, *Antiquers*, pp. 149–54, 255–62.

12. March 25, 1958, Hall of Everyday Life in the American Past, Exhibition Files, Division of Domestic Life, National Museum of American History, Washington, D.C.

13. Ibid.; "Conceptual Script for Revision of the Hall of Everyday Life in the American Past," April 9, 1973. The "revision" did not depart substantially from the concept that had originally shaped the Hall.

14. Dell Upton, "The Virginia Parlor, National Museum of American History, Smithsonian Institution: A Report on the Henry Saunders House and Its Occupants," July 1, 1981; and Upton, "Architectural Survey of the Delaware Log House," June 1, 1982 (Reports for the National Museum of American History, Smithsonian Institution).

15. "Preface to a Preliminary Proposal," February 20, 1974, pp. 1, 3, Hall of Everyday Life in the American Past, Exhibition Files.

16. The Hall's inclusion of women, daily routines, and other topics appears in the exhibition script, Files of the Division of Domestic Life.

17. Fitzgerald, *America Revised*, pp. 10–11, 56–58, 73–84.

18. Ibid., pp. 11–12, 47–70.

19. See especially Jesse Lemisch, "The American Revolution Seen from the Bottom Up," in Barton J. Bernstein, *Towards a New Past: Dissenting Essays in American History* (New York, 1969), pp. 3–45.

20. Edmund S. Morgan, "Slavery and Freedom, The American Paradox," in *The Challenge of the American Revolution* (New York, 1976), p. 140; Lemisch, "American Revolution from the Bottom Up," p. 4; idem., "Jack Tar in the Streets: Merchant Seamen and the Politics of Revolutionary America," *William and Mary Quarterly*, 3rd ser. 25 (1968): 371–407.

21. David Cobb to Robert Treat Paine, February 24 and June 10, 1776, *Robert Treat Paine Papers*, 1776 xeroxes, Massachusetts Historical Society. See also Cobb to Paine, July 22, 1776, ibid.

22. The literature on the many Revolutions is extensive. Among the most important works are Staughton Lynd, *Class Conflict, Slavery, and the United States Constitution* (New York, 1967); Eric Foner, *Tom Paine and Revolutionary America* (New York, 1976); and the essays in Alfred F. Young, *The American Revolution: Explorations in the History of American Radicalism* (De Kalb, Ill., 1976).

23. John Adams is quoted in Edmund S. Morgan, "Challenge and Response: Reflections on the Bicentennial," *Challenge of the American Revolution*, p. 197.

24. The phrase describing marriage was Pamela Sedgwick's, quoted in Mary Beth Norton, *Liberty's Daughters: The Revolutionary Experience of American Women, 1750–1800* (Boston, 1980), p. 42.

THE WAR AT HOME

Samuel Colton,
Merchant of Longmeadow,
Massachusetts

*I*t was late in the night when the crowd began to gather. Some men had disguised themselves with blackened faces, others were wrapped in blankets "like Indians." All of them were angry enough to venture out on a cloudy, rainy midsummer's night in the little village of Longmeadow, Massachusetts. Late July was harvest time, and in ordinary years, long days' work in the fields discouraged late-night excursions. But this was 1776, and the times were far from ordinary. Only three weeks earlier, the thirteen continental colonies had declared themselves independent of the British Empire. For over a year, American soldiers and militiamen had been fighting redcoats on the battlefield. And warfare and independence were only the culmination of many years' events that took men's minds from harvest and turned them to political matters. It no longer seemed odd, then, to trade sleep for politics, though on this July night, Longmeadow men gathered not to fight redcoats but to rebuke their own neighbor, the merchant Samuel Colton.[1]

As the merchant later reported, the crowd "forcibly Brake open his Store Locks" and, by the light of their lanterns, poured into the shop that lay along the western side of Colton's mansion. Inside the house itself, the merchant and most of his household lay asleep. Witnesses and participants disagreed about what happened next. Colton later accused the crowd of "Ransacking and Searching his House from top to bottom," putting his family "in great Fear and Terror." But by most accounts the crowd was fairly orderly, avoiding destruction and indiscriminate looting. They had come for one thing: a particular stock of West Indian goods. The crowd searched the store, bypassing shelves laden with imported cloth and earthenware; drawers packed with ribbon, buttons, and pins; barrels of nails; hardware, axes, scythes, and other tools. Swiftly they found their objective: triumphantly they seized the merchant's supply of rum, molasses, sugar, and salt and carried it away.[2]

The perpetrators of the midnight raid were soon discovered. Roused by the noise, Lucy Colton, Samuel's wife, had recognized several faces among the crowd. She had seen Nathaniel Ely, deacon of the Congregational church; Azariah Woolworth, neighbor to the Coltons; and Festus Colton, her own cousin and brother of Samuel's first wife. The stolen goods were equally easy to find. The crowd delivered their prize to the town clerk—another Colton—who openly sold it over the months that followed. Eventually, Nathaniel Ely offered the proceeds from those sales to Samuel Colton and, when the merchant refused the money, simply left it on a table in Colton's house.[3]

The midnight raid in Longmeadow was obviously not an ordinary burglary. Crowd members acted with restraint and even tried to pay Colton for his losses. Moreover, despite blackened faces and Indian disguise, members of the raiding party made little real effort to hide their identities. The leaders of the crowd included some of the town's most upstanding and respected citizens. Crowd members had property of their own and lived in a society based on private property. They frowned on stealing, but they did not regard what they did as theft. Indeed, even to many people not directly involved, the raid resembled a legal proceeding more than it resembled a crime. When the matter reached the ears of the state government five years later, over 120 people from Longmeadow and nearby towns sided with the raiders.[4]

To Samuel Colton, however, the raid was both an injustice and an outrage, for those guilty of "Ransacking" his store, "plundering and carrying away what they saw fit," were his neighbors. It added insult to injury that they pretended to legal authority, and that they left enough molasses, rum, salt, and sugar for the Colton family's private use. If legend can be trusted, Samuel Colton never spoke to those neighbors again.[5]

$\mathcal{W}$hat happened that night between Colton and his neighbors? How could conscientious, law-abiding citizens convince themselves (and others) that taking Colton's goods was justified?

To begin with, the raiders had a specific economic grievance against Samuel Colton. Despite protests from his customers, the merchant had raised prices on his West Indian imports, and it was only those imports that the crowd appropriated. Accordingly, when the town clerk sold the merchant's goods, he charged what local people consid-

All the tokens of a genteel and prosperous life—a glass of wine, a Georgian mansion, a ship laden with imported goods—bespeak the wealth and fashion of this Connecticut valley merchant.

ered a "reasonable price" for it. Although Colton quibbled about the matter, even he acknowledged that his prices provoked the raid.[6]

In many respects, moreover, the raid represented a traditional response to grievances about prices. For centuries, in seasons when grain supplies ran short and bread became more expensive, England had witnessed similar events, when crowds of poor people took marketing into their own hands. Their targets were farmers who sold their grain to exporters rather than supplying consumers in their own neighborhoods, or millers and merchants who withheld flour from the market in order to raise the price. Though the authorities called them "rioters," English crowds rarely turned violence against people; usually, they acted with discipline and restraint, and they often paid their victim a price they considered fair for what they took. On such occasions, the English poor expressed their belief that such necessities as grain and flour were not strictly private property, that in the face of hunger and distress suppliers had an obligation to make such necessities available to the poor at an affordable rate. And although the English authorities disapproved of such "food riots," some well-to-do and educated Englishmen thought that common law and custom stood on the rioters' side. So a venerable tradition of thought supported the crowds' interpretation of social and economic justice. In America, shortages of grain were less common, but when they struck, crowds sometimes followed the English precedent, breaking into warehouses and stores to take control of flour and grain.[7]

No doubt participants in the Longmeadow raid knew that they acted in a tradition that was centuries old. Yet no one was starving in Longmeadow in 1776—at least, not for want of molasses or rum. Moreover, few of the raiders would be counted among the ranks of the local poor, and none of them, it seems safe to say, had done anything like it before. The tradition of "food riots" shaped the crowd's action, but that tradition did not account for it completely.

By 1776, of course, Americans were familiar with other sorts of crowds. For over ten years, ever since the British Parliament first laid taxes on goods shipped into the colonies, patriot crowds had been busy in many cities, harassing British soldiers, tar-and-feathering British sympathizers, and boycotting tea importers. In 1773, respectable Bostonians had dressed up like Indians and dumped imported tea into the harbor rather than pay a tax on it. When the raiders in Longmeadow put on Indian disguise, they expressed a sense of unity with the people behind the Tea Party. As far as the raiders were concerned, the break-in at Colton's store was a part of the Revolution.[8]

This is the story of Samuel Colton, his relationship with his Longmeadow neighbors, and the part of the Revolution that most deeply changed his life. That part of the war was fought, not by soldiers, but by civilian crowds, town meetings, and local committees elected in counties and towns to coordinate the struggle at home. It was on the homefront, rather than the battlefield, that most supporters of American liberty contributed to the patriot cause. In Longmeadow and other towns, civilian men and women worked to supply troops in the field and to prevent British sympathizers from supplying the other side. Equally important, patriots carried out the Revolution by trying to reshape relationships in their own communities. As many Americans saw it, gaining independence from Britain was only half the battle; the other half involved creating an American society that would make independence worthwhile. The men who broke into Samuel Colton's store in 1776 considered their action a necessary part of that struggle.

So the Longmeadow raid and the conflicts that give rise to it can shed light on the meaning of the eighteenth-century movement for liberty, as it was experienced and interpreted not by political and military leaders but by more ordinary Americans. The raid reflected larger social and economic changes taking place not only in Longmeadow but throughout much of eighteenth-century America. Colton and his neighbors came into conflict over more than molasses, sugar, rum, and salt. Behind the raid lay important ethical disagreements over such matters as prices, profits, and the rules of economic exchange. The raid signaled concern about the obligations of individuals to the communities in which they lived. It raised troubling questions about the effect of trade and commerce on American character and American community. Long after political independence had been secured, these issues remained important to Americans who lived far from the Connecticut River and who had never heard of Samuel Colton.

Longmeadow had always been a place for both farming and trade. For thousands of years, Algonquian-speaking people had lived in the Connecticut River valley, planting corn and other vegetables, fishing and trapping along the riverbanks, and trading with people who lived as far away as the Hudson River valley and Narragansett Bay. In the 1630s, English settlers followed the Indian paths from Boston to where the Agawam Indians, their numbers recently lessened by smallpox, farmed and lived. The Agawams refused to part with the richest of their planting lands, those along the western bank of the Connecticut River. But for "eighteen fathoms of wampum, eighteen coats, 18 hatchets, 18 howes, [and] 18 knifes," the whites purchased land along the eastern bank, where they set up their homes. They chose a site eight miles north of the boundary of Connecticut Colony and ninety miles above the point where the river emptied into Long Island Sound.[9]

The river attracted settlers. It was a kind of highway that could connect the new settlement, called Springfield, with Boston and the wider world. In an age when travel over land was arduous and slow, wind and water were preferred means of transport, trade, and communication. Such considerations were critical to the man who was Springfield's wealthiest and most prominent settler, William Pynchon. Quickly establishing himself as middleman in the lucrative fur trade, Pynchon amassed a fortune. He received beaver and other pelts from Agawam and Woronoco hunters and shipped them to England to be manufactured into hats and clothing. As time went on, the Pynchons and other traders found new products to export, and new markets as well. For them, the river was a road to profit.[10]

The river trade was important to many besides Pynchon, for he hired laborers, canoers, and teamsters to pack and transport beaver pelts, and he ran a general store where Indians and whites could buy tools and textiles. The beaver population dwindled late in the 1660s, but trade on the river continued. For most of the Pynchons' fellow settlers, though, the river's main attraction lay elsewhere: in the rich alluvial lands along its shores. The fertile soil readily produced such staples as Indian corn, oats, barley, and hay. Settlers grew flax for making linen and a variety of fruits, especially apples for cider and currants for jam. Rich meadowlands, nourished by floodwaters every spring, provided grazing for cattle and pigs. Upland were forests that yielded timber for houses, firewood, and fences to protect cornfields from hungry livestock. Settlers who came as farmers cared less about the world overseas to which the river offered access than about their local community. While the Pynchons and other traders catered to English markets, the majority of settlers planted orchards and fields,

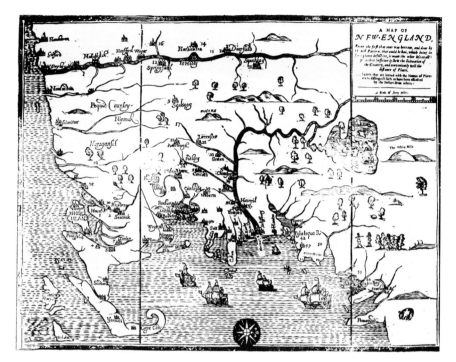

John Foster's "Map of New England," 1677, shows Springfield and other Connecticut River settlements along the top. The first map drawn, engraved, and printed in America, it still presents Europe's point of view: the direction north is oriented to the right.

produced for their own families' consumption, and concerned themselves with purely local events.[11]

Samuel Colton's great-grandfather George Colton was among the majority attracted to the Connecticut River valley for its rich lands. Along with a handful of others, he moved onto the "long meddowe" three miles to the south of Springfield in the late 1640s. There he prospered. George married a Hartford woman, who bore eight children who lived to maturity. Most of them stayed in the Longmeadow area and produced families of their own. By the end of the century, the community included over thirty families—a fair number with the surname Colton.[12]

In 1703, male heads of village households petitioned the Springfield town meeting for permission to leave the tract they had originally settled. Floodwaters from the river threatened to inundate the meadow where they lived. Cattle had already been killed and people were endangered. Equally important, Longmeadow residents found themselves so far away from the Springfield meeting house that it was difficult to travel to church on Sunday. Could they move up the

This map, drawn about 1900, shows the home lots laid out in 1703 for Longmeadow settlers to build their houses on. Marshlands lay to the west along the river, farmlands to the east.

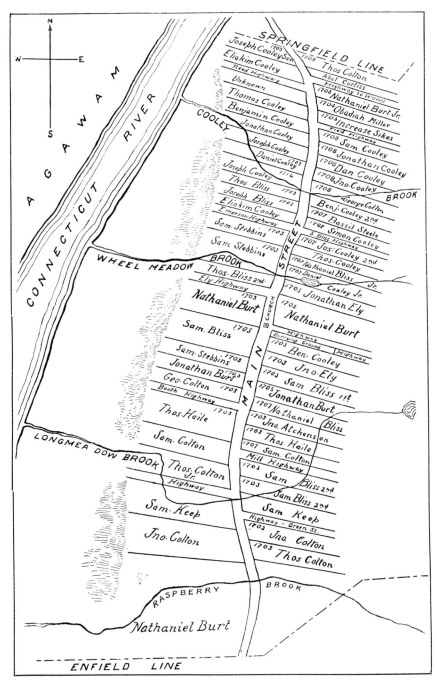

MAP OF HOMELOTS AT LONGMEADOW.

hillside and build new houses there? The Springfield town meeting decided that they could. It appointed men to measure out home lots, and allotted them to families with the stipulation that those families build houses on them within a few years.[13]

The move got townspeople settled on dry land, but it did little to lessen the distance to church. In 1715 Longmeadow received permission from the Springfield town meeting to build its own meeting house and hire its own minister. Longmeadow continued to share the same town government as Springfield, but it began electing a local "precinct committee" to oversee payment of the minister's salary and other parish affairs. Over the years, Longmeadow residents sought permission to set up as a separate town. The colonial government thought their numbers were too small, but people in Longmeadow felt themselves to be a community distinct from Springfield in many ways.[14]

Like the inhabitants of other rural villages, Longmeadow residents created many ties with each other. For the most part they worshipped together, socialized with one another, and cooperated on local projects like hiring a schoolteacher and building a meeting house. Families in Longmeadow followed the pattern of most New England settlers when they set their home lots close together rather than spreading out onto farms. Having their houses close was convenient for women, who often went next-door to share work and talk with neighbors and kin. If it was less convenient for men, who traveled out to their fields and back every day, that did not seem too important. What mattered to New Englanders was living in a community.[15]

Having neighbors brought economic advantages as well as social ones. Families tended to their own affairs—men working their own lands, women managing their own households—but few households were self-sufficient. Couples worked and planned to gain security for themselves and to give their children a "competence" in life, and to reach those goals, people naturally looked to each other when their own skills fell short. In the midst of a village, it made sense to rely where possible on neighbors rather than do everything for oneself. Some farmers learned blacksmithing, coopering, or shoemaking. Some women churned butter for the neighborhood or spun yarn for families who didn't own a wheel. A few artisans plied their crafts full-time, producing "spoken goods"—articles custom-made to suit their neighbors' requirements. Some men ran gristmills, sawmills, or tanneries. Households concentrated on certain areas so that together they provided the range of skills that rural life required.[16]

The result of this specialization was a complicated network of local exchange. Farm goods, labor, and craftsmen's products changed hands as a daily occurrence: wheat for a cow, flax for the use of a team of oxen, a day's labor for a homemade shirt. Many exchanges took a long time to complete, as people paid for labor in the fall with wheat harvested the next summer, or got shoes for the winter by promising a calf come spring. So at any one moment, most people stood in debt to some of their neighbors while others in turn were owing to them. The situation gave no cause for worry—people knew they would be dealing again. Far from being lone and independent frontier families, settlers in Longmeadow were closely involved with their neighbors' lives and fortunes.[17]

Interdependence sometimes caused conflict, but it also generated expectations and rules for governing social and economic life. As New Englanders saw it, the chief threat to harmony was that private ambition might conflict with the welfare of the whole community. When

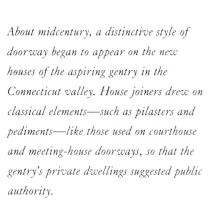

About midcentury, a distinctive style of doorway began to appear on the new houses of the aspiring gentry in the Connecticut valley. House joiners drew on classical elements—such as pilasters and pediments—like those used on courthouse and meeting-house doorways, so that the gentry's private dwellings suggested public authority.

"Crooked-back" chairs—so named for their curved backs—were popular seating chairs of the middle and upper classes in New England. Often bought in sets of six or more, they were used in the better rooms of the house.

that happened, they thought, the general good should take precedence over any individual's self-interest. Longmeadow settlers could not just relocate their homes from the flooding meadows nor form a church nearby to suit their own convenience. The town meeting, composed of white male heads of households, had to authorize most projects, and individuals had to wait until it did.[18]

In making such decisions, the town routinely considered benefits to individuals less important than the welfare of the group. Ideally, town meetings preferred to act by unanimous accord. When Nathaniel Burt and his partners wanted to build a sawmill on Longmeadow Brook, the meeting stipulated that the mill must "prejudice no man's proprietys." Similarly, in the winter of 1709 the town agreed to pay Thomas Colton (Samuel's uncle) thirty shillings to provide schooling for Longmeadow children, but insisted that Colton forgo all payment "if it occasion strife or disturbance amongst his neighbors at Longmeadow." The records do not reveal what disruption the town anticipated, or whether anyone in Longmeadow did object. They make clear, however, the town's commitment to averting disputes by making sure that people took their neighbors' needs and opinions into account.[19]

Similar limitations on individual self-interest were the ideal for governing economic exchange. After all, Longmeadow settlers inher-

Colton's scroll-pediment doorway was more elaborate than many that graced the houses of more prominent "River God" families.

ited ideas about economic fairness akin to those expressed in the food riots of English and American crowds. To make flour available at a reasonable price, Springfield regulated millers' profits, allowing only a set "toll" for each bushel they ground into flour. The principle held for farmers and craftsmen too; no one was to charge what the market would bear in times of dearth or duress. Even in good times the whole purpose of trade, as one Massachusetts minister said, was "mutual" advantage, and not the profit of one party to a transaction at the expense of the other.[20]

At times, of course, Longmeadow people failed to live up to their ideals, but they also took active steps to put them into practice. Like other New England towns, Springfield elected local officials to prevent fraud and ensure fairness in exchange. On one occasion, seeing that James Osborne "doth prejudice him self and his family by disadvantagious bargaynes," the town meeting instructed selectmen to oversee all of Osborne's transactions worth more than ten shillings. Such care for neighbors reflected self-interest as much as community altruism; if the Osbornes became destitute, the town would have to provide support for them. At the same time, the closeness of community life allowed people to see clearly the unhappy consequences that bad bargains carried for some local families. When social conscience and inherited ideals failed, then Longmeadow residents were prepared for town officials to intervene.[21]

Neighbors could also use unofficial means to control each other's behavior. In order to continue trading with one another, each party had to leave a transaction at least tolerably satisfied of its fairness. A man might deliver rotten shingles instead of sound ones, a woman might pass off fourteen ounces of butter as a pound, but neither could simply walk away anonymous. Farmers and craftsmen depended on keeping good personal reputations in the neighborhood; word of any sharp dealing would travel far and fast. Even in Boston, a city of 15,000 people at midcentury, housewives who purchased country produce for their families relied on word of mouth to distinguish trustworthy retailers from sharpers and to keep sellers honest. Such informal methods of control were even more effective in smaller towns, where inhabitants were tied to one another as neighbors, brethren, and kin. People could appeal to their neighbors' consciences, or call on church elders to intervene, or pass word of their grievances to everyone in town—or else just threaten to do so. All these recourses gave town inhabitants leverage over one another's behavior. The standards of neighborly dealing made sense in the context of village life. As Samuel Colton would discover, however, those standards could cause problems for the international merchant.[22]

From first settlement, many Americans used wooden utensils for eating and drinking, but those who could afford it, like the Coltons, used pewter.

In the 1700s, pewterers had shops in American cities, but colonial artisans still sold imported Engish pewter along with their own wares. The plate and mug pictured here are both American-made.

"*Marchant*" Samuel Colton was born in 1727 in a house built by his father a little to the south of Longmeadow Common. Both Samuel and his sister, Margaret, were late children. Margaret had arrived seventeen years into her parents' marriage, her brother three years later. The children were cast on their own relatively early. Their mother died nine years after Samuel's birth, and their father died eight years later, in 1744.[23]

Early independence must have been a mixture of burden and blessing for the children. Freed from management of her father's household, Margaret, aged twenty, married within a few months and moved with her bridegroom to New Castle, New Hampshire. Samuel remained to establish himself in Longmeadow. He was seventeen years old, bereft of immediate family, but surrounded by relatives.[24]

His prospects for worldly success were good. Like most young men in New England, Samuel had only a local education. He did not attend either Harvard or Yale, institutions where the sons of the well-to-do or socially prestigious might acquire broader intellectual horizons and a wide circle of acquaintances. Nor did he inherit the political connections that would assure him entry into the ranks of the Massachusetts governing elite. The families who dominated the Connecticut River valley were a cut above the Coltons. In Springfield, the Worthingtons ranked among these "River God" families. They had influence with powerful personages in England and with the colonial governor appointed by the king. That patronage reinforced the wealth, privilege, and prestige that supported their power in their own communities. As Samuel Colton surveyed his prospects in 1744, he recognized that he stood outside that favored circle. Though the Coltons were among the wealthiest families in Longmeadow, their political power and political connections ended at the town border.[25]

Still, young Samuel could count his blessings. He inherited a great deal of property. When Longmeadow's tax assessors evaluated families' holdings in the 1720s, they listed five Coltons among the top eight taxpayers in the district. Prominent among those was Samuel senior, one of the two men in town to own a black slave. His estate included a house and an orchard, lands that produced grain and flax, as well as twenty cows and some oxen. One-third of the estate went to sister Margaret for a dowry, but the lands and many other assets went to her brother. Lucky in having only one sister, young Samuel could enjoy his father's holdings essentially intact.[26]

This gave him a great advantage over others of his generation, many of whom suffered from New England's growing shortage of available land. Measured by Old World standards, the first white settlers had allotted to themselves what seemed abundant acreage. They also kept common lands in reserve, set aside for grazing animals and for future division among new settlers and the children of the old. At the time, such measures had seemed enough and more than enough. But life in the New World had its unexpected ironies: a healthy climate and increased fecundity. People lived longer, married earlier, and lost fewer children in infancy. There were more heirs to provide for than anyone had expected. With each generation, families divided their estates among male heirs and, to supplement their dwindling holdings, parceled out the common lands in private grants. Over the years, then, the farms of the parents grew ever less adequate to sustain the children.[27]

At the same time, years of agriculture were beginning to tell on the soil of the river valley. Western Massachusetts farmers did not yet practice such techniques as crop rotation, systematic manuring, or the cultivation of legumes to replenish the soil. As a result, many fourth-generation children faced a difficult situation: their fathers' lands could not be divided further and still provide a living for a householder and his family. Young men faced pressure to learn new trades to supplement the meager produce of small farms, to migrate to the frontier, or else to remain among family and community but accept smaller holdings and dimmer prospects than their fathers had enjoyed. Samuel Colton was lucky. He could choose between more enviable alternatives.[28]

Young Samuel's ambitions were apparent from the outset. He remained under the legal guardianship of his uncle Ephraim until the age of twenty-one. He boarded with his uncle for four years, taking with him Tom, the slave inherited from his father. Late in 1748

Samuel reached his majority. He took possession of his substantial inheritance, moved into his father's house, and began farming his extensive lands. Within a year he had hired half a dozen local men to work the fields, care for the livestock, tend the orchard, and mow in the meadows. Samuel managed the farm, but his own interest was not primarily in agriculture. In 1749 he traveled to Boston, and he started an account book to record a few dealings with neighbors. He sold them apples, buttons, ribbons, and fabric, and he took livestock in exchange.[29]

In 1753 he sent a crop of tobacco to Boston, probably as partial cargo on a ship belonging to an established merchant operating along the Connecticut River. He probably entered the West Indies trade in the same way. Merchants based in the commercial towns of the valley had established links with the owners of sugar plantations in the West Indies. New Englanders supplied the lumber that made barrels, hogsheads, and other casks in which Caribbean colonists shipped molasses and rum. They exported the pork and beef packed in brine with which white planters fed their black slaves. Farmers who owned more land than they needed to provide for their families countered the declining productivity of the soil by using the excess to raise livestock for export. Colton probably numbered among them. He got his foot in the door of the West Indies trade and made money by selling West Indian rum wholesale to his cousin Simon, who ran a tavern. Within a few years, Samuel Colton was spending much of his time running a store out of the house his father had built.[30]

Soon, however, his father's house proved too small to contain either Samuel's mercantile business or his ambitions for social standing. In 1753, at age twenty-six, he hired local housewrights and joiners from nearby Connecticut towns to build him a new house. The project took about two years to complete. The builders put up a two-and-a-half-story mansion, with a gambrel roof and spacious halls decorated with dark wainscoting. In 1753 he paid for the sawing and framing of timbers, the carting of stone for the foundation, and the making of brick for chimneys. In April of 1754 Colton paid John Steel for "Bording the Ruf of the house." In May workers did the shingling, and in July joiners Oliver Eason and Parmenus King began to finish

This wooden box, covered with horse or cow hide, might have been made in either America or England.

Colton's house had two rooms on either side of a central hallway on each floor.

the outside work on the side and front of the house. The joiners made Colton an elegant and imposing doorway: a paneled door framed by carved pilasters and capped by a graceful swan's-neck pediment and ornamental rosettes. To set off the entry, Colton spent an extravagant twenty-nine pounds sterling for "Stepstones for my fore door." The result was an impressive entranceway in the Connecticut valley's decorative Georgian style. The house presented an elegant face to Colton's neighbors, announcing its owner's wealth and taste and making many Longmeadow houses seem plain by comparison.[31]

All the while, Colton moved away from farming and toward greater involvement in trade. He held on to his lands, but rented some out to tenants and left work on most of the rest to hired laborers. His own time was increasingly devoted to commerce: making connections in foreign markets, establishing a source of credit in Boston, and mastering the intricacies of shipping, marketing, and finance. His house reflected Colton's commitment to trade: it included a large shop in the ell along the rear, with fireplace, shelves, and "forty sashes" in front of the shelves for light and display. When Colton moved into the house in 1755, a bachelor of twenty-seven, the store marked him as primarily a merchant.[32] Twenty years later, it would be the site of the late night raid.

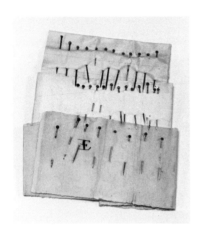

Pins, simple but necessary commodities, brought many women to stores like Colton's.

Building a house may also have reflected Colton's intention of starting his own family, but Samuel moved much more slowly into matrimony than he had into merchandising. Business took his time and attention through his twenties. At age thirty-two, he was half-a-dozen years older than the average New England bridegroom when he married Flavia Colton, the daughter of his wealthy cousin Simon. When she took Samuel's hand, Flavia was eighteen years old—four or five years younger than the typical New England bride. She was also six or seven months pregnant, but in that she was more conventional. Late in the century in some New England towns, as many as two-thirds of all brides were pregnant at their weddings. Such early pregnancies were not completely acceptable, but neither were they scandalous. Sadly, the Coltons' marriage proved ill-fated; Flavia's child died two days after birth, and only three years later Flavia died as well. There is little to suggest the texture or feeling of the relationship or its importance in Samuel Colton's life, but he did not marry again for several years. When he did, he chose kin once again. In 1765 he married Lucy Colton, Flavia's cousin.[33]

Lucy became full-time manager of the household and, on occasion, part-time manager of the store. She had eight pregnancies and bore four children who lived to maturity. She managed a household that contained many people besides her husband and offspring. Slaves and hired farmhands lived in the house. Other people boarded with the Coltons while they rented some of the merchant's farmland. Artisans sometimes stayed with the family while they produced for the household. Caesar, probably a free black, spent two months with the Coltons making bottoms for chairs. Moses Pane lived in while he mended the family shoes. Late in one of Lucy's pregnancies, Susana Chandler joined the household, spinning cotton thread and probably helping with the new baby. William Hancock boarded with the merchant for over a year while he rented the use of Colton's blacksmith shop and anvil. Samuel's nephew moved in to learn bookkeeping from Samuel's cousin. Both relatives paid their keep by clerking at the store. The patriarch of the household, "Marchant" Samuel Colton presided over a substantial domain.[34]

In the 1750s and 1760s, the Colton store became a center of eco-

Within the print:

How blest the Maid whose bosom no headstrong passion knows,
Her days in Joy she Passes, her nights in soft repose.

KEEP WITHIN — BE SURE. TO AVOID MANY TROUBLES. WHICH OTHERS INDURE: KEEP WITHIN COMPASS. AND YOU SHALL — COMPASS

A Virtuous Woman is a Crown to her Husband.

ENTER NOT INTO THE WAY OF THE WICKED, AND GO NOT IN THE PATH OF EVIL MEN.

This contemporary English print advised women to live carefully and discreetly and to "Keep Within Compass." Its message reflects a double standard in sexual matters: during courtship, restraint was the duty of the woman more than the man.

Below: brass candle snuffer.

The eighteenth-century merchant kept his invoices, bills of lading, and accounting records in his desk, a piece of furniture that was as important for storage as for writing. Although many men and some women were literate, few people besides merchants needed desks, commonly using tables for writing surfaces instead.

nomic and social activity in Longmeadow, attracting customers from numerous neighboring towns. Colton stocked it with a wide array of items. He continued to provide his cousin Simon with rum at wholesale, but the greater part of his business was in retail. Success depended on supplying a large number of customers, each of whom bought relatively few items at the store. Colton's account book yields a picture of the nature and extent of his local business. Colton sold "a setting out," including "punch bowles," to Esther Farrington. Daniel Burbank spent money on a looking glass and an "Almanack." Lydia Hitchcock traveled from Brimfield to buy cambric and "sowing needles." Westfield inhabitant Ezekiel Fosdick purchased a "tub of butter and sundries." Experience Hancock wanted some "shugar," as well as a "porringer and earrings." Longmeadow's Congregational minister, Stephen Willams, paid Colton twelve shillings for shoe buckles and also bought "two gallons of rhum" and some tobacco plants. Deliverance Atchenson got some "rub stones" for honing knives and a snuffbox. Hannah Parker bought some whalebone and a string of beads to wear. Eunice Hale bought "ribin" and "½ thousand pins." The widow Chandler rode up from Enfield for knee buckles, a silk tie, and some "camfire." And a lot of farmers needed plows and other tools and wanted such West Indian goods as rum and sugar.[35]

Colton received very little cash for his sales. Most people paid the merchant with home products and surplus from their farms. Colton accepted corn, wheat, flaxseed, tobacco, beef, and pork for his goods. He took dried apples and shipped them to the West Indies. He took payment in flax and sent it to Britain. Nathaniel Ely once paid him 4,380 barrel staves, which Colton probably sent to the sugar islands. A less well-to-do customer paid him with a "musksquosh skin" and a pair of "blue yarn socks." Many of Colton's neighbors exchanged their labor for store goods. He paid the carpenters who built his house in credit at his store, and other artisans received payment in the same way. He could use goods in the store to enlist agricultural laborers to work his lands and to pay teamsters and canoers for packing and hauling cargoes.[36]

Most of Colton's customers must have regarded their dealings with the merchant the same way they regarded dealings with one another. They gave their own surplus produce or labor for what they wanted. They had little need for cash. If they wanted rum in March but would not have wheat to pay for it until later in the year, they could count on Colton to extend them credit. If they worked on Colton's farm at harvest, they could take payment in store goods through the following year. Their indebtedness to him, or his to them, never seemed different from their debts to each other. Indeed, the merchant did not seem very different from them, for they all knew him outside his role as storeowner. To many, he was also a relative, fellow church member, or friend. For them, dealing with Samuel Colton was neighborly dealing.[37]

Yet Colton's situation differed from that of his neighbors. As a merchant, he produced little; instead, he transported the products of others from place to place. Unlike his neighbors, he had direct business relationships with people far outside the Longmeadow area. He did a lot of business with Boston merchants, who supplied his store with imported European goods. Colton acquired two ocean-going ships, the *Speedwell* and the *Friendship*, that ranged beyond Boston and

American potters produced inexpensive and practical stonewares and earthenwares for use in American homes. Mugs, pots, jugs, porringers, and other vessels were often sold in merchants' stores.

involved him in economic relationships outside Massachusetts. On one voyage, for example, the *Friendship* carried hoops and staves for barrel making to the West Indies, and took on spices, sugar, rum, and molasses. From the Caribbean the ship sailed to Bristol, England, where it exchanged part of its tropical cargo for earthenware, nails, and glass. It returned by way of Portsmouth, New Hampshire, to leave off some of these items for retail before it finally sailed south past Boston, around to the Connecticut River, and home.[38]

At the *Friendship*'s every port of call, Colton had business connections. Some of those might have grown out of family ties; sister Margaret and her husband had moved near to Portsmouth and might have put Samuel in touch with retailers there. But at other ports, Colton depended on more professional relationships in which neighborly norms did not apply. A Boston merchant might extend Colton credit, but that was not at all the same thing as the personal trust with which the Longmeadow merchant accommodated his neighbors. The

A set of measures represents only a few pounds out of the hundreds of tons of pewter Americans imported from England each year.

local lender routinely listed his customers' obligations in his ledgers without interest for years; the merchant in the metropolis assessed his Connecticut valley correspondent 6 percent annually.[39]

So Colton became a middleman between his customers and a world that included West Indian planters, African slaves, Irish linen makers, English earthenware manufacturers, and Boston creditors. Because of that, he could not draw the line at importing goods. He began importing different sorts of economic relationships and rules for exchange. He started charging interest on unpaid accounts at the store: 5½ to 6 percent on small accounts, 6 to 6½ percent on larger ones. He came to press for payment in cash, since it let him pay his own creditors most directly and gave flexibility to his affairs. In his account books he wrote instructions for his clerks to follow: "If not paid quickly, charge more," he put next to one account. "If paid in cash, make some allowance," he wrote next to another. By his own involvement, Colton brought his customers into greater participation in the practices of the Atlantic market.[40]

Such activity benefitted many. Colton offered his neighbors desir-

Innovations in technology, work organization, and marketing revolutionized the British ceramics industry in the eighteenth century. The result was an outpouring of moderately priced, as well as expensive, refined earthenwares and stonewares.

On these two pages are shown a variety of imported wares: a creamware mustard pot and (with spout) coffee pot, a plate of white salt-glazed stoneware, and tin-glazed earthenware plates with Oriental, floral, and geometric designs.

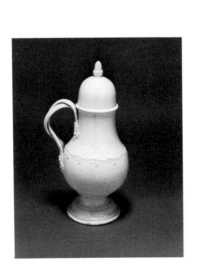

able items they could not get locally. Many women preferred buying cloth to the constant task of spinning, for example. And access to the West Indies market for livestock allowed Connecticut valley farmers to keep their heads above water even though their land was wearing out. But participation in the market also had its costs. One was loss of local control, as they all grew more dependent on distant economies, markets, and events. If the demand for molasses rose in England, or the price of slaves fell, Samuel Colton felt it—and so did his customers. Colton brought his customers into dependence on strangers, people not susceptible to the influence of the local church or neighborhood. Merchants in Boston did not need to worry about their reputation in Longmeadow. People in the West Indies or Britain would not be bound by the Springfield town meeting.[41]

Few New Englanders thought through the meaning of these developments. There is no evidence that Longmeadow area residents complained about (or even fully understood) their increasing inability to control their own economic destinies. Yet the trend toward greater dependence persisted. Up and down the river valley, families worried about the shrinking acreage of their farms and the diminishing productivity of their fields. Some stood by as their children left for fresh land in distant frontier settlements. Others watched helplessly as their children, left landless, ended up working for wages on someone else's farm. And all the while they saw some men, like Samuel Colton, grow more and more wealthy. Colton bought up other people's farms and, by the end of his life, owned land in Enfield, Somers, Ludlow, and Wilbraham as well as in Longmeadow. He may have joined others among the well-to-do in speculating in unsettled lands, driving prices up and threatening to close off opportunities for others. Inescapably, colonists in the Connecticut River valley saw the gap between rich and poor growing wider. Yearly they encountered larger numbers of "strolling poor," transients without permanent attachments to any town at all. Americans recognized that their society was becoming less equal—and more like hierarchical England and Europe.[42]

Not all these developments could be blamed on men like Samuel Colton, but some of them could. In the middle decades of the century, Americans saw a growth in unfettered greed, a decline in the sense of mutual obligation that many ascribed to the effects of commerce. Americans' fear of losing an accustomed control, local and collective, over their own lives was an important part of what took them into revolution against Britain in the 1770s. It was also an important part of what made a crowd of Longmeadow citizens break into Samuel Colton's store on a midsummer night in 1776.[43]

*P*eople in the Connecticut River valley were slow to become involved in the patriot movement that led to revolution against Britain. In the 1760s, agitation over imperial relations remained largely confined to Boston and other eastern maritime centers. But during the 1770s,

residents of Springfield and other valley towns began to listen to the arguments of patriot leaders.[44]

Three aspects of the patriot argument convinced many that the dispute with England was relevant to their own lives. First, Britain seemed to have forgotten the rules of mutual dealing and common concern. For years the British Parliament had regulated the trade of the colonies—forbidding commerce with foreign nations and the use of foreign ships, for example—but generally such restrictions had advantages for English and Americans alike. Since 1764, Britain had taken a new tack; Parliament placed customs duties on colonial imports solely for the purpose of raising revenue for the British Treasury. As many colonists saw it, the English proposed a tax to skim the profits off the top of American earnings. British taxpayers might benefit, but colonial traders and consumers would suffer. By levying taxes, it seemed, England was pursuing its own interest rather than considering the welfare of the empire as a whole.[45]

It made matters worse that Americans had no way to make their objections to English policy heard. Every year Massachusetts towns elected representatives to their own colonial legislature, the General

English entrepreneur Josiah Wedgwood perfected creamware during the 1760s. He produced a dinner service for Queen Charlotte, then called the ware "Queensware," which appealed to a status-conscious clientele in both Britain and America.

Court in Boston. Ordinary voters did not have much say in the policies set by the Court, but if their representatives passed measures that seemed harmful or unfair, voters could express their disapproval and, if worst came to worst, elect someone else to change things. By contrast, not a single member of Parliament had to worry about American votes. Members of Parliament lived an ocean away from Massachusetts, and they could hardly feel any loyalty to or neighborly concern for distant colonists. The men in Parliament were strangers, and it was dangerous to let English strangers vote away American money.[46] Said one patriot pamphleteer: "Those who are governed at the will of another . . . and whose property may be taken from them by taxes, or otherwise, without their own consent, and against their will, are in the miserable condition of slaves."[47] Parliament could not tax the colonies, patriots said, because it did not represent them. That was a fundamental principle of the British Constitution; if that constitution consisted of customary practices rather than a written agreement, it seemed no less binding for that. In petitions to England and in pamphlets written for their fellow colonists, the patriots repeated this vital principle: If Parliament's taxes were unconstitutional, then resisting their enforcement was no crime.[48]

Finally, some Americans thought the heart of the problem lay not in Britain but in the colonies themselves. Wasn't it reliance on imported goods—satins and silks, tea and chocolate—that made Americans vulnerable to English greed to begin with? After all, Parliament's customs duties wouldn't hurt if Americans could learn to do without. And wasn't it only hunger for fancy imported baubles and pretensions to English "style" that made Americans prefer expensive imported goods to the plain but honest products that could be made at home? Too many Americans, the argument ran, displayed the same self-seeking and ambition that led Parliament to tax the colonists. Too many sought gain while their neighbors tightened their belts. Too many had closer ties to Great Britain than to the communities in which they lived.[49]

In defense of American liberties, patriots petitioned Parliament and began organizing their own neighbors. They urged colonists to stop importing goods. English merchants and manufacturers would be

Coarse shoes made of leather or fabric were made in Massachusetts households, but silk shoes such as these had to be imported from England or, possibly, Philadelphia.

Another sign of gentility was a decorative snuffbox, like the one shown below, filled with the fashionable addiction of the day.

New England metalworkers made goods for sale locally or regionally. They marketed their wares directly from their shops, through traveling traders, and through storekeepers like Samuel Colton.

Pictured here are a pewter pitcher, a brass brazier with wood handle and scalloped rim, a copper bed warmer, and a pewter close-stool pan.

hurt by a boycott, and those powerful interests might lobby Parliament to repeal offending laws. Equally important, ending trade would decrease Americans' dependence on the British by stimulating home manufactures. Boycotts would have the double virtue of affecting British policy and changing American lives.[50]

The patriots enjoyed some success with the boycott, but by early in the 1770s it was clear that they were failing to change Parliament's determination to tax. Meanwhile, in the colonies, the unity so essential to successful boycotts proved in short supply. The "Sons of Liberty" and other crowds used intimidation to make dissenters join in. The very need for such measures seemed to prove the patriots right. The Boston Tea Party was necessary only because, tax or no tax, some Americans would have bought imported tea. Some apparently cared more about having such luxuries than defending the rights of their community.[51]

Parliament's response to the Tea Party moved American resistance to a new level and roused towns in the Connecticut River valley into action. To punish Boston, Parliament voted to close down the harbor, abolish the Massachusetts General Court, and outlaw most town meetings. Throughout the colony, towns responded with outrage. In Springfield, voters announced themselves ready to join any "reasonable pact" for ending trade with Great Britain. In the summer of 1774, the thirteen colonies sent delegates to a Continental Congress in Philadelphia to formulate such an agreement.[52]

Like earlier boycotts, the Congress's Continental Association aimed at hurting England and at charting an alternative plan for American society. The Congress set a date for merchants to stop importing and for everyone else to leave off using British goods. Traders might sell their stock on hand, but they shouldn't raise prices as imports became more scarce. Meanwhile, artisans and farmers should be busy at their labors. Farmers could raise sheep for wool, housewives could spin it into thread, and weavers could turn it into cloth. People could drink home-brew instead of East India Company teas. Rather than rely on overseas commerce, colonists should rely on their neighbors and themselves. The Association encouraged mutual sacrifice for the public good. It was an exercise of "public virtue"—it banned rituals that people associated with the pretensions of English and American upper classes: tea drinking, of course, but also horse racing, gambling, and even fancy funerals. It called on Americans to back out of the Atlantic market and develop local production and trade.[53]

People in Longmeadow and the rest of Springfield were active in joining the Association. The town elected a Committee of Inspection to see that everyone complied with the boycott. Ordinary citizens outside the committee also watched over their neighbors to see that they followed the rules. They made sure that no one drank tea. They made sure that no merchant imported goods or raised prices on imports already on hand. They reported violators to the committee,

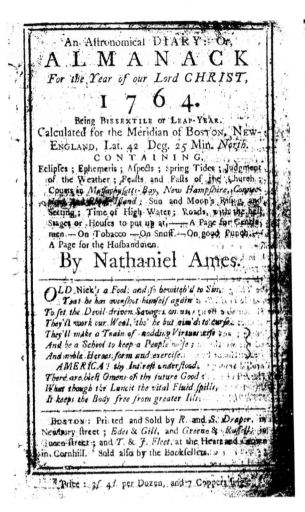

New Englanders consulted yearly almanacs to learn about the weather and the rising and setting of sun and moon, and to find aphorisms, moral advice, and, occasionally, political opinions.

which in turn confronted the accused and threatened to publish their names in the newspaper if they did not reform. Meanwhile, some men drilled with the local militia. In the spring of 1775, news came from the east that fighting had broken out between British and Americans at Lexington and Concord. Minutemen, under the command of Andrew Colton, marched off to support the patriot side. Men barred from military service by age or inclination helped the war effort by collecting supplies for the army, or serving on the committees that debated political policy, or paying for clothing and blankets and guns. Women, barred by gender from military service, took over men's

THE WAR AT HOME

work in farms and stores, made clothing for soldiers, and sacrificed in countless ways to support the cause.[54]

From most of this activity, Samuel Colton held himself aloof. He served the town in the early 1770s, sitting on the precinct committee to take care of local business and on a committee "to seat the meeting house," a job that required fine social judgment, since it involved assigning people to pews according to their standing in Longmeadow. But the merchant took little part in the resistance movement that was unfolding around him. He could hardly welcome a movement that opposed international trade, that sought to replace reliance on imports with reliance on American goods. And like most "River Gods" in the valley, Colton had little sympathy for a movement that promoted popular political activity instead of leaving control in the hands of wealthy and prominent men.[55]

Conservatives throughout the colony objected to the Association's committee politics. As a Loyalist woman described the situation, "The resolves of the Continental Congress are now executing in the several Provinces, and political inquisitors are appointed in each town to pry into the conduct of individuals." Even worse, men and women not on committees were prying too. In nearby Worcester County, where upper-class leaders opposed the Association, fifty-two blacksmiths pledged to withhold their labor from anyone who failed to sign it. In the town of Wrentham, near Boston, a crowd of 400 to 500 people gathered outside the house of a man known for buying tea and intim-

At some funerals of the well-to-do, bereaved families gave memorial jewelry to friends and relatives of the deceased. The giving of funeral rings was banned by the Continental Congress as part of the colonies' boycott of English imports and disavowal of "extravagance" in 1774.

97897

LIBRARY
COLBY-SAWYER COLLEGE
NEW LONDON, N.H. 03257

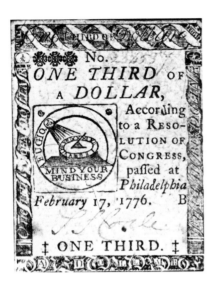

Coins from many nations circulated in the American colonies. Yet specie got drained away to pay debts to British merchants, so colonial and revolutionary governments issued paper bills.

idated him into a public promise to reform. Similar "Mobs and popular Tumults" occurred throughout the province.[56]

In Longmeadow, the conservative minister Stephen Williams wrote in his diary: "I understand that this wild Spirit of liberty (as tis called) prevails & Spreads and insults are offered to one and another that are branded Tories. . . . When will people be wise—when will they be prudent?" His fortune, social position, and involvement in international trade encouraged Samuel Colton to share Williams's opinions. Colton ridiculed the "Furious Zeal" with which patriots enforced the Association. He dismissed as absurd the idea that everyone who drank a cup of tea was a Tory. As some people in Longmeadow saw it, Colton "early shewed an unfriendly Disposition to the Liberties of his Country." As Colton himself put it, he was not "liberty mad" like his neighbors.[57]

In Springfield and other towns, some merchants who opposed the boycott simply shut up shop. Some left off trade for the rest of the war. Colton apparently stopped importing during the boycott, as required. Then, when resistance turned to revolution in 1775, the patriots scrapped their trade embargo in order to procure goods to feed, clothe, and arm the military. Colton's reservations about liberty did not prevent him from taking advantage of the new economic opportunities. He sold a ton of rye flour and tobacco to the American army camped at Cambridge. He dealt with patriot governments, as he later boasted, extensively and often on credit. No one begrudged the merchant a profit on these exchanges. Yet some of his neighbors did resent it when he began to exploit wartime shortages of domestic necessities. In 1775 Colton raised the price on "Liver Oyl," prompting customers to accuse him of a lack of patriotism.[58]

The Springfield Committee of Inspection investigated, but was

divided on the matter. Nathaniel Brewer and Edward Chapin, members of the committee from Longmeadow, thought Colton was opposing the patriot cause. Apparently committeemen from Springfield disagreed, because Colton got away with it. In 1776, encouraged by his success, Colton took a fatal step: he raised the prices on West Indian goods—sugar, salt, molasses, and rum.[59]

As the merchant was quick to point out, he was not the only trader in the area to raise his prices. A new Committee of Inspection had been elected in May, one lacking both Brewer and Chapin and so possibly more sympathetic to the priorities of merchants. But if official committee members looked the other way, other townspeople still objected. The Association might no longer strictly hold, but the values it embodied remained important. Americans were not supposed to be lining their own pockets. Moreover, to pay for the war, American governments had recently issued paper bills, whose value rested on general confidence in the success of patriot arms. British agents actively worked to undercut the money's buying power by counterfeiting it. British sympathizers took the bills at a discount when they took them at all. The bills were depreciating, so raising prices helped the other side. According to some of Colton's would-be customers, he refused to sell West Indian goods except for hard money, which would not depreciate in value. By doing so, he demonstrated that his primary concern was for profit, and flaunted his disdain for the cause and for his neighbors' opinions.[60]

On July 11, 1776, Stephen Williams recorded the upshot in his diary: "A number of people . . . manifested uneasiness with those that trade in rum, molasses, & sugar &c.," he wrote. The crowd explained their anger in a note to the firm of Jonathan and Hezekiah Hale:

Sirs: it is a matter of great grief that you should give us cause to call upon you in this uncommon way. Every man whose actions are unfriendly to the comon Cause of our country ought to be convinced of his wrong behaviour and made to reform, or treated as an open enemy. We find you guilty of very wrong behaviour in selling at extravagant prices, particularly West Indian Goods. This conduct plainly tends to undervalue paper Currency which is very detrimental to the Liberties of America. We therefore as your offended Brethren demand satisfaction of you the offender by a confession for your past conduct and a Thorough reformation for time to Come.

In the future, the crowd concluded, the Hales should not exceed equitable prices: six shillings for a gallon of rum, three shillings for a gallon of molasses, ninepence for a pound of sugar, and six shillings for a bushel of salt. The Hales had an hour to think it over. When the crowd returned for their answer, the merchants prudently decided to give in. Samuel Colton, who also received an ultimatum about lowering prices, decided differently.[61]

In response, a crowd took possession of Colton's goods and stored them in a barn nearby. When the merchant suddenly relented and promised to abide by their price limitations, the crowd returned what they had seized. Colton seems to have made a public apology on this occasion: the merchant said later that he had arranged "a compromise"; the Reverend Mr. Williams wrote that the merchant "made a prayr in publick." But even the minister had doubts about Colton's sincerity: "Oh Lord Give to us as a community to *forsake* Sin as well as *confess* it," he added.[62]

Indeed, the merchant's change of heart proved all too temporary. A few days later, he raised prices again. Impatient with "moderate measures," the Longmeadow crowd laid their plans, blacked their faces, and broke into the Colton store to set matters right.[63]

Predictably, Stephen Williams disapproved of the raid. "I don't see the justice or equity of it," he wrote, and he thought that some other townspeople shared his view. But nobody did much about it, and it was not very clear what there might have been to do. Crowds had closed down the courts of justice, because the courts represented the English king and Parliament's laws, so Colton could not take the case to court. He did appeal to the Springfield Committee of Inspection, who sympathized with his plight and "adviz'd to an immediate restitution of the Goods." When the raiders ignored that advice, Colton referred the case to a convention of local committees meeting in nearby Northampton. The convention, he later claimed, urged the raiders to return his possessions and "to abstain from all Violation and Invasion of private Property" in the future. But Longmeadow raiders did not

The several Printers throughout the United States are requested to insert this notice, and continue it in their papers six weeks.

—————

A HINT.

THIS country has been reduced to the brink of ruin by the infamous practices of Monopolizers and Forestallers. They have lately monopolized the STAFF of LIFE. Hence the universal cry of the scarcity and high price of WHEAT, RYE INDIAN-CORN, FUEL, &c. It has been found in Britain and France, that the people have always done themselves justice when the scarcity of Bread has arisen from the avarice of Forestallers. They have broke open magazines—appropriated stores to their own use without paying for them—and in some instances have hung up the Culprits who have created their distress, without judge or jury. Hear this and tremble, ye enemies to the freedom and happiness of your country. Hunger will break through Stone-Walls, and the resentment excited by it may end in your destruction.   MOBILITY.

ENOUGH to get here from the Coast of Spain.

Likewise, 15 Bags of Pepper Dust; a Quantity Litharge of Lead, 16 Pieces of Cannon, one and two pounders.

—————

TO THE PUBLIC.

WHEREAS some infernal Liar, and Enemy to me, with a view to Injure my Character, has most wickedly propagated that I the Subscriber lately offer'd in Salem for a Quantity of Coffee, 3s. per lb. with a design to Monopolize that Article, and thereby enhance the Price, I declare the Assertion to be False, and that I've made no offer for that Commodity, neither have I convers'd with any Person whatever respecting it.

I offer a Reward of FIFTY DOLLARS to any Person who will inform me who this Slanderer is, that I may have an opportunity (if he has his Deserts) of bringing him to that Post, to which he (as I suppose) had impudence to Nail my Sign.   MARTIN BICKER.

Boston, 21 April, 1777.

—————

NOTICE is hereby given, That Thomas Rogerson, a Molatto Lad, who was some Time ago taken in a Vessel from the West-Indies, has Permission granted by the Governor and Council at Providence, to pass from Bristol to Newport, that he may Return to his Friends——

care what committees or conventions said. After all, the weight of local opinion (if not authority) was on the raiders' side.[64]

Moreover, even patriot authorities were divided over the principles of the Colton case. As prices rose throughout 1776, towns expressed their belief that Congress "intended that no unreasonable advantage should be taken" in transactions, and that "all should be sold upon reasonable terms." Early in 1777, the new Massachusetts government, now consisting of town representatives without a royally appointed governor, seemed to confirm that idea. In January the state passed a law to set price ceilings for goods and labor. The limit for rum was two shillings per quart; the limit for beans, six shillings per bushel; the limit for tow cloth, two shillings threepence per yard—and the list went on and on. In Northampton, thirty-eight valley towns met to establish uniform prices throughout the county and urged the suppression of Tories who used their "utmost endeavors" to destroy the value of state and continental money. Henceforth profits in Longmeadow would be limited by law. In his business Samuel Colton would

In the resistance movement against England, newspapers spread ideas and named the names of loyalists. During the war, they aroused patriots to action against those who monopolized goods in order to raise prices.

Patriots used images as well as arguments to win Americans over to their cause. In "Boston Cannonaded," first published in London, the British ministry, armed with the Port Bill that closed Boston harbor, forces tea down Boston's throat.

have to defer to the needs of the war effort and the needs of his neighbors.[65]

There was little for Colton to do except let the matter of the raid drop. He pursued his private business and nursed his sense of injury for several years. Toward the end of the 1770s, Massachusetts gave up setting prices by law. With the courts about to reopen, the raiders stood in danger. Late in 1780, Colton prepared to sue the raiders for the theft of his goods.[66]

The leaders of the raid—Nathaniel Ely, Azariah Woolworth, and Festus Colton—appealed to the state government to grant them im-

munity from prosecution. Both sides to the dispute made their case to the General Court in writing. Colton and the raiders gave somewhat different accounts of the break-in. Both sides defended their own motives and impugned the motives of the other. Colton and his neighbors differed most profoundly over two related points: they had different ideas about the rules of trade; correspondingly, they had different interpretations of the Revolution itself.

As the merchant saw things, he was the victim of theft, clear and simple; "there was no Colour for the People at large Interposing and in this violent outragious Manner Depriving any man of his Property." Colton explained why he had raised the price on liver oil in 1774. During the months of the nonconsumption pact he had stored the oil, and some of it had leaked or wasted away. The obvious thing to do was to recover his losses by passing them on to consumers. The merchant did not bother to give his reasons for hiking the price on West Indies imports. He merely said that the "stipulated PRICE" demanded by the crowd was too low. He did not see how his raising prices excused the raid. He had merely followed "the ordinary course of . . . business."[67]

But the raiders insisted that it was not fair for Colton to take advantage of his neighbors' needs. It was true that they had led a crowd of townspeople and seized Colton's goods, but they had taken his property to prevent him from using it "in such a Manner as essentially to injure the whole." Colton had preferred his own private profit to the welfare of the community. Private property had its rights, but it still had to yield to the larger good.[68]

The principles of the Revolution were vital to the raiders' case, for those principles distinguished the raid from an ordinary crime. "All Power having originated from the Body of the People," it followed that the people could act in their own defense. In times of crisis, power "reverted back to its Source and Fountain." Although at times the people delegated authority to committees, at other times they acted for themselves. In Longmeadow, the people had acted "to hinder some Members of the Community from acting contrary to the General Welfare just as their Humor or Malice should direct." Regulating Colton's prices was consistent with the Revolution.[69]

Colton could hardly say that he thought the Revolution itself was regrettable, but he did dismiss the early war years as a time of "madness and Extravagances," of "mobs and tumults." His main claim was that the Revolution was irrelevant to understanding the raid. He hotly denied all charges of Toryism; he had never hoped that the British would win. His decisions about prices were not political. They came "from *interested* motives rather than from a Principle of Enmity and Opposition to the American Cause." He had not favored the British, but only favored himself.[70]

There was the crux of it. From the outset the patriot movement had joined together two components. Patriots wanted to defend American property against parliamentary taxes. At the same time, they fought for the ideal—traditional, and now revolutionary—that the good of the whole community should outweigh individuals' narrow desire for profit. What made Colton "unfriendly" was his commitment to profit, even at a time of general hardship. Colton's defense—that he had only "continued in the ordinary course" of his business, that he hadn't even considered politics—didn't make sense. To many, "the ordinary course of . . . business" was exactly the problem. In charging him with Toryism, the raiders did not claim that Colton had rooted for the British; they claimed he had acted like a merchant instead of a neighbor.

Two members of the Springfield Committee wrote to ask the government to support Samuel Colton's case. They had not participated in nor approved of the raid in Longmeadow. On the other side, 126 people from Longmeadow "and Places adjacent thereto" signed a petition attesting to the truth of Ely's, Woolworth's, and Festus Colton's description of events. The petitioners included sixteen Coltons and many of the merchant's associates. The state government may have been convinced by the numbers, or by the fact that Colton could find support only from people outside his own village. Or perhaps it was too soon for state legislators to forget that, in the eyes of many of their constituents, "the madness and Extravangances" of the early war years expressed values central to the Revolution. In February 1781, the General Court voted to indemnify the raiders against Samuel Colton's lawsuits.[71]

The state's decision fed the merchant's bitterness toward his neighbors. He continued to run his store, but Lucy Colton took over more and more of the work. Soon after the state's decision about the raid, Colton was overtaken by illness. His account books show that palsy increasingly affected his writing. He died in 1784, leaving Lucy to manage the store until her own death fifteen years later. Colton left one of the most valuable estates of any Springfield resident, but in a sense he died in defeat. His state and his neighbors had judged against him.[72]

The issue of the Longmeadow raid was not really settled in the

"A Prospective View of the Town of Boston," published in that city in 1770, portrays a town of church steeples and international commerce.

1780s. Colton was only one of many Americans who had reservations about liberty. After his death, men of Colton's sort would gain increasing power in the state and nation. They were conservative men, well-to-do, and more concerned with accumulating property than with neighborly dealing. At the same time, other Americans held on to the ideas that had given meaning to their participation in the Revolution. Many continued to believe that individuals had obligations to their neighbors that should come before the dictates of private interest and marketplace. After the Revolution, Americans continued to struggle over the line between the rights of property and the liberty of the community.[73]

THE FARM AND THE MARKETPLACE

The Springer Household of Mill Creek, Delaware

If it were not for a band of English kidnappers, people named Springer might never have lived in Delaware. Born into a prominent Swedish family in 1658, Carl Springer was an unwilling immigrant to the New World. He grew up in Stockholm, studied in Riga, then traveled to London to further his education under the guidance of the Swedish minister. He had nearly completed his work in English and arithmetic when, late in the 1670s, he was abducted and shipped to Virginia. As he later remembered the experience: "I was kidnapped and, against my will, taken aboard an English ship. And against my will I was carried to America, in the West Indies, to Virginia. And when I got there I was sold off like a farm animal that is driven to market. Thus I was sold, to labor, and held in very slavery. . . ."[1]

The temporary "slavery" that Virginia imposed on Swedes and other Europeans differed markedly from the lifelong slavery the colony imposed on Africans, but for Carl Springer, a five-year term as an indentured servant still proved hard to bear. The work, he later said, was "unspeakable" and the Virginia climate devastating. "In summer it was *Extra Ordinary* hot during the day, and my work was mostly in the winter, clearing land and cutting down the forest and making it ready for planting *Tobacco* and the Indian grain in the summer. I had a very hard master. . . ." When he gained his freedom in 1683, he heard rumor of a settlement of Swedes living along the Delaware River in the English colony of "Pensellvenia." With little in his pockets but anxious to put Virginia behind him, Springer set out on foot to travel four hundred miles to the north.[2]

The community that welcomed him had been established for forty years. In the 1630s, investors in the "New Sweden Company" had built a fur trading outpost called Fort Christina a few miles from the Delaware River. Swedish settlers followed in the 1640s. Within a generation, both the fur trade and the colony had been taken over twice—first by the Dutch in the 1650s, then by the English a decade later. Despite their changing fortunes, the Swedes had cut away the forests and planted farms along the riverbanks. They chose farming rather than "traffick," according to William Penn, and preferred to make "enough rather than plenty." When Springer arrived in 1684 there were roughly a thousand people of Swedish descent living in fewer than two hundred households in the Delaware valley.[3]

Carl Springer quickly put down roots in the community. He became a founder, warden, and vestryman of its central institution, Holy Trinity (Old Swedes') Church. He took up land in the area, married a local woman, and established himself as a yeoman farmer. He wrote to his mother describing his success: "I have two plantations that I have bought, and on one of them I live, and plough and plant, sowing all kinds of seed during the year. I also have livestock for the needs of my household, and so live, thank God, that I and mine suffer no want."[4]

Not every Swede did so well on the Delaware: if Carl Springer owned two plantations, someone else unable to afford land probably lived as a tenant on one of them. Yet Springer did not define success solely in terms of the economic well-being of his own household. He also cared about the spiritual life of his family and his countrypeople. He devoted time, money, and labor to the construction and welfare of Old Swedes' Church. For five years after the colonists' minister died, Springer read sermons to his brethren and led in singing psalms.[5] In 1693 he wrote to Sweden asking for Bibles, catechisms, and other Swedish readers, and stressing the colonists' desire for a Swedish pastor. He described both the bounty of the American land and the colonists' fidelity to Swedish ways:

Wee are for the most part husbandmen, and plow and sowe and Till th[e] ground, and wee use yet the good ould fashions in meate and drink; this Land is a mighty fruitfull good and plentifull Contry and here doth growe all sorts of grains in greate plenty; and this River, out of it is sent and shipt away all sorts of grains every yeare . . . , and heare is also great plenty of all sorts, beasts, fowls and fishes; and our wifes and daughters follow spinning of flax and wool, some with weaving, so that we have great occasion to thanck the Almighty God for his manyfold mercies and benefits. . . . We also live in peace, friendship, and amity with one an other. . . ."[6]

Amity was no easy accomplishment. Governed by the English proprietor William Penn, and living alongside Dutch and English settlers, the Swedes struggled to maintain a distinct identity and way of

Ships brought immigrants, European goods, and "the freshest advices," or news, to the New World. Colonial printers used woodcuts of ships to announce recent arrivals in port.

THE FARM AND THE MARKETPLACE

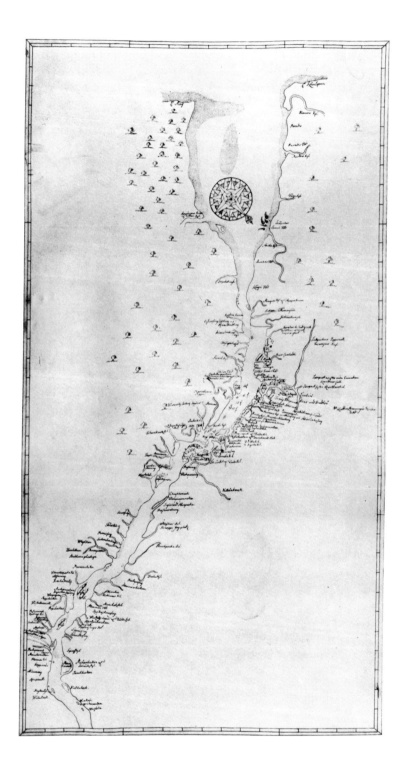

The Swedes' River, or the Delaware, from Swede Peter Lindestrom's Geographia Americae, *compiled between 1654 and 1656. For many years, Europeans held only a toehold in America, living in settlements along the waterways. Mapping the New World was one part of taking possession of the land.*

Slowly, Europeans cut away the great forests of America, taking trees for timber and clearing the land for cultivation.

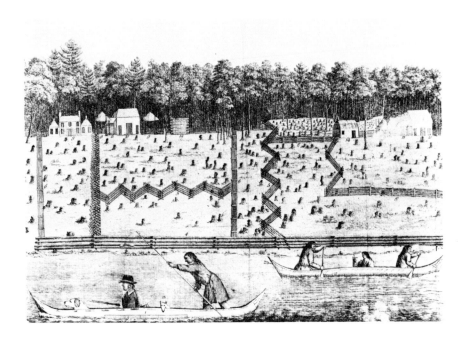

life. No one was more fervent in that struggle than Carl Springer. Despite his cosmopolitan background he held fast to parochial values. When one Swedish minister spent too much of his time preaching in the English churches nearby, Springer registered his objections. Like a great many other settlers in America, he deeply valued ties of common language, background, and culture. Like many others, he sought both material security—the chance to work for himself and his household—and a wider network of social relations to give meaning to his life.[7]

Over the next century, generations of Springers continued in Carl Springer's footsteps, tilling the strong clay soil of New Castle County, tending livestock, and raising families of their own. In many regards, Thomas Springer, who farmed the Mill Creek tract after the Revolution, followed the same way of life that his great-grandfather Carl had established. He too planted "all kinds of seed" and raised animals on a family farm. He too enjoyed material success; by his late thirties, in 1798, he stood in the top 10 percent of all taxpayers who lived in his section of the county. Yet by Thomas's day, the "lower counties" of Pennsylvania Colony had become Delaware State, and society in the river valley community had changed. Swedes no longer formed a tight-knit, separate culture; neither ethnic nor religious ties bound the Springers to many of their neighbors, and forces from an increasingly wider social and economic world shaped the everyday life of Thomas and his household. The Springers' story is the story of a family farm in the midst of change, commerce, and the early stirrings of industrialization.

From his childhood, Thomas Springer's future as a farmer was planned. His father, Charles, already had three sons and a daughter in 1762 when he learned that his wife, Ann, was expecting another child. Charles took his responsibilities as a father seriously: he worked to provide his sons with the skills and the wherewithal to support households of their own, and to provide for his daughter "as girls ought to be reasonably done by," with a dowry in expectation of marriage or a sufficiency to survive in the household of a relative while single. Parents passed on property in a number of forms: linen, furniture, and other household goods, livestock, tools, and black slaves. Yet above all else, the property that mattered in Delaware was land. Accordingly, Charles laid his plans for his fourth son, Thomas, even before the child was born. In 1762, he purchased 170 acres of farmland along the "westerly bank" of Mill Creek and a "parcel of Marsh land" nearby. When Ann delivered a baby boy, Charles set the Mill Creek tract aside for his son's future use.[8]

Thomas learned from his father the skills he would eventually need to run his own farm. He learned about the needs of the land, the care of horses, sheep, and cows, and the growing cycles of different crops. Thomas watched his father deal with millers, artisans, and storekeepers. As he developed specific skills, he also began to form expectations for his own future life. Someday he would be working his own land, building his own household, and establishing his own independence.

Gaining that independence took a little time. Thomas was the fourth in line and had to wait for his three brothers to be "settled off" on their own land. Each brother's departure left more work on the

Settlers built rough roads for cart and wagon travel. Most farmers could make their own wagon bodies but needed an experienced wheelwright or blacksmith to produce the undercarriage and wheels.

Wheelwrights used a "traveler" like the one below to measure the circumference of a wheel, choosing the heaviest wood available to make wheels strong enough to withstand ruts, rocks, and tree roots.

farm to those who remained. Dependent on his children's labor, Charles, now in his fifties, might have been somewhat reluctant to let his last son leave the family farm. When Thomas reached the age of twenty-one, in 1785, he was still living in his parents' house. For the next several years he worked on his father's farm but probably claimed part of his time to devote to improvements on the Mill Creek tract. He may have cleared and even planted some land on the tract. Sometime in the 1780s he built a simple log building (or "tenement") there, and perhaps a small log barn to house a few animals.[9]

We don't know if Thomas begrudged the time he spent working for his parents, but it was normal for rural people to start out working for family or for someone else. Fathers with land routinely kept title to much of their property until death, making sure they would be secure in old age. Other fathers lacked the resources to provide for all their offspring. So, most rural children expected to spend their twenties working at home, as tenants on another's land, or as paid laborers in the household of an established farmer, trying to accumulate enough money to buy land of their own. Knowing that his father's prosperity secured his future, Thomas Springer probably took his obligations to his parents in stride.[10]

The death of Thomas's mother hastened her youngest son's move toward independence. Charles remarried in 1787. His new wife, Elizabeth Graham Rice, was a moderately wealthy widow with children of her own—seven of them under the age of seventeen. By marrying Charles Springer she gained a father for them as well as a companion for herself. Charles too gained more than companionship, for his new wife's wealth solidified his financial position, and her children would contribute labor in the household and on the farm for many years.[11] His father's remarriage may have deepened Thomas's desire to get out of his father's house. More to the point, it gave Charles the security to let his youngest son go.

In 1788, Thomas bought two small parcels of land that abutted the Mill Creek tract, and soon he was living there on his own. He built a proper log house, about 19 by 23 feet in size, with a single room on each floor. About the same time, he got married. His wife was named Elizabeth—the records do not tell us her last name. She moved into

The Springer house along Mill Creek in 1962, after the roof and wood siding had been removed to reveal the original rafters and planked log walls.

the log house sometime about 1790 and had two baby daughters shortly thereafter.[12] Finally, in 1792, Thomas was able to buy 104 acres of the Mill Creek tract from his father. Charles charged him less than the market price for the land, and he allowed his son to owe him part of the price. With his father's help, then, by age twenty-nine, Thomas was settled on 129 acres of his own land as the head of his own small family. He was an independent householder, listed alongside his father and brothers as a "yeoman" in the records of New Castle County and Delaware State.[13]

From those records—land deeds, tax lists, probate inventories, the federal census—emerges a picture of the Springers' daily life during the 1790s. The scene includes many patterns common to pre-industrial communities. In the eighteenth century, as before, households were the site of production of foodstuffs and goods. It followed that

Families needed all hands, however small, to produce their many household necessities. This 1780 print is called "Wethersfield Girls Weeding Onions."

many households contained laborers as well as immediate family members. In 1798, a tax assessor listed Thomas as the owner of four slaves—an uncommonly large number for the northern part of Delaware, where most white families owned no slaves at all.[14] Ace, a young adult, was probably the Springers' most valuable laborer. In addition there were Sara and Amelia, one a young girl between the ages of eight and fourteen, the other slightly older. There was also Will, about sixty years old, perhaps the same "Will" who had appeared in the estate of Evan Rice, the first husband of Thomas's stepmother, a few years earlier.[15] But no evidence has survived to tell us how the Springers' slaves were acquired, how they were related to one another, or how they experienced life on the Springer farm. They probably lived together in the log tenement.

The 1800 census reported three young white people—a female and two males, aged sixteen to twenty five—in the Springer household too.[16] These might have been servants, or perhaps Thomas's step-brothers and stepsister—children of Evan and Elizabeth Rice—or possibly relatives of Elizabeth Springer. We do not know their relationship to Elizabeth and Thomas, or whether they lived in the log house with the Springers or shared the tenement with the African-American slaves. For an "independent" yeoman, though, Thomas Springer clearly depended heavily on the labor of many others.

Not least, he counted on the labor of his wife. From their youth Thomas and Elizabeth had learned separate skills, and with adulthood they assumed responsibility for different domains. White women were less likely than men to travel far from the homestead visiting artisans' shops and stores, and they rarely worked in the fields. Elizabeth might do men's work at harvest, at apple-picking time, or whenever her husband's absence required her to act in his place, but most of the time her realm was the house, the kitchen, the yard and its animals, and the garden she probably planted nearby. White people commonly assigned jobs more flexibly to their African-American slaves; black women probably performed "men's work" more often than white women. But over all the division of labor by gender applied to blacks as well as whites.[17]

These social and economic arrangements were far from egalitarian. Household members—bound and free, young and old, male and female—stood unequal to one another in legal status and more: they enjoyed different amounts of control over their everyday labor; they made different contributions to the household and benefitted from its prosperity in different degrees. As yet only African-American slavery—perhaps the most glaring and recent of these inequalities—had come under attack in Delaware. Ace appeared on the Springer inventory in 1804 as having "nine years left to serve"; apparently he had made some arrangement to buy his freedom. For the most part, however, the Springers remained untouched by the antislavery fervor that swept much of the state in the 1770s and 1780s. And few people in the Springers' day questioned the right of age to rule youth or male to rule female.[18]

Under Thomas's direction, the household practiced a brand of diversified farming. Like most other farmers in New Castle County, Thomas produced a variety of crops: oats, hay, and Indian corn to feed livestock, vegetables to feed the household and exchange with neighbors, and wheat both for home consumption and for distant markets. But Thomas differed from the majority of nearby farmers in his dependence on livestock. In 1798, farmers in the Springers' section of the county owned, on average, $132 worth of animals—a sum that might represent a half-dozen cows, a dozen sheep, and one or two horses, along with poultry and hogs. By contrast, Thomas's holdings were worth $644. Only one other landholder in the area possessed more valuable livestock than Thomas, and the vast majority owned animals valued at less than half as much. To a degree, then, the Springers specialized in raising livestock. Thomas's choice of crops reflected the importance of animals to the household's economic success: in the one year we know about, he devoted the most acreage on his farm to oats, slightly less to corn, then wheat, rye, potatoes, clover, and timothy, in that order.[19]

Some thirty acres of the Springers' land remained unimproved—probably woodland, forested with oak, hickory, poplar, walnut, maple, and ash, and providing forage for farm animals. From the forest the Springers could gather firewood for cooking their meals and heating their home, lumber for building, and in season, berries, nuts, and maybe mushrooms. Another ten acres was grassy marsh, yielding a grass particularly fine for cattle. There was also an apple orchard and outbuildings, yard, and—almost certainly—a vegetable garden near the log house, leaving in all roughly ninety acres for cultivation.[20]

In one year, the records show, Thomas planted about half of those ninety acres. Like other farmers throughout the East, he probably

A view of a rural landscape in the mid-Atlantic states, from the Columbian Magazine, *1780.*

found the "freshness and richness of the soil" declining and adopted techniques for saving the soil and its nutrients. Few Delaware farmers practiced a systematic rotation, but they knew that fields could not support the same crop for many years running and that the land needed years of rest. It was approved practice to leave about half of the acreage used for cultivation fallow in any one year.[21]

Some of the Springers' unplanted acres might have been pasture. Thomas grew timothy and clover, perhaps to replenish his arable land, though his workers cut and stacked some for fodder as well. His large holdings of livestock made it possible to manure tired soil and to impose stricter crop-rotation schemes. His choice of crops, numerous animals, and command over the labor of others all suggest that Thomas might have followed the lead of English farmers who sought a balance among animals, fodder crops, and grain to increase their land's productivity. He might have been a rather progressive farmer; his father's wealth gave him that choice.[22]

Relying as they did on the land and its products, the Springers' lives followed a seasonal pattern. Winter was a slow time for farmers, when the most pressing tasks were cutting firewood, keeping animals fed, clean, and warm and doing small chores like mending tools and harnesses. Delaware's cold winters kept the Springers inside the house as much as possible during December, January, and February. Some-one had to venture out of doors to tend the cattle and horses in the log

Basic tools of the farm: a venerable plow; a hay knife; a wedge (for splitting firewood); a burl maul and a beetle, both used for driving fence posts and stakes.

barn and the sheep in the fields, but it seems likely that Thomas often delegated those tasks. He could use the slack season to travel to nearby towns—New Castle to register a deed or settle other legal affairs, Wilmington for commercial dealings with storekeepers, visits to artisans' shops, and socializing at Francis Dunlap's tavern. In the winter months, Thomas had time to walk his fields, surveying the acres planted with wheat and rye the previous fall and figuring how to use the rest of his land in the year to come.[23]

In March, when Mill Creek had thawed and buds and blossoms began to appear on the trees, it was time for spring planting to begin. The first crops were oats for feeding livestock and flax for making linen. If he was dissatisfied with his last year's crop, or if he wanted to experiment, Thomas might trade with neighbors for a new batch of seed. Most often, however, farmers simply used the seed saved from their previous season's harvest. Thomas, Ace, and Will sowed the seed broadcast over the plowed ground. Agricultural experts recommended plowing again to cover the seed over with fresh soil and fresh nutriments. But it was easier to attach a harrow, an A-shaped frame fitted with spikes, to a draft animal and lead the animal up and down the fields, cutting more shallowly into the earth but raking soil over the seeds in wide swathes at a time. Most Delaware farmers preferred the latter method.[24]

As soon as oats and flax were in the ground, May brought the job of planting Indian corn. Once they were planted, Thomas could leave his oat and flax fields alone, but cornfields required weeding through the spring and summer months. Thomas might choose a new and grassy field for planting corn; it would require frequent plowing between the corn rows that year, but he had the labor—slave and free—to do it, and then the field would be clear and ready for wheat in the fall.[25]

In June and July came the heaviest labor of the year. It was harvest, time to bring in the ripened wheat, barley, and rye planted the fall before. Using a sickle, one man could cut about an acre of wheat a day. All male hands were called on to work the fields in the long days of midsummer, and perhaps some female hands as well. Amelia and Sara most often helped Elizabeth with household work and manufacturing, but they might be pressed into service in the rush of harvest. When weather made speed essential, white women worked in the fields as well, but the Springers' wheat harvest was not extensive enough to make that a frequent occurrence. To prevent infestation by flies, the harvested grains had to be threshed as soon as possible. It was common practice to "tread out" wheat with horses, whose heavy hooves broke the fibrous chaff away from the grain. The men of the Springer household probably used the same method to thresh barley. They flailed oats and rye by hand, or left these crops to straw for the cattle.[26]

Interspersed with other summer labor was mowing in the meadows. From late June through early autumn, rural men used scythes to cut grass, timothy, and clover. The common practice was to pile both hay and grain in tall stacks or long ricks, housing only oats and clover in the barn. The most well-to-do farmers could afford to hold their wheat for a good market price, but most could not risk spoilage nor delay sale to millers and grain merchants. We do not know if the Springers waited for the market or, like the majority, sold their surplus in late summer.[27]

Finally, with fall came new tasks. In September the men sowed wheat and rye fields. The household harvested apples in the orchard for Elizabeth to use in baking and making conserves and for Thomas to use in making cider. There might be second and third cuttings of meadow grass to store as winter fodder for cattle. In the years he kept sheep, Thomas had to make special preparations for their winter comfort. Dr. James Tilton described one method: some farmers took mown grass from the marshland and laid it out on horizontal poles set about four feet from the ground, creating a shelter for sheep to eat away by spring.[28]

In different years, Thomas Springer owned various numbers of sheep, cows, and and horses. In 1796, he bought nine sheep from a relative's estate to provide both mutton and wool. Two years later, local tax assessors listed his holdings at $644 worth of livestock—a sum that must have included at least a few horses for pulling the plow and for driving the "chaise" later listed among Thomas's possessions. Yet his holdings reflect more than the ordinary needs of farming. One rough indication of the extent of Thomas's holdings comes from the enumerated holdings of his neighbor John Ball. In 1804, Ball's estate inventory listed the following livestock:

16 sheep	22.00
2 calves	6.00
8 milch cows	96.00
2 Bulls	18.00
3 2-yr. old calves	18.00
1 bay horse	45.00
1 old black horse	4.50
1 3-yr old colt	35.50
1 old mare	2.00
7 shoats	7.00
poultry	8.00

In all, Ball owned $262 worth of animals—only 40 percent of the value of Thomas Springer's holdings.[29]

Unfortunately, when appraisers listed Thomas Springer's estate, in December of 1804, it included only seven horses (most of them old) and "1 red cow," worth $182 all together. Thomas had sold off his nine sheep and a great many other animals. Luckily, other evidence

The Columbian Magazine *of October 1786 offered this romantic image of the industrious farmer, the backbone of the young republic.*

suggests what sort of animals Thomas owned. A "Barrel churn," pails, and milk pans listed among the Springers' possessions indicate dairying; two spinning wheels suggest that the household processed wool. In addition, the low valuation of livestock in the winter of 1804 might have reflected seasonal variations in the number of animals Thomas owned. There was good reason not to keep large numbers of cattle on hand in the winter. A single cow ate about forty pounds of hay a day, and a good farmer added vegetables and grains to the feed—boiled potatoes, turnips, bran, buckwheat, lentils, carrots, corn. Therefore, *Poor Richard's Almanac* told farmers, "If you live within thirty miles of a good market, you will find it much cheaper to sell all your calves for veal and keep up your stock of milch cows by purchasing such as are brought from distant parts at a low price."[30]

The Springers lived only six miles from Wilmington, and they may have taken Poor Richard's advice. Farmers in the southern two counties of Delaware bred cattle in the forests and marshes, then drove them north to be fattened for marketing in Wilmington and Philadelphia. Moreover, ships outbound from Philadelphia often stopped at the town of New Castle, near the Mill Creek farm, to take on livestock for export. The Springers might have taken advantage of the rich meadows along the creek and their proximity to town to specialize in fattening cattle from the south.[31]

*S*ketching Elizabeth Springer's everyday life and work is a little bit harder than piecing together Thomas's. Eighteenth-century women appear less often than men in the official records that historians rely on. Even "free" women like Elizabeth enjoyed few political and legal rights; they could not vote, sue in court, or, when married, possess real estate of their own. Unfortunately, we have no letters or diaries that tell us about Elizabeth Springer's early life, her decision to marry Thomas, or her personal experience of marriage and motherhood. But we do know that her life was shaped by her role as the wife of a yeoman farmer. In the eighteenth century, a woman's status depended on the men to whom she was legally attached. Contemporary women knew that their husband's situation determined their own: as one woman put it, marriage was "*the* important Crisis, upon which our Fate depends." From her husband's position, then, we can try to draw the outlines of Elizabeth's everyday experience. On the basis of Sara and Amelia's position as slaves, we can try to imagine the nature of their daily labors.[32]

Women's work in the Delaware countryside had seasonal rhythms and variations much like men's. In the spring, most women planted a garden near the house, where they grew peas, cabbage, and other vegetables through the summer for family use in the fall. Dairying was another seasonal job for women. It began after calves were born in the spring and continued through the hot months of the year. Milking took place twice a day, in the early morning and again in the evening.[33]

European settlers made splitwork baskets of oak, ash, and hickory for use in the fields and in household activities, and for storage. They exchanged techniques and designs with American Indians, who also had a basketmaking tradition.

THE FARM AND THE MARKETPLACE

"Straining and Skimming," an engraving
published in Baltimore in 1819, shows an
idealized view of dairying—no cramped
quarters, no flies or dirt. Women in the
Springer household performed the same
tasks, but they worked on a smaller scale
and under less immaculate conditions.

Some women saved the "strippings"—the milk that came last from
the udder and that contained the most butterfat—in a separate pail.
The next step was to pour the milk into wooden or ceramic pans to
separate, and put the pans aside. The Springers may have used shelves
in the log kitchen for the purpose, but since the milk had to cool it
would have made more sense for them to build a small springhouse
by the creek. Depending on the temperature, it took from eight to
twenty hours for the cream to rise. With the cream skimmed off, there
was milk to use in baking, to feed the pigs, and for the family to
drink. The cream went into the barrel churn, often mixed with salt,
saltpeter, sal ammoniac, or a mixture of sugar and water to keep it
fresh-tasting. When enough cream had accumulated, it was time for
churning.[34]

One contemporary writer counseled that dairying was "too ticklish
a business to be trusted to servants," but in practice women followed
their own ideas and experience about that. It seems likely that Elizabeth left much of the tedious work to Sara and Amelia. The barrel

churn represented a distinct improvement on the older plunger type, producing more butter in less time, but bringing the cream to butter still took hours. After churning, butter needed to be pressed, either by hand or with a wooden utensil, to remove the remaining liquid. Dairywomen added salt to preserve the butter, put it in a pot, and stored it in some cool place in the summer and in the flour bin in winter. From a good dairy cow, a woman could get about two gallons of milk a day, with enough cream for one pound of butter.[35]

Even in urban areas of Delaware many families kept cows and produced milk and butter of their own, so that large-scale dairying ventures were few. Yet it does not seem likely that the Springers' dairying was just for family consumption. With their location near markets, their valuable livestock, their barrel churn, and their female labor force, it seems probable that the Springers sometimes marketed butter. Perhaps Elizabeth could exchange some butter locally, although the Balls nearby owned "milch cows" and other families in the neighborhood owned livestock too. Wilmington and New Castle provided larger markets, and merchants operating in the port cities of the region exported some butter as well. We can only speculate about the scale of the venture, but—especially if Thomas fattened livestock for sale—marketing butter would have been easy enough for the Springers to do.[36]

Dairying often tailed off in the fall, but then other work took its place. Rural women helped in the slaughter of small animals, then salted pork and bacon for use in winter and early spring. They preserved fruits and vegetables, often in wide-mouthed stoneware jars sealed with animal bladders or skins and stored on kitchen shelves. In all these jobs, Elizabeth Springer could call on the help of Amelia, Sara, and her young daughters as they grew. Here, as in other tasks, it was in Elizabeth's interest to train the young women to take over the jobs she found most difficult or boring.[37]

The women of the household worked with one another and with local artisans to produce cloth. Imported cloth was available; Wilmington merchants stocked English broadcloth, shalloon, and other fabrics, which the Springers could get in exchange for farm surplus. But store-bought cloth could be expensive, and Thomas owned his

THE FARM AND THE MARKETPLACE

"Stephen Miner, Hereby informs his
Customers and Others, That he weaves
Coverlids of all Sorts,—makes them and
knots the Fringe, all in the neatest
Manner, for one Dollar each." Ad in the
Connecticut Gazette and the Universal
Intelligencer, March 3, 1775.

THE SPRINGER HOUSEHOLD OF DELAWARE

Household women cooperated with local craftsmen to produce textiles like this overshot coverlet, made of linen, cotton, and wool and dated 1787. "Hackling" was one step in processing linen: pulling fibers through the metal spikes separated the short fibers, or "tow," from the long ones, called "line." The hackle and cover below are dated 1773.

own sheep. The animals were washed and sheared during the summer. To make woolen cloth, women first had to clean and card the fibers. Then they spun the wool into yarn, feeding the short fibers into a spinning wheel, twisting them and holding them taut and steady enough to produce yarn of an even gauge. The Springer women passed on the yarn to a professional weaver—possibly John Robinson, a close neighbor—who possessed the loom and the skills to transform it into cloth. From the weaver the cloth went to Robert Johnson's fulling mill, where it was soaked in water and pounded with heavy hammers powered by a water wheel. Fulling tightened the weave of the cloth and softened the finish. When it was returned from the mill, the cloth was almost done. There was probably a professional dyer in Wilmington, but if Elizabeth preferred she could make her own dyes by gathering, pounding, and then boiling roots, bark, berries, or flowers in her large kettle. It was arduous work, but, like Thomas, Elizabeth had help and she may have felt the results worth it, either because she preferred the colors produced by her own recipes or because she saved the cost of a dyer.[38]

In some years the Springer women probably made linen rather than wool. Household spinning of flax took place "in almost every private family" in the state of Delaware. Like producing woolen cloth, producing linen was a cooperative project between private home and skilled craftsmen in the neighborhood. Women processed the flax plant by removing the seed pods, breaking off the outer stalk, beating the flax to remove the chaff, and finally spinning and reeling the fiber itself. The yarn went to the weaver and dyer from there.[39]

From homespun wool and linen or imported materials, rural women cut and sewed clothing for the household. They also produced textiles for household use—curtains for the windows, linen towels, and bed hangings. There was everyday mending too. Elizabeth must have welcomed the chance to delegate much of this labor to Sara and Amelia, working herself on the parts of the process about which she was particular or in which she could show skill and taste. From a very young age, her two daughters, Mary and Ann, could help by taking on some of the spinning. Elizabeth might have taught her girls quilting and a little fancy needlework as well.[40]

As with dairy products, it is hard to judge how much of the Springers' wool, yarn, or cloth reached the wider marketplace. They could trade wool to neighbors who owned no sheep or else sell it in town. According to James Tilton, in 1788, a fleece would sell for six to eighteen shillings; that it had a common price indicated that fleece was

Saxony-type spinning wheels, introduced into America early in the eighteenth century, had foot treadles and a bobbin and flyer device to make drawing, twisting, and winding linen fibers easier. Combining linen with wool produced linsey-woolsey, the fabric used in the blanket at left.

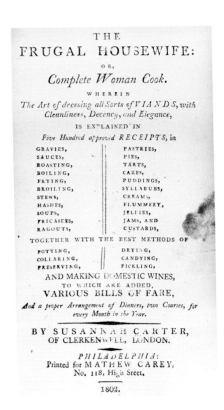

THE
FRUGAL HOUSEWIFE:
OR,
Complete Woman Cook.
WHEREIN
*The Art of dressing all Sorts of VIANDS, with
Cleanliness, Decency, and Elegance,*
IS EXPLAINED IN
Five Hundred approved RECEIPTS, in

GRAVIES,	PASTRIES,
SAUCES,	PIES,
ROASTING,	TARTS,
BOILING,	CAKES,
FRYING,	PUDDINGS,
BROILING,	SYLLABUBS,
STEWS,	CREAMS,
HASHES,	FLUMMERY,
SOUPS,	JELLIES,
FRICASEES,	JAMS, AND
RAGOUTS,	CUSTARDS,

TOGETHER WITH THE BEST METHODS OF

POTTING,	DRYING,
COLLARING,	CANDYING,
PRESERVING,	PICKLING,

AND MAKING DOMESTIC WINES,
TO WHICH ARE ADDED,
VARIOUS BILLS OF FARE,
*And a proper Arrangement of Dinners, two Courses, for
every Month in the Year.*

BY SUSANNAH CARTER,
OF CLERKENWELL, LONDON.

PHILADELPHIA:
Printed for MATHEW CAREY,
No. 118, High Street.

1802.

Eighteenth-century housewives and female laborers knew how to stew, bake, broil, fry, and roast, and could learn fancy cooking from books like The Frugal Housewife.

The rack on the toaster shown at right could be turned to expose both sides of the bread to the cooking fire.

commonly exchanged. The Springers could also market yarn. When Thomas Springer died in 1803, his largest debtor was Mordecai McKinney, an entrepreneur who opened a complete water-powered woolen manufactory in nearby Stanton in 1809. There were no woolen manufactories in the area in the late 1790s, but McKinney and other men may already have been engaged in processing cloth, putting out wool to rural women, who would clean, card, and spin the fibers, then return them to the wool merchant for weaving, finishing, and sale. Some fullers in the 1790s began to add dyeing, napping, and shearing to their services, and merchants became increasingly involved in coordinating the process of cloth production. At least one farmer in northern Delaware owned "a spinning house" on his property a few years before factories were built. Elizabeth, Amelia, and Sara may have spun yarn for wool dealers too.[41]

Cooking's daily routine cut across the changing work of the seasons. Like many Delaware farm families, the Springers had an outside kitchen, a small log building that removed heat and servants from the log house. Here the Springer women tended fires and cooked three meals a day. Meat was central to the household diet. As James Tilton wrote in 1788: "Few men breakfast without a portion of meat, and it is an universal practice to dine in the middle of the day, upon a full meal of meat, with bread & vegetables. The meanest slaves have this indulgence." Rural women roasted fresh mutton, poultry, and fish in the summer and fall and boiled salted meats the rest of the year. They often used vegetables from the garden to make a sauce for the meat.

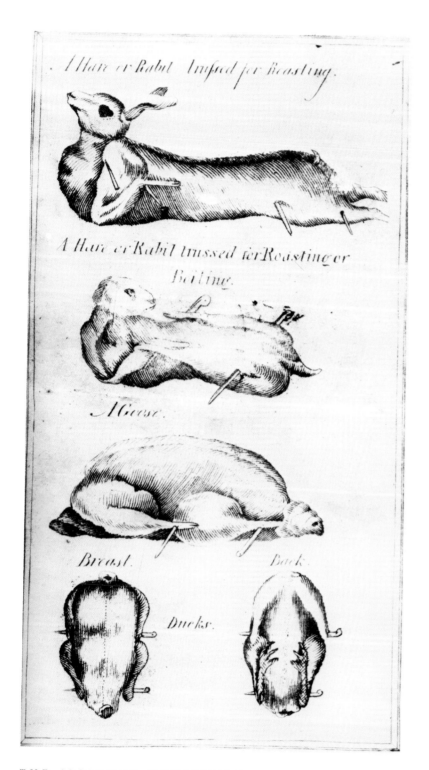

Left: an illustration from The Frugal Housewife. *Above: a lidded pot with feet to raise it above the coals. Below: a wooden bucket, useful for many kitchen tasks.*

Households frequently baked bread; there was wheat bread for the family, and possibly cornbread for the slaves.[42]

One other life pattern cut across all other women's work in the eighteenth century. Married women could expect to become pregnant about once every two years. If all went well during her pregnancy, a woman kept working at household tasks until very close to her lying-in time. If she had servants, slaves, or older daughters, she might be able to afford a few weeks of recovery after childbirth before returning to work. Most women breastfed their infants for a year or so. Then,

"A Man-Mid-wife or a newly discovered animal," London, 1793, depicts a striking change. Helping to bring children into the world had long been a job for midwives; male physicians who attended births seemed new and even preposterous.

The forceps in this obstetrical kit helped in the safe extraction of an infant during a difficult delivery. The perforator, blunt hook and crochet, and bone crusher enabled a doctor to remove a stillborn child or destroy a child that endangered its mother's life.

Written treatises like the one below about the "management" of pregnancy began to replace the oral tradition of midwifery.

soon after the baby was weaned, another pregnancy became likely. In all, eighteenth-century women were likely to spend some twenty years in a cycle of bearing, nursing, and raising children. In fact, Elizabeth Springer bore her two daughters, Mary and Ann, in quick succession shortly after her marriage. If she had other pregnancies in the late 1790s, either she did not carry to term or the children died in infancy. Both were common tragedies for women of the day, though no records survive to tell us more about Elizabeth's experience. Motherhood meant nursing, teaching, and loving her daughters, and passing on the household skills that would enable them to run homes of their own in the future.[43]

Mary and Ann learned a variety of skills proven by time and many traditional attitudes toward household life. Work on the Springer farm varied in pace and intensity from season to season and from day to day. Some days Thomas, Will, and Ace probably labored until nightfall; on others they probably finished at midday. In some seasons women pitched into the rush of harvest; in other seasons there was time for a slower pace. This was a fundamental characteristic of preindustrial living, when people worked to finish the task before them rather than punching a time clock.[44] Moreover, like farmers from time immemorial, Thomas had to worry about early frosts and late

A

TREATISE

ON THE

MANAGEMENT OF PREGNANT

AND

LYING IN WOMEN,

AND THE MEANS OF CURING, BUT MORE ESPECIALLY OF

PREVENTING THE PRINCIPAL DISORDERS

TO WHICH THEY ARE LIABLE,

TOGETHER WITH SOME

NEW DIRECTIONS

CONCERNING THE

DELIVERY OF THE CHILD AND PLACENTA

IN NATURAL BIRTHS.

ILLUSTRATED WITH CASES.

By CHARLES WHITE, ESQ. F.R.S.

Man Midwife to the Lying in Hospital, in Manchester, in England, &c. &c.

First **Worcester** Edition.

PRINTED at WORCESTER, MASSACHUSETTS,
BY ISAIAH THOMAS.

Sold at his Bookstore in WORCESTER. Sold also by said THOMAS, and ANDREWS, Fault's Statue, Newbury Street, BOSTON; and by said THOMAS, and CARLISLE, in WALPOLE, Newhampshire.

MDCCXCIII.

The Springers' neighborhood, on a redrawn map from 1799, showing mills, towns, churches, and roads. The Springers lived next to J. Stroud's mill on Mill Creek.

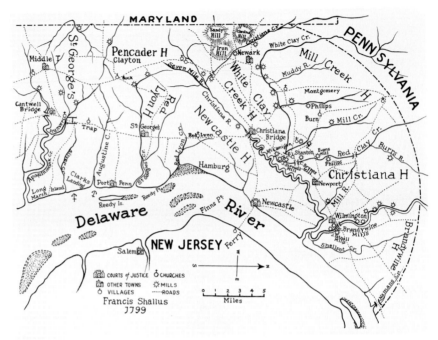

rains. But to a traditional anxiety over the weather he added a concern for the market price of wheat and livestock. In subtle ways, engagement with the marketplace altered the meaning of Elizabeth's work as well. She tended to traditionally female tasks, but like her husband, she produced in part for a new and growing market. In some regards the Springer household was "self-sufficient"—they grew much of the food they ate and produced many of the goods they used. Yet they relied on neighbors to grind grain and process cloth, and on the wider Atlantic marketplace as well. If Mary and Ann learned traditional ways, they also grew up in a household adapting to change. To understand those adaptations, we have to look more closely at the world surrounding the Mill Creek farm.

*T*he Springers lived in a section of the county called Mill Creek Hundred. In 1798, tax assessors there counted 455 taxpayers—free males aged twenty-one or older and women who headed households of their own. Of that number, 255, or 56 percent, owned neither land nor houses. Some of the landless were in the same position that

THE FARM AND THE MARKETPLACE

Register

Of Samuel Colton's FAMILY He was MARRIED

BORN September 7th 1729

Flavia Colton She was born August 31 1741

& by her hath the following Child viz.

NAMES	BORN	DIED
Nameless child	February 1st 1760	February 3d 1760
Flavia the mother	died April 6 1763.	Samuel Colton married
again October 16th 1765 to Lucy Colton		she was born June 24
1742 and by her had	the following children	
Adna	August 31 1767	Sept 9 1767
Still Born	November 20 1768	
Flavia	October 1 1769	August 5. 1815
Margaret	Nov 18th 1770	December 29 1770
Margaret	October 19th 1771	Jan 7 1817 1818
Lucy	June 8 1773	October 18 1804
Samuel	Sept. 8 1775	August 25 1777
Samuel	Feb 4 1778	June 17 1811

Flavia was married October 11 1787 to Col Alexander Field

Margaret was married September 11 1794 to David Booth

Lucy was married January 29 1794 to Dr Benjamin Stebbins

Samuel was married March 6 1799 to Anne Gregory Warriner

Mr Samuel Colton DIED November 5 1784

Mrs Lucy Colton DIED December 7 1799

Above: Nine-year-old Slowi Hayes, daughter of an affluent Boston merchant, made this silk sampler in 1788 to record the different stitches she learned. Most girls learned ordinary sewing, and poor girls did mending work to augment the family income.

Right: Sabra Waterman of Norwich, Connecticut, made this hooked bed rug in 1794.

Previous page: This Colton family register records a high infant mortality characteristic of the era.

After its adoption in 1782, the Great Seal of the United States appeared in decorative arts of many kinds, as in the center of this pieced-work and appliqué quilt.

The Smithsonian's Connecticut River valley room, possibly from Samuel Colton's house.

Left: Skill in embroidery enhanced an upper-class young woman's marriageability. Rachel Breck Hooker worked this design in silk in the first decade of the nineteenth century.

Below: Made of wood with a painted face and inset glass eyes, this expensive English doll from the early eighteenth century wears a silk gown with apron and a lace cap.

Left: Life on a farm could include afternoon tea as well as the varied and difficult round of daily agricultural labor. The possessions of a farm family ranged from a fine pewter teapot to serviceable storage jars to utilitarian tools.

Opposite: Many cooking pots and pans had legs so they could be set directly on the fire; long handles helped protect the cook from the heat of the hearth. Pictured here are (clockwise from left, items on the floor): iron pot, frying pan, peel (for placing bake goods in the hot oven), iron pot, pine-stave bucket, toaster, posnet (a cooking pot with feet), and (in the middle) gridiron, for putting pots on. All are American, and most are from the eighteenth century.

Above: William Bailey, maker of this copper teakettle, worked in York and Lancaster, Pennsylvania, and in Baltimore, Maryland, between 1770 and 1800.

Below: Hand-forged iron skewer-holder and skewers, for securing meat on a spit.

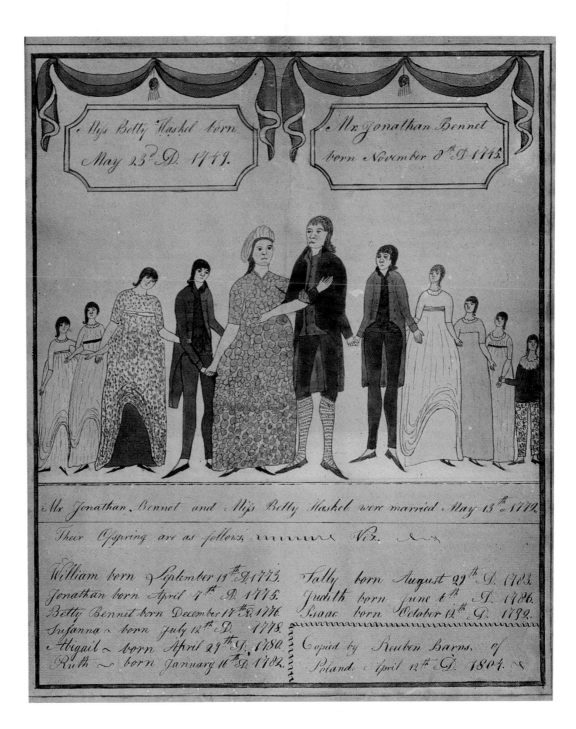

Miss Betty Haskel born
May 23rd D. 1749.

Mr. Jonathan Bennet
born November 8th D. 1745.

Mr. Jonathan Bennet and Miss Betty Haskel were married May 13th 1772.

Their Offspring are as follows, Viz.

William born September 19th D. 1773.
Jonathan born April 7th D. 1775.
Betty Bennet born December 17th D. 1776.
Susanna born July 12th D. 1778.
Abigail born April 29th D. 1780.
Ruth born January 16th D. 1782.

Sally born August 29th D. 1783.
Judith born June 6th D. 1786.
Isaac born October 12th D. 1792.

Copied by Reuben Barns, of
Poland April 12th D. 1804.

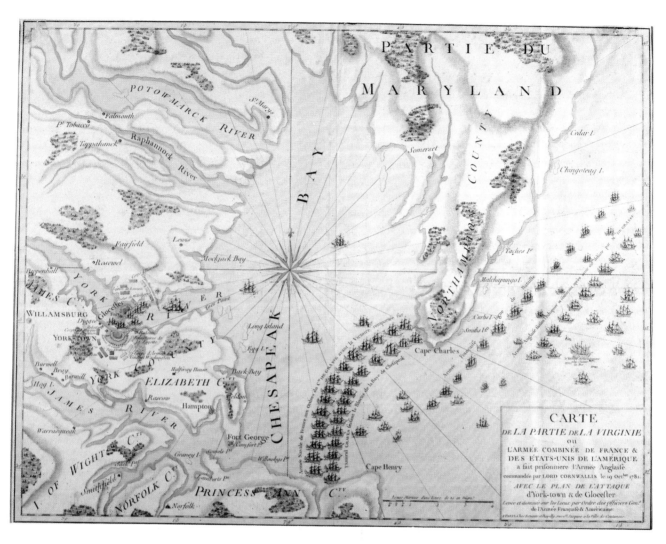

Opposite: Illuminated family records were popular art forms that commemorated births, deaths, and marriages. This Bennett family record, an 1804 watercolor from Poland, Maine, underscores the degree to which pregnancy and childraising filled many eighteenth-century lives.

Above: Isle of Wight County, site of Henry Saunders's plantation, appears just south of the James River on this French map depicting the battle of Yorktown in 1781.

Above: The Old Plantation, *a watercolor by an unknown artist (c. 1800), shows a celebration involving dance and music in a slave quarter. It illustrates the survival of African forms (the stick, drum, and possibly the dance itself) among slaves who lived some distance from the manor house in the background.*

Opposite, top: Thomas Coram's Residence and Slave Quarters of Mulberry Plantation *(Carolina, c. 1800) shows an early eighteenth-century mansion house and rows of one-room slave houses. The West Africans' familiarity with rice-growing contributed to the development of rice culture in Carolina.*

Opposite, bottom: Market Folks *by Benjamin Henry Latrobe, 1819, depicts distinctive Afro-American dress and basketry in what is probably a southern port city.*

Market folks

Africans brought with them many remembered traditions, but few African artifacts. In recreating the things of everyday life, they had to use American materials and often suit European tastes. They elaborated on traditional forms and created new, African-American ones as well.

Left: Ceramic jars like this were made and used by women all over Africa. This large jar was used for storing palm oil, a cooking oil made from the seeds of palm trees.

Below: Wooden scoop and gourd dipper.

Above: These African instruments include a lyre from the Congo, now Zaire, probably early twentieth century; a balaja or balafo (xylophone), collected near Monrovia, Liberia, nineteenth century; a kendo (bell), Western Congo people, the Congo (Zaire), nineteenth century.

Left: This nineteenth-century Akan drum from Elmina in the Gold Coast, now Ghana, resembles a drum made of American cedar and deerskin, found in Virginia in the eighteenth century and now in the British Museum.

Above: Map of Philadelphia, c. 1796.

Opposite: Old Lutheran Church, Philadelphia; and High Street, Philadelphia, with the procession in commemoration of the death of General George Washington: both by William Birch, ca. 1800.

"You will consider Philadelphia, from its centrical situation, the extent of its commerce, the number of its artificers, manufacturers and other circumstances, to be to the United States what the heart is to the human body in circulating the blood."
Robert Morris, 1777.

Pennsylvania Germans sought the religious toleration associated with Penn's colony, but prized their Old World language and culture. In the New World, their craftsmen combined striking decorations and fine workmanship in all their products, even the most utilitarian.

Above: Two views of a painted chest, Pennsylvania, eighteenth century.

Right: The special events of life—births, marriages, and baptisms—were celebrated in fraktur, documents using a distinctive, centuries-old form of writing and ornamentation.

Thomas Springer had been in a decade before: they were the sons of landed farmers but not yet established on their own. Thomas's young friend Joshua Johnson, for example, had only fifty-two dollars' worth of livestock to his name in 1798, but the tax assessors listed him next to his very successful father, Robert, owner of a brick house, sawmill, gristmill, fulling mill, and 111 acres of land. Joshua might be impatient to have property of his own, but owning land was just a matter of time.[45]

Others among the landless were artisans, such as carpenter Joseph Robinson, tailor Thomas Dixson, and wheelwright David Parker, men more likely to invest in the tools of their trade or a few head of livestock than in land. Yet many apparently had neither artisans' skills and tools nor landowning fathers. Some men without land worked as tenants on other men's farms, paying an annual rent by handing over a share of their harvest or a portion of their livestock. Many must have been laborers, living in the households of others.[46]

Some people owned almost nothing. A handful of women owned substantial farms, like Mary Beason and widow Hannah Moore, but most widows lived closer to Pheby Hughes's standard of living: she had a house, a barn, twenty acres of land, and only eight dollars' worth of livestock. Among the most impoverished men were free blacks—"Black Sam" and "Black Frank" owned virtually nothing— and there were white men on the bottom too. In 1798, the bottom half of the taxable population controlled only 16 percent of the hundred's taxable wealth. The fact that he owned land at all set Thomas Springer apart from many others of his generation. It made him more successful than most other free men in the hundred in 1798, and more successful than some of them would ever be.[47]

Thomas's 129-acre farm put him in the top 35 percent of all those with land in the category of total acreage. Not quite 40 percent of the landowners had less than 100 acres, and another 25 percent owned between 100 and 129 acres. On the other side, many landowners held substantially more land than the Springers did: about 16 percent of the landed had between 130 and 199 acres, and another 17 percent owned between 200 and 400 acres. A few—just seven taxpayers— owned more than 400 acres.[48]

In total wealth, Thomas Springer stood better than the great majority. His land, his slaves, and his livestock holdings put him in the upper 10 percent of all taxables in 1798. Moreover, his land was valued more highly per acre than the average land in Mill Creek Hundred, reflecting its location along a waterway, its proximity to Wilmington market, and the improvements that Thomas, Will, and Ace had made on the farm.[49]

With the Mill Creek farm, the Springers acquired neighbors. As the deed to the land put it, the farm began at "a marked corner Maple near to Mill Creek being a corner of this and Land of the Reverend William McCannon and the Land of Captain Montgomery." From there the Springers' holding ran down the creek "to a Gum on the corner of this and Land of Andrew Reynolds." The boundary ran south and west after that, to "a corner for land belonging to the heirs of Simon Paulson Decd . . . to a Whiteoak tree . . . in the line of land of John Ball."[50] The deed defined a neighborhood as well as a plot of land.

In addition to the McKennons, Montgomerys, Reynoldses, and Balls, there were other close neighbors. In 1790 Samuel Stroud, an established mill owner, had bought thirty-three acres of the original Mill Creek tract from Charles Springer. The purchase included a narrow strip of land that cut from the creek through the farm—then being worked by Thomas—to act as a millrace, conveying water to power a mill. In the nineties the Strouds constructed a three-story mill, 35 feet by 47 feet in size. By 1798 it was owned and operated by Joshua Stroud. On the other side of the Springer homestead was Milltown, a crossroads village consisting of a sawmill, a gristmill, a few houses, and a small store. During Thomas Springer's lifetime, most of these buildings belonged to Caleb Harlan and his family.[51]

Members of the neighborhood did not all share a common background or a common faith. Swedish, English, Scots, and increasing numbers of Irish lived in the area. The Reverend William Mc-Kennon, next-door to the Springers, served as minister at Red Clay Presbyterian Church. The Harlans were Quakers, while the Springers maintained ties with Immanuel (Episcopalian) Church. Neighborhood households were not knit together by the bonds of common worship, but there were many other social ties. Close neighbors might also be relatives by blood or by marriage. Thomas Springer's brother Jeremiah and his second cousin Charles lived nearby, and Elizabeth Springer may have had kin in the neighborhood too. The Balls, Giffins, Strouds, and Springers all had ties by marriage as well, so that many neighbors were also in-laws at one remove or another.[52]

Rural life created other connections. Women in the eighteenth century formed deep bonds by helping each other through the difficult hours of childbirth. Except in the few urban centers, doctors rarely supervised women's labor. Most women depended on neighbors to bring herbs and medicines, their own experience, and emotional support to ease the ordeal of giving birth. Catherine, Ann, and Sarah Harlan, Nancy Ball, Elizabeth McKennon and her two daughters, and Mary Reece Springer, wife of Jeremiah, made up part of the female community who might have attended Elizabeth Springer in childbirth—and whom she might have attended in turn.[53]

Women also visited one another's homes on more ordinary occasions, taking sewing and young children with them in order to work in company and talk together. There were more formal occasions for

Although most children played with simple, homemade toys, a few expensive English imports found their way to America. When assembled, the puzzle shown below left, made about 1790, shows portraits, names, and brief biographies of English kings and queens. The puzzle is one token of well-to-do Americans' continuing ties to English culture in the years after the Revolution.

Teapots and kettles grew more and more common in household inventories through the 1700s, reflecting Americans' enjoyment of an English practice.

visiting as well. One contemporary observer reported that in Delaware, "the genteel people generally indulge in the parade of tea, in the afternoon." The Springers' teacups and sugar dishes suggest that from time to time Elizabeth emulated the genteel. On such occasions she could serve her guests her fanciest baked goods or perhaps imported nuts or other delicacies.[54]

Much of Thomas Springer's socializing probably took place in public settings. Francis Dunlap's tavern in Wilmington drew many of the men from the Springer neighborhood, and many also patronized Wilmington stores. Caleb Harlan, Jr.'s store in nearby Milltown was small—it recorded "no neet profit" in 1798—but it must have been a handy place for Thomas to pick up a few necessities and talk with the Harlans. From time to time, Thomas had to travel to nearby mills to have wheat and corn ground into meal for the family's use. At mills and artisans' shops, men gathered and shared news and information.[55]

On many occasions when men or women met together, social exchange and economic exchange were combined. Early in the 1800s, many of the Springers' immediate neighbors had occasion to describe some of their ordinary economic dealings. When Andrew Giffen sued John Ball's estate, the neighborhood testified about the two parties' transactions. Their testimony affords us a glimpse of neighborhood exchange in the Springers' area, and offers one insight into the ways the Springer household's daily activities connected them with people outside.[56]

The dispute arose following John Ball, Sr.'s death, when his nephew and executor, John Ball, Jr., pressed Giffen to repay a longstanding debt of over two hundred dollars. Giffin admitted that he had borrowed money long ago, but thought he had paid off the debt over the years by delivering "divers sums of money" and "divers Articles of property," and by performing "work and labour" for Ball. As Giffin saw it, his payments more than satisfied the original debt. He thought that the Ball estate owed him for "a Beef Cow, Half a Stack of Hay, 13 bushels and a half of corn, 600 pounds weight of Hay, 3 bushels wheat, a Cart Saddle, a Barrel of Cyder, 2 days work drawing logs, 3 yards of linen, 2 items of Cash—1 dollar and 10 dollars."[57]

THE FARM AND THE MARKETPLACE

To settle the matter, Giffin entered an "Amicable Action" in the New Castle court. A justice of the peace referred the dispute to three local referees: Caleb Harlan, Jr., John Hall, and James Stroud. The investigators listened to the other side of the case too. John Ball, Jr., who had lived a decade in his uncle's house, testified that Giffin had already received remuneration for all the items he had listed. Ball said his uncle had paid for Giffin's apples and cider by pruning Giffin's orchard. Moreover, "the three yards of shirting linen were given to the sd Testator [Ball] in consideration of a hieffer calf" that Ball gave Giffin's daughter. Finally, "the drawing of logs charged" by Giffin had only constituted payment for the use of three of Ball's horses "for two days treading out wheat."[58]

American-made red earthenware, plain or with decorative glaze, was less durable than the refined wares imported from England—but also much cheaper.

The referees found Ball's account the more convincing one and decided that Giffin still owed the Ball estate $209.85. As interesting as the outcome of the dispute, however, is what it tells us about relationships in the Springers' immediate neighborhood. To begin with, those relationships were of many years' standing. Most witnesses in the Giffin-Ball case testified that they had known Giffin for twenty or twenty-five years ("since he came into the country"), and most had known John Ball, Jr., for the ten years since he had joined his uncle's household. Joseph Ball, age sixty-seven, said he had known Giffin for almost a quarter of a century, and John Ball, Sr., for at least half a century. Neighborhood exchange took place between acquaintances if

Some eighteenth-century Americans owned imported furniture, but most bought from local and regional craftsmen who practiced in cities and towns. Furniture makers turned, sawed, planed, and often carved or painted wood tables, bedsteads, chairs, chests, and other furnishings. The fan-back Windsor chair shown above right is one of a fine set of six from the Delaware River valley area, 1780–1800.

not always between friends. Giffin and Ball had traded cows, linen, labor, and money over the course of many years.[59]

Second, other members of the household were involved in the two men's longstanding economic dealings. Ball gave a calf to Giffin's daughter in exchange for three yards of shirting linen; women as well as men engaged in local exchange. Finally, only a few of these local transactions involved cash or immediate payment. People exchanged hours of work, the products of their labor, the use of tools or animals, and money. The result was a complicated relationship between Giffin and Ball. When we add in the trading that took place among all the families of the neighborhood, we see an intricate network of economic exchange. How common and accepted these practices were appears in the testimony of another witness in the case: James Ball told the court that he knew none of the particulars of the dealings between Giffin and John Ball, Sr. He knew only that they "did neighbor with each other, by borrowing & lending, etc." Economic exchange was so common a part of local life that it made sense to call it "neighboring."[60]

The "borrowing and lending" of the Springers' neighborhood was neither casual nor unimportant: Giffin's dealings with just one of his neighbors amounted to several hundred dollars' value—well worth a

THE FARM AND THE MARKETPLACE

lawsuit. But neighboring apparently was something different from simple buying and selling. Borrowing and lending was a sort of economic exchange in a social context. It was economics mixed with kinship, friendship, or long-standing social relationships between households.

The Springers took an active part in this local network. When Thomas died in the early nineteenth century, his executors had to settle forty-seven small accounts—debts owed and credits due to near neighbors like Andrew Reynolds, the Strouds, Samuel Paulson, and Charles Springer and to many others in the hundred. The Springers must have produced some of their surplus crops and manufactures with their Mill Creek neighbors in mind. At least two neighbors specialized in milling and probably welcomed farm produce from nearby. In turn, Elizabeth could get honey from Nancy Ball's bees; like Andrew Giffin, Thomas might have called on John Ball's skills at pruning apple trees.[61]

The Ball-Giffin dispute underscores one other aspect of life in rural Delaware. Witnesses in the case were very familiar with the details of their neighbors' transactions. Day-to-day deals were often struck in public, so members of different households were often privy to one another's business. It made sense for neighbors to referee each other's disputes, not because they were impartial, but because they commonly

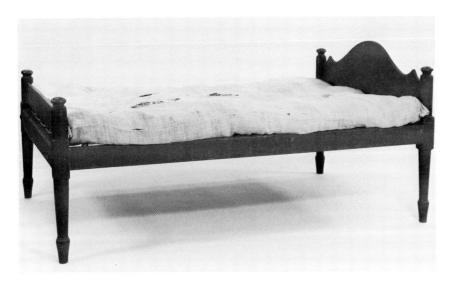

had informed opinions about the neighborhood already. Local men could be expected to know what was going on or else whose word to trust about it.[62]

It was an attitude toward neighbors reflected in the Springers' two-room house. Judging from the inventory, Thomas and Elizabeth slept upstairs, as did at least one of their daughters. They also used the space for storing clothing and extra bedding, and perhaps for spooling yarn. Another bed sat in the common room downstairs, along with the family's best chairs and tables, a looking glass, a linen chest, and a corner cupboard filled with queen's ware, teacups, and wine glasses. How the Springers arranged these furnishings is hard to say. Some of the items they owned had quite specific uses: a dining table, a breakfast table, and a tea table. People whose houses had several first-floor rooms commonly set such specialized items in different rooms. By contrast, the Springers lived more of their lives in a single setting. By building a separate log kitchen, they removed some work (cooking) and some people (slaves) from that setting. By building a second-floor space for sleeping, they claimed some privacy. Still, for the most part visitors to the Springers could step right into the midst of household life.[63]

The Springers' experience "buying and selling" took them out of their own neighborhood and into an expanding Atlantic market. They dealt directly with mere acquaintances in nearby towns, and indirectly with people in distant cities and countries. The products of their farm might travel to Europe, the West Indies, South America, or even China. Household members stayed closer to home, of course, but though their lives were rural, they were not necessarily isolated. The Limestone Road passed right by the Springer homestead and was a major route from Stanton, Delaware to the Pennsylvania state line. It was a short journey for Thomas into two nearby towns.[64]

One of the towns was New Castle, dismissed in 1760 by an English traveler as "a place of very little consideration." Twenty years later, the town consisted of "a Parish Church, a Presbyterian Meeting-House, a Court House, a Gaol, a Pillory, a Pair of Stocks, one old Cannon for Signals or rejoicing Days and a Pound for Hogs." Nor was the village likely to grow very rapidly, for there was "no Wharf or Dock, where ships can ride out of the strong Current." Yet New Castle was the city where growing numbers of Irish immigrants entered the country to settle farms in the region. Forty miles below Philadelphia, it was a stopping place for overland travelers between that city and Baltimore, and a port where outbound Philadelphia ships stopped to take on livestock and inbound ships stopped to pick up pilots. Equally important, it was the political capital of the county, the seat of courts of justice, and a center for legal affairs. Thomas Springer had to travel there to register his will, record land deeds, and cast his vote for local officials like the county sheriff or for president of the United States.[65]

There were shops in New Castle, but the most important economic center of the region was Wilmington, six miles east of the Springer farm. Originally founded—as "Fort Christina"—by the New Sweden Company in the 1630s, the town remained small for a century's time. In the 1730s Wilmington took on a new name and new life. Its growth depended in part on its location. Settlers began pouring into Lancaster and Chester counties in Pennsylvania, pushing the farming frontier to the west. Soon farmers in the region began producing surplus wheat. Many found the shortest route to market was to send it overland in wagons to the Christiana River near Wilmington, where it was loaded into shallops, twin-masted freighters that sailed east to the Delaware River and then north to Philadelphia. Wilmington's location made it a center for the transhipment of grain.[66]

By the 1770s, Wilmington merchants dealt with many parts of the Atlantic market. For the most part they carried staples: bread, flour, beef, pork, and lumber for the West Indies; potash and flaxseed for Ireland; and a variety of goods (including rice and indigo acquired through trade with the southern colonies) for England. They brought in rum, molasses, sugar, and coffee from the West Indies, linens and glass from Ireland, china and tinware from Britain, as well as Indian cottons, Chinese tea and silk, Eastern spices, and European wines. They distributed these foreign goods, English manufactures, and items produced locally or by Philadelphia artisans to the inland farmers of Delaware and Pennsylvania. Around this commerce developed a community of local artisans, including shipbuilders, coopers, and

BANAN and BURKE,
are just returned from Cork, in the Henry, of White-Haven, Henry Jefferson, Master, and have for Sale on board said vessel, at Brownejohn's Wharf, the following articles, viz.

BEST mess pork in barrels and half barrels,
Do. mess beef in barrels and half barrels,
Mould candles, and soap,
Rose butter, of the first quality,
Ox tongues, in half barrels,
Pigs tongues, in ditto,
A parcel of earthen-ware,
Best London-bottled PORTER,
A parcel of best quills,
Fifty dozen of prime CLARET,
A few puncheons of Antigua RUM,
Mens and womens shoes,
A parcel of best boots, and a few saddles,
Linen and worsted stockings,
A parcel of the best Irish linens,
A parcel of womens callimanco and silk petticoats,
Sixty suits of mens best superfine cloths, suitable to every season,
A parcel of stamp'd linens,
A parcel of check, and check trowsers,
A parcel of lawn and silk handkerchiefs,
With other articles too tedious to mention.
And as they are determined to return immediately

Foodstuffs, clothing, cloth, and liquor were available at importers' stores.

Travel over land improved, but roads remained rough, and water continued to be the preferred means of transport into the nineteenth century.

Salt was a precious commodity, often stored in a box like the one below and hung by the fire to keep dry.

Wilmington and New-Castle Mail.

THE SUBSCRIBERS respectfully inform the Public, and the Citizens of Wilmington and New-Castle in particular, that they have established a Stage for the purpose of carrying the Mail between the aforesaid places, and also for the conveyance of passengers and baggage....It will leave New-Castle for Wilmington, every morning between 6 and 7 o'clock, and arrive at D. Brinton's Tavern, in time for passengers to take the 8 o'clock Stage for Philadelphia.

THE Stage will occasionally return to New-Castle in the forenoon, when a sufficient number of passengers offer, and back to Wilmington, and leave there every day for New-Castle after the arrival of the Philadelphia Stages.

Passengers may rest assured, that this establishment will be much safer and more expeditious than any heretofore established between those two Towns; having the best horses, and a careful driver.

JOSEPH BRINGHURST, P. M. *Wilmington.*
DAVID MORRISON, P. M. *New-Castle.*

Wilmington,
Delaware.

others closely tied to commerce, and "hatters, coppersmiths, Booksellers, &c."[67]

Around midcentury, another element contributed to Wilmington's growth: millers began using the powerful waters of the Brandywine River to grind grain on a large scale. Early in the 1780s, there were seven mills within 150 yards of one another along the river. In most mills, two pairs of grindstones were connected to a single set of gears, so that one pair could cool while the other ran. Wagons brought in Pennsylvania wheat, and ships could anchor right off the banks of the city's merchant mills. Millers reached out for supplies from farms in New Jersey, Maryland, Virginia, and New York. By 1788, said James Tilton, it was "a prevailing opinion in Delaware that we have the largest and most perfect manufacture of flour, within a like space of ground known in the world."[68]

The output of the mills was indeed prodigious. By the 1790s, mills along the Brandywine were grinding 300,000 to 500,000 bushels of wheat every year, and entrepreneurs were still buying up expensive millsites and building more mills. Wilmington merchants expanded their trade accordingly, shipping more and more grain to the West Indies and sending both flour and wheat to Philadelphia for local consumption, for export, and for making ship's biscuit and bread. In the last decade of the century, the French Revolution increased the demand for wheat and other grains in both Europe and the West Indies. Thomas Springer's surplus wheat eventually reached distant consumers.[69]

The expansion of their operations changed the millers' relationship with farmers in the area. Milling had always been a part of life in rural Delaware, but it had been a part-time occupation of farmers with lands located on the riverbanks. The men who established mills along the Brandywine in the late eighteenth century were rarely farmers too. Increasingly they specialized, and when they branched out into new ventures their pursuits were seldom agricultural. Many millers took over much of their own shipping, so that they became flour merchants as well as mill owners. Moreover, by 1785, the Brandywine millers were getting to be quite well-to-do; said one traveler, "these mills belong to 11 people and bring them an immense income." Although the cold of winter sometimes froze millraces in Wilmington, otherwise the mills operated all year long. And "in active or busy times," wrote James Tilton, "the mill grinds perpetually night and day." Late in the 1790s a French traveler remarked upon the novel principles by which one family ran their milling business: "Their Mill is not employed for the public but solely for their own private service. It is called a flour Manufactory."[70]

Such changes made a difference in the lives of Delaware farmers. In 1783, complaints about the behavior of Brandywine millers reached the ears of the state government. Over forty farmers from the Brandywine and Christiana hundreds petitioned the legislature. In the past, the farmers said, they had customarily taken wheat and corn to the mills "to be ground into Meal for the use of their families, paying therefor a stated Toll." Yet recently mill owners had come to prefer the "very great advantage arising to themselves by purchasing large quantities of Wheat and Manufacturing the same into Flour for distant Markets." As a result, the farmers charged, mill owners had "neglected and even refused grinding the Corn belonging to the adjoining

Inhabitants for the supply of their respective Familys—by which means the Inhabitants are subjected to great inconvenience and often distress."[71]

The farmers considered it a "Matter of Right" to have access to local mills. Mills, they thought, had been built "as well for the ease and convenience of the Neighbouring People and the private emolument of the particular Owners," so millers should work both for their own self-interest and for the welfare of their neighbors and neighborhood. Milling represented a sort of quasi-public venture to Delaware farmers; a mill was not quite a private business. Apparently the state agreed with that assessment, for the legislature set fines for millers who refused to grind grain for local use at least one day out of every week. Farmers expected millers to continue neighboring, to keep borrowing and lending in the local market as well as buying and selling in the wider world. There is evidence, however, that many

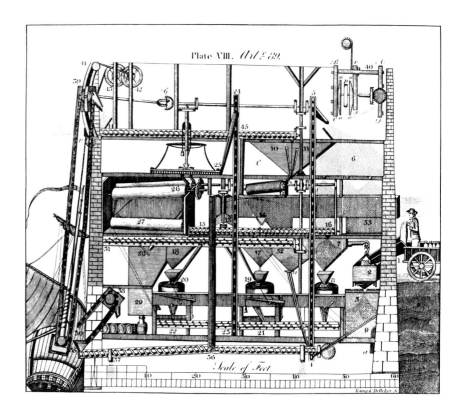

Delaware resident Oliver Evans patented a mechanized grain elevator and "hopper boy" and illustrated them in The Young Mill-Wright and Miller's Guide, *1795.*

THE FARM AND THE MARKETPLACE

Brandywine millers preferred profit to neighborliness; within a very few years the legislature had to increase the fine for turning away local customers. [72]

No similar complaints survive from farmers in the Springers' part of the county. Perhaps millers in the area did not withdraw so fully from neighboring. Yet they did withdraw from agriculture; many of the millers in Mill Creek Hundred owned too little land to be farmers as well. Some branched out into other pursuits. A few took advantage of their location along the water to run a sawmill, paper mill, or fulling mill too. At least one put capital into livestock and owned a springhouse for butter making. Moreover, like Brandywine millers, Mill Creek millers developed connections outside the immediate neighborhood. The Harlans' son William carried on the family's dealings in Philadelphia; Joshua Stroud acquired another mill in New London, Pennsylvania. The Stroud mill next to Thomas Springer's land boasted the latest technological improvements: a grain elevator to take wheat to the mill's top floor, and a "hopper boy," a revolving rake to spread the meal out to cool and then gather it up again. These devices increased the volume of flour produced and reduced the labor needed. In Mill Creek as in neighboring hundreds, the world of selling and buying threatened to change relationships in the community. [73]

Not surprisingly, millers in the hundred could be distinguished from farmers around them by their wealth. In 1798 there were seventeen men in the area who owned a mill or held an interest in one. Nine of them were assessed in the top 5 percent of all taxables. Most of the rest fell into the top 15 percent. Moreoever, millers acted increasingly to make their wealth visible. To the eye, Mill Creek Hundred presented a landscape of houses made of logs and houses made of stone. Yet many country millers built themselves houses like those in Wilmington: houses made of brick. Late in the century, millers were three times more likely than farmers to live in brick houses. Building these substantial homes, millers marked their distance from their neighbors, expressing both material prosperity and cosmopolitan taste. [74]

Thomas Springer did not live to build a house of brick—and

maybe he would have chosen not to build one, anyway. Yet in some measure he and Elizabeth oriented their lives toward the city of Wilmington and beyond. The Springers seem to have found opportunities in many of the changes that threatened other farmers. Thomas could accept the growing power of millers with equanimity because his household was relatively independent of them. The Springers did grow some grain, but they concentrated on raising livestock. The household found several ways to gain from the market: fattening animals, producing butter, selling wool, yarn, and meat. They could live with one foot in a local network of exchange, the other in a wider market. In large part, what made this strategy possible were the inherited advantages that gave Thomas land, livestock, and control of others' labor. He had managed to gain "independence" in the first place only with the help of his successful father, and he prospered only by depending on the work of Elizabeth, some white servants or relatives, and four African-American slaves. Such affluence was out of the reach of many young men in the Springers' neighborhood. In material terms, Thomas and Elizabeth Springer were among the lucky ones.

Just after the turn of the century, Elizabeth Springer died. We do not know the cause. Left with two young daughters and a household to run, Thomas decided to remarry. He chose twenty-two-year-old Margaret Wells. Margaret's father had died five years earlier, and her mother passed away in 1801. Marriage to Thomas Springer made sense to her. They were wed in 1802. Margaret brought her share of the family inheritance into the marriage. There is some evidence that she brought an eight-day clock—listed as the Springers' most expensive possession a few years later—into the household, where it was prominently displayed in the downstairs room. Margaret took over Elizabeth's duties as household manager and mother of Ann and Mary. In 1804, Thomas fell ill. He died in the fall of that year, having lived forty years. He provided as best he could for his family. He left Margaret "the white-face cow" and the proper legal settlement for widows: a one-third interest in his estate for life. He appointed Joshua Johnson as a guardian for Ann and Mary during their minority, and instructed his executors, Joshua Stroud and Jeremiah Springer, to sell the farm for his children's support.[75]

THE FARM AND THE MARKETPLACE

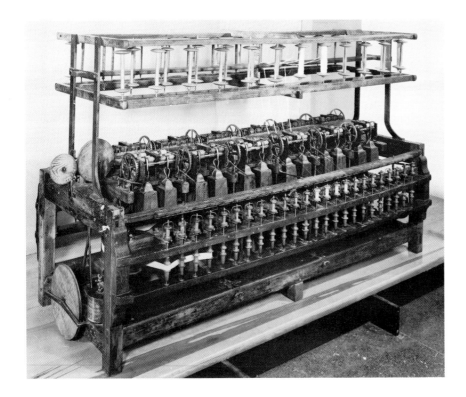

In eighteenth-century England, a series of inventions allowed workers who spun and carded fibers to increase their output, first in the home, then in the factory. In the 1790s, American entrepreneurs also moved labor into factories and expanded production using machines like this spinning frame.

The household broke up quickly. The slaves Will and Ace were sold away from the family. They probably joined the stream of unfree labor moving to the south and west, eventually to grow cotton to supply textile mills along the Brandywine and elsewhere. Amelia and Sara were left to the Springer girls by Thomas's will. Margaret must have gone to live with relatives for a few years. Mary and Ann may have joined their stepmother, but it seems more likely that they settled in with closer relatives in the Mill Creek area. In 1806 Margaret married again and moved into New Castle as Mrs. George Peirce, Esq., leaving many rural routines behind.[76]

Mary Springer remained closer to the land. In 1808, when she was still in her teens, she married Robert McMurphy, son of a farmer and gristmiller. She and her husband ran a farm and a tavern "on the State road leading from New Castle to Dover on the North side of Black Bird Creek." The growth of cloth manufacture freed Mary from the spinning wheel, but she must have used most of the other skills she had learned growing up on the Mill Creek farm. Ann Springer was to experience town living like her step-mother. She moved to Middletown, Delaware, and married Richard Craddock in 1814. The two sisters remained close: when Mary's husband wrote his will, he appointed Ann's husband as his executor. By 1820, Robert McMurphy had died, and Mary McMurphy and Ann and Richard Craddock had all left the state. It is nice to speculate that they moved south and west, perhaps following growing numbers into Kentucky and beyond. A man named David Eastburn bought the Mill Creek farm at auction in 1805. Within a few years he rented it out to a tenant farmer.[77]

THE FARM AND THE MARKETPLACE

THE AMBITIONS OF
A TIDEWATER PLANTER

*Henry Saunders of
Isle of Wight County, Virginia*

$\mathcal{A}$lmost half a century after the merchant Samuel Colton paid local artisans to build a house on the Connecticut River, and several years after Thomas Springer raised a log house on Mill Creek, a planter named Henry Saunders directed his slaves to build a house in Isle of Wight County, Virginia. Like the Springer log house, the Saunders house was small—it stood just a story-and-a-half high, with two small rooms on each floor. Like the Colton house, the Saunders house reflected its owner's ambition for standing in the community. Henry Saunders followed the example of a wealthy neighbor when he chose brick for the two gable ends of his dwelling and fashionable paneling for the interior. The house expressed Saunders's desire to leave his mark on the landscape of southeastern Virginia.

This is the story of Henry Saunders, his community, and his ambitions. It is important to know at the outset that Henry Saunders was no ordinary Virginia planter. While he never reached the ranks of the greatest planters of his society, at the peak of his landholding and slaveholding career he was better off than 90 percent of the white men in his county. But there is also a much more spectacular fact about him: late in the year 1808, Henry was convicted of murdering his wife, Anne. He was sentenced to serve eighteen years in prison and jailed at the state penitentiary in Richmond, where he died. It is a shocking fact, and a tantalizing one, for time and happenstance have closed it to us. Just after the Civil War, fire destroyed the records of Nansemond County, where Henry's trial took place. We know that at least twenty-one neighbors testified against him at that trial, but we don't know what they said under oath, or what Henry said in his own defense. We don't know what happened between Henry and Anne, and we don't know why it did.

In light of this tragedy, the question arises: how much can we learn from Henry Saunders's life about the lives of his more ordinary neighbors? In fact, we can learn a fair amount. Little of what we know about Saunders's life illuminates the murder itself, but evidence survives about such matters as his land purchases, his slaveholding, and his appointment to the militia, experiences that place him in the common world of Virginia's white men. It is also worth remembering

Benjamin Henry Latrobe, a critic of slavery, recorded one view of the institution in 1798, using pen, ink, and watercolor. He called it "An Overseer Doing His Duty."

that the twenty-one neighbors who testified at Henry's trial must have had knowledge of the Saunders household, knowledge that came from social visits and business contacts and that reflects the Saunderses' membership in the Isle of Wight community. It is true that that community eventually cast Henry out. But his crime did not take place outside his society; as we shall see, it was a society in which violence had its place, where affluent men like Henry Saunders learned pride, self-assertion, and to expect to have their own way.

𝒫erhaps the first Englishman to step south of the James River was John Smith, who, in 1608, visited the Warrascoyak Indians in what later became Isle of Wight County. The Warrascoyacks provided Smith with fourteen bushels of corn to feed the starving settlers at

Jamestown. It was not the last instance of friendly dealings between Native Virginians and the newcomers, but within a very few years a less amicable pattern became the norm. The English people's hunger for corn quickly became hunger for land. By 1620 some had set up farms below the James, settling first along the riverbank at Lawne's Creek, then farther east at the mouth of the Warrascoyack River (Pagan's Creek).[1] In 1622, an Indian attack pushed back white settlement, but the English continued to immigrate, now with renewed determination to wipe out the native population or at least push them out of the way. The Warrascoyacks, Nottoways, and other peoples, their numbers thinned by smallpox and warfare, made treaties and traded with whites, striving to keep their own way of life and some of their hunting grounds in the face of continued white expansion.[2]

The white population grew, in spite of the extraordinary toll taken by deadly diseases in Virginia. Typhoid fever and other illnesses combined with malnutrition to kill many new immigrants, especially those who had the misfortune to arrive in summertime. Those who survived the first devastating year of "seasoning" could still expect to suffer from debilitating diseases and to face early death. Yet year by year English people continued to pour into the colony, and slowly they began to shape a distinctive society. New Englanders would settle in close-knit villages, but Virginians chose to settle some distance from one another on plantations. Spreading out across the countryside was not the original plan. Like other English, those who landed in the Chesapeake area thought of towns when they thought of civilization. But soon after landing they discovered another possibility: tobacco, a plant grown by Native Americans, could be cultivated, cured, and sent to England to create and then feed habits of smoking and snuff. They discovered that if a planter devoted all of his time to tobacco, if he could command the labor of others, and if he was lucky, he could make a fortune. As early as the 1620s, Virginians began to stake out plantations and build an "empire," as King James put it, "on smoke."[3]

"Smoke" made some planters rich, but it also created inequality and discontent. It took a lot of work to raise a tobacco crop. Just a few harvests exhausted the soil, so new land had to be cleared all the time, and the plants themselves needed constant care. To become rich, a man needed laborers who would work very hard for very little pay. Virginia's ambitious planters imported English servants, mostly young men under indenture to work from four to seven years to pay for their passage to the New World. In America, these men found that Virginia law, made and enforced by the emerging master class, offered little protection against abuse and exploitation. Even servitude in England was benign compared to the severity and degradation of servitude on the Chesapeake. Virginia employers beat their servants like animals, sold them to new masters at their own convenience, and occasionally even gambled them away at cards or dice like any other piece of property. If servants ran away, the law simply extended their terms of service. When they lived long enough to finish their term and gain freedom, they found that most available land lay out at the edge of white settlement, where they could expect resistance from Indians. The government was no help, because its leaders were content to see scarcity of land force many people back into servitude. So ex-

Tobacco, along with patent medicine, was among the first products marketed by brand name. Sellers of both claimed that their products had curative properties.

THE AMBITIONS OF A TIDEWATER PLANTER

As these eighteenth-century English tobacco labels illustrate, consumers a continent away still associated the weed with black labor and white leisure.

servants and other poor whites had to eke out a living at the margins of the society, hoping to gain a few acres or farm as a tenant rather than become a servant again.[4]

The Saunders family started out among the ranks of the discontent. In 1677, one John Saunders appears in the record as a "notorious actor in the late rebellion."[5] The rebellion in question was Nathanial Bacon's, an uprising of whites who coveted Indian lands, scorned the royal governor's efforts to distinguish friendly from unfriendly tribes, and resented the high taxes levied to pay the expenses of the rich men who ran the government. Bacon and his followers went off to kill Indians, and maybe to fight the king's governor too. After months of bloodshed and disorder, England sent an armed ship to sail up and down the James, convincing many rebels of the advantages of loyalty to the governor.[6] John Saunders was apparently among them; he was fined two thousand pounds of tobacco for his part in the revolt, then pardoned. By 1681 he was in sufficiently good standing with the government to receive a share in a grant of 1,650 acres of land near Kingsdale Swamp, at the county borders of Nansemond and Isle of

These familiar, powerful illustrations from early eighteenth-century manuals advised slave traders how to make the most economical use of space.

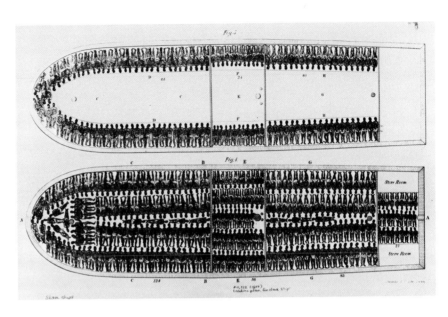

Wight—a few miles south of the site where Henry Saunders would build his house one hundred years later.[7] By the turn of the century, this generous grant had been divided among many heirs; in 1704, eight Saunderses headed households in Isle of Wight and Nansemond counties. Henry's grandfather was prominent among them. With 700 acres, he owned more than 80 percent of the landowners in the area did. Most other Saunderses owned between 100 and 200 acres, enough for a modest plantation. They generally settled into a pattern of small farming, raising tobacco, corn, and other crops, and practicing carpentry, coopering, and other trades on the side.[8]

Virginia as a whole was settling down by the early 1700s. It was still a society of rich and poor, and still a society where the ambitious made good by exploiting the labor of others. But more and more of the exploited were African slaves. Although a few Africans had lived in Virginia since the second decade of the seventeenth century, it was seventy years before black slaves began replacing white servants as the colony's main source of labor. By then it had become harder to entice English immigrants to Virginia; Pennsylvania, founded in the early 1680s, was a better "poor man's country," offering better treatment and more opportunities to indentured servants.[9] In addition, a decline in the death rate made it more profitable to buy a slave for life than to hire a servant for a few years. Black labor offered one other advantage: since slaves never became free, they would never turn into a stream of intractable, unhappy, land-seeking poor. They would not stir up conflict with the Indians, set up on their own to grow tobacco and depress the price of the crop, or demand a more democratic government. Of course, they *would* revolt, run away, or resist the demands of their owners in other ways. And they had no incentive to work hard at all. To make them work, masters applied the tactics they had developed to force work from their white servants: they used violence and terror.[10]

The switch to slave labor changed white society in unforeseen ways. It deepened the differences that existed among Virginia landowners. Slaves cost more than servants, so only those who could spare enough capital imported them.[11] The three workers that Henry Saunders's well-to-do grandfather imported in 1698 were probably African, but other, smaller farmers still had to be satisfied with white servants.[12] As slave women gave birth, their children became property too, concentrating control of slave labor in the hands of the rich. Only a few owned enough slaves and enough rich land to live in leisure and opulence. Late in the seventeenth century, William Fitzhugh told English readers that a well-located farm and eight to ten slaves would yield "a handsom, gentile and sure subsistace."[13] He made it sound easy, and perhaps it was—for the propertied class who could afford so much land and so many slaves. The great majority of white Virginians could not. They toiled in the fields themselves, owned one or two

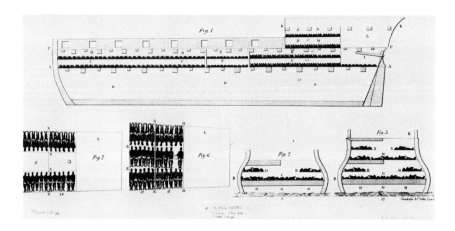

The "middle passage" was the time blacks spent between capture in Africa and arrival months later on an American plantation as slaves.

slaves or none at all, lived in cramped, ramshackle houses, and depended on their wealthier neighbors to extend them credit, help them market their crops, and tide them over in times of crisis. Most Virginians were plain folk and remained divided from wealthy "gentlefolk" in important ways.[14]

At the same time, the switch to slave labor created new ties among whites, despite their differences. Ambitious planters no longer had to extort labor from other whites; they had blacks to exploit instead. If small planters sometimes resented their more fortunate neighbors, they were apt to feel a sense of commonality with them too. Ways of thinking developed that expressed and created this new unity: not all English people started out convinced that all Africans were inferior to all English, but soon enough, slaveowners promoted that idea. In the late decades of the seventeenth century, Virginia's government passed laws explicitly aimed at separating whites from blacks; these laws provided that white servants should be treated better and prohibited the interracial marriages that had seemed fine to many white Virginians for several generations after they first met Africans. Whites' feelings of racial superiority grew: however poor they might be, they were not slaves. The creation of a settled white community, then, took place only in relation to Virginia's black one.[15]

Virginia's slave community also went through a process of settling down in the 1700s. West Africans imported into the colony came from different countries, spoke different languages, and brought different cultural expectations. All had been painfully uprooted from their homes and subjected to the brutalities of the Middle Passage across the Atlantic. It took time to put down roots in Virginia: Africans created a pidgin language to talk with other slaves, learned English from whites, and devised ways of understanding and shaping their new situation. They and their Afro-American children created a way of life to counter the violence being done them and limit the exploitation of their labor. As the century wore on, more blacks were Virginia-born. More lived on large plantations, spending some of their time apart from whites in separate quarters, where, drawing on African traditions and on their experience under slavery, they formed a culture of their own. So in Isle of Wight (and throughout eastern Virginia)

"Group of Negros, as imported to be sold for Slaves" illustrated a 1796 book about the armed rebellion of African slaves in Dutch Guiana thirty years earlier.

THE AMBITIONS OF A TIDEWATER PLANTER

From the fifteenth through the nineteenth centuries, Europeans brought an estimated 13 to 30 million Africans to the New World. Relatively few—probably less than 1 million—were imported into what became the United States.

there grew two communities, profoundly linked with one another and profoundly opposed. Differences in wealth divided the white community, but the creation of racial slavery united them. The white world Henry Saunders inherited at midcentury was grounded in a black world, dependent on black labor, and shaped by black culture in profound ways.[16]

$\mathscr{H}$enry Saunders's father owned five black slaves when he died in 1761. The appraisers of his estate tell us as much about white attitudes as about black lives; they calmly listed slaves' names, then assigned them market values. Most valuable was Tom, "a Negro man," listed at £60. There were two women: Mage, appraised at £45, and Joan, either sickly or more elderly, appraised at £20. Finally, there were two children. Jubilee, a boy appraised at £45, was already a strong working hand on the plantation. Joan, listed at £12, could not have been much more than a baby.[17]

At two hundred years' distance, it is tempting to imagine family relationships among Saunders's five slaves. Might young Joan have been the daughter of Mage and named, perhaps, for her grandmother Joan? Could Tom have been her father, and Jubilee an older brother? It is possible. But twentieth-century assumptions often distort eighteenth-century lives. Slaves lived not where they wanted but as their masters chose. White people generally kept very young black children with their mothers—the children, by law, belonged to their mother's owner. But whites felt little need to allow men to live with their wives and children or to respect other ties of family or friendship, no matter how precious those ties to blacks themselves. No law required whites to respect black families when selling or bequeathing the people they considered their property. Therefore, it is unlikely that the Saunders blacks were a simple family unit. Blacks belonging to some of the Saunderses' neighbors—the thirty slaves on Brewer Godwin's farm, the seventeen on Benjamin Eley's—had a better chance of living with mother and father and amongst brothers and sisters and other relatives too. By contrast, the Saunders farm was pretty small. If Joan was the offspring of either Mage or the elder Joan, then the odds are that her father lived on a neighboring plantation and was allowed to visit the family once a week on Sundays.[18]

Blood relationships and marriages were important to black Virginians: they named their children after family members and traveled long distances to see relatives whenever they got the chance.[19] Also important were the ties formed within households, among the people who lived and worked together, sharing knowledge and resources in

THE AMBITIONS OF A TIDEWATER PLANTER

daily life. Mage, Joan, Tom, and Jubilee all probably took part in caring for young Joan and for each other.

In part this practice was a heritage of West African life. Despite their differences, many Africans shared a few basic traditions that survived in the New World. Many came from cultures that assumed every member of a community to be related to everyone else, so that everyone shared responsibility for overseeing the young, the old, and the infirm. Their vulnerability in Virginia encouraged West Africans to keep that expectation of mutual responsibility and pass it on to their African-American children. Whatever their biological relationship, the blacks at the Saunders place had to look out for one another.[20]

Yet no bonds of their own making could protect slaves for long against the disruption of their domestic arrangements, and the death of Henry Saunders, senior, in 1761, broke up his black household. His widow, Martha Saunders, was left with two minor children, Henry, junior, and a younger child, Sarah. Young Joan stayed with Martha and her children and shortly after Henry senior's death another child was born to either Mage or Joan, for the executors of the estate paid a midwife for assisting at the delivery and Martha Saunders noted down care of "young negroes" as one of her household expenses.[21] Over the next decade, some of the older slaves might have continued working on the Saunders farm, but Martha hired at least some of them to nearby planters who wanted an extra hand or two for a season. If the slaves were lucky, the hire might reunite them with kin or friends on other plantations. To be hired by a small planter meant living close to whites; to be hired by a large planter meant living in a separate black community, in slave quarters at some distance from the "great house" where whites lived, spending some of one's time in relative freedom from white supervision. Whatever their feelings about their living situation where they were hired, the Saunders slaves knew it to be temporary. The usual practice was for hire to end a few weeks before Christmas, when hired slaves would return to their owner's household. For a decade of Henry Saunders's youth, Tom, Joan, Mage, and Jubilee probably spent most of the year living apart from one another.[22]

To counter the pain of such separations, blacks created networks of

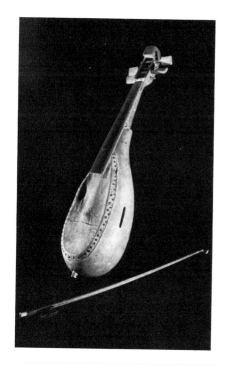

Afro-Americans drew on the designs of both European violins and African stringed instruments to make the gourd fiddle. This fiddle, from early nineteenth-century Maryland, is of the type commonly made in the eighteenth century.

African women made baskets of intricately coiled design, some woven so tightly they could hold water, some so sturdy they were passed from generation to generation. Africans brought the skill of coil basket-making to the New World and passed it on to their Afro-American children. Here, a nineteenth-century Afro-American bread basket.

relatives and friends throughout their neighborhoods. White Virginians had laid out roads so they could travel and visit from house to house; blacks traveled these roads as well, and as newspaper ads for runaway slaves show, when they lacked permission to travel they used their own pathways to reach the quarters of neighboring plantations. To limit the disruption that whites caused in their lives, black Virginians forged broad alliances with one another, counting on mutual protection and support, building loyalties beyond the household and beyond the narrow nuclear family.[23]

In 1771 Martha Saunders decided to remarry. She asked the court to confer upon her the one-third of her husband's estate that legally belonged to her during her lifetime. Accordingly, in February the court of Isle of Wight awarded her ownership of Tom and Joan. The court did not specify which Joan, so perhaps by then one of the slaves with that name had left the household. When Martha married planter John Carstephan and went to live at his farm nearby, she probably took the two with her.[24] A few years later Henry took the rest of the slaves and set up a farm of his own. After ten years of instability, the Saunders blacks were able to set up family and household lives with a little greater security. Yet the slaves still had no guarantees against renewed disruption and pain.

An Afro-American "fanner" basket also from the nineteenth century, used in the processing of rice. After threshing, the rice was tossed up with the fanner; the kernels would fall again to the basket while the husks would blow away.

One more appearance in the records illuminates the lives of the Saunderses' black household. In 1773, Mage was taken to the county courthouse and charged with breaking into Moses Eley's house and taking fifteen or sixteen pounds in Virginia money and "sundry other articles." Mage claimed that "she was in no wise guilty" of the theft, but the testimony of "Sundry Witnesses" convicted her, and the judges sentenced her to hang. Things looked bleak. Then, on June 3, while she was in jail, she reported to the sheriff that she was pregnant. The sheriff could not determine whether she was telling the truth, but he wrote to the governor to suggest a stay of execution or, as was sometimes granted in such cases, a reprieve.[25]

The records do not reveal whether Mage was really pregnant, or even what the governor finally decided about hanging her. But the episode dramatizes two key elements of African-American life in Virginia. White owners had tremendous power over slaves and were willing to use violence to keep it, whether acting as legislators and judges in cases like Mage's, patrolling as militiamen to prevent slave meetings and uprisings, or acting as individual owners with whip and chains to discipline their workers. But blacks were able to create space for themselves because they knew that their labor was valuable to whites and because that value put limits to the violence whites would do. Even in order to hang black criminals, white authorities had to take account of their value as property: slaveowners would not testify against slaves in capital cases if it meant losing their valuable property. The law required the county court to estimate Mage's value (£46) when she was sentenced to hang, and then to recompense the Saunders estate for her loss. By claiming that she was pregnant, Mage gave white authorities a chance to save that expense, consider the gain of a black child, and prove themselves lenient and humane. She offered them a chance to serve their own self-interest and their own self-image too.[26]

Mage's was merely an extreme version of a defense used daily by slaves who never crossed white men's laws and slaves who never got caught at it. Joan, Tom, young Joan, and Jubilee did not need the example of Mage's conviction and bid for survival to understand the rules of the game. In daily life they learned early of white power— that they had to plant tobacco and corn, tend cattle, and do other work for the whites who owned or hired them. At the same time, they knew they were vital: their labor formed the basis of the Saunderses' livelihood, and they could use that fact as leverage to gain some control over their lives. They could cooperate with one another in working slowly, pretend to be sick, or run away to the woods or to another plantation at harvest, when their work was most crucial. These tactics, or the threat of their use, might wring concessions from white owners. Masters generally recognized Sundays and a few religious holidays as time off from work, and many allowed their slaves to raise some livestock and cultivate small gardens of their own on the land near their quarters. White owners often liked to think of these concessions as evidence of their own kindness to their workers; the workers saw it differently, considering these arrangements to be rights rather than privileges. The master who tried to change things could expect to meet with disobedience from his hands. He could respond with severe punishment but, especially in the face of united resistance, if he wanted to keep the plantation going—and to think well of himself at the same time—he had to consider slaves' wishes. Whites could not simply dictate their relationship with blacks; instead, they had to negotiate and compromise.[27]

$\mathscr{Y}$oung Henry Saunders, born about midcentury, grew up on the privileged side of this relationship. We have only a few glimpses of his boyhood life, mostly from the records of the county "Orphans Court," the body that officially oversaw the inheritance of fatherless minors. Henry's mother, Martha, kept track of her expenditures for the children. One year, she noted, she paid for clothing for Henry: one "fine Hatt" worth eight shillings; an ordinary hat worth three shillings; a pair of leather breeches; linen and oznabrig (another fabric) and the labor involved in making a coat and pants. Another year she supplied Sarah with the materials to sew her own clothes: linen, holland, and durants. About 1770 Martha paid for "schooling and board" for each child. This education must have been rudimentary—Martha spent only as much on Henry as on Sarah, and girls were not expected to need much learning. Henry probably learned reading, writing, and basic figuring. Lessons available outside the classroom were just as important. As a youth he learned that being white meant he could aspire to live off the labor of blacks. And being male meant he, and not his sister Sarah, would inherit the bulk of the estate. When he came of age, sometime in the mid-1770s, Henry took over his inheritance—then four or five slaves and about 250 acres of land—and set up as a young planter.[28]

Henry devoted most of his time to making a living. For him, as for his father and grandfather, the demands of the farm ordered daily life. Four or five slaves were not enough to free him from labor; although he could delegate the most onerous tasks, he put his own back to farm work too. Raising tobacco was a year-round and often day-long job; its demands were, in fact, a good deal more burdensome than those of the crops cultivated by farmers in the northern colonies. Where wheat could be grown in irregular rhythms of intense toil and extended leisure, tobacco required constant attention. Even before one crop reached the market, the next one had to be in the ground. Ideally, this meant breaking new land as soon as the winter frost had passed, the strongest workers cutting trees, all hands working after hours to burn off wood, brush, and roots. In March or early April work moved to a separate seedbed, where the ground had to be dug and raked and finally sown with tobacco seed. While the seeds sprouted and took root, attention returned to the new ground cleared for the crop itself. It was heavy work with a hoe to break up the earth, then draw it into small hills, roughly knee-high, set in neat rows and flattened at the top. Once the seedlings were strong enough, sometime in May or June, the workers waited for a good rainfall, then quickly transplanted the seedlings to the hills. There followed a long growing season, during which Henry and his slaves built more hills to feed the young plants and hoed between the rows to prevent weeds from choking off their growth. "He who would have a good crop of tobacco," advised one contemporary, " . . . must not be sparing of his labour, but must keep the ground constantly stirring during the whole growth of the crop."[29]

Summer brought other tasks. Workers went from plant to plant, pinching off the main stems ("topping") and extra sprouts ("suckering") to leave all nourishment for the valuable leaves. Some years worms infested the tobacco and had to be picked carefully from the leaves. As summer turned to fall, a novice like Henry Saunders might consult a neighboring "crop master" or his most experienced hands: harvest should begin only when the leaves reached full ripeness but end before the first autumn frost. Everyone available pitched in to the tasks of harvest. The most skillful and experienced hands cut leaves, harvesting ripe plants first, leaving less mature ones a little more time. The other hands gathered the leaves into bunches (or "turns"), attached them to a stick, and carried them to a nearby "tobacco house," a wooden building where the sticks were hung and the leaves suspended to cure. For the most part, air cured the leaves, although in moist seasons planters built fires to smoke them dry. A slave or two on nearly every large plantation had some coopering skills and made hogsheads (barrels) to take the crop to market. When the crop was cured, workers stripped the leaves from the sticks, rolled the leaves into bundles, and packed them firmly into hogsheads. By then preparations for the next year's tobacco were under way—clearing new land or, when necessary, penning livestock on older fields to manure the tired soil.[30]

Into this annual round of work Saunders and his slaves fitted many

These scenes of a tobacco house show the various stages in processing and inspecting the leaves as they are prepared for sale.

How planters moved tobacco to market depended on their access to good roads or waterways.

other jobs. Farmers in southeast Virginia produced goods besides tobacco for market. They raised cattle and swine for meat for the West Indies and gathered pitch and tar for use in shipbuilding from the forests and swamps of the region. Many of these products went through the hands of merchants in Norfolk, a city that became a center for trade with Barbados and other Caribbean islands. West Indian planters enjoyed a lucrative market for their sugar crop, so they devoted as little land and labor as possible to the production of food. It seems likely that Henry Saunders and his slaves produced some crops or livestock for the West Indies trade, along with substantial acres of corn to feed farm animals and to feed themselves. On most Virginia plantations, slaves grew garden vegetables for consumption on the farm; they hunted and fished in nearby woods and streams to supplement their own diets and supply the tables of their masters. And they did basic carpentry work, building shacks, tobacco houses, and furniture. Still, with a handful of slaves, Henry Saunders could only get so far toward self-sufficiency. Larger plantations came closer. They could spare one or more of their slaves exclusively for skilled craftwork: tailoring, shoemaking, or blacksmithing. Smaller planters like

On the wharves that lined Virginia's rivers, the product of a year's labor in the fields became a commodity on the world market.

Henry Saunders were more dependent on the skills of their neighbors and the wider marketplace for shoes, blankets, and clothing materials for themselves and their slaves.[31]

Of course all planters, big and small, depended on the world market for tobacco. If that made them competitors with each other, it also drew them together on common ground, for they all had to worry about weather, market prices, and getting their crops from the field to the buyer. There were a number of ways of moving tobacco—in carts and wagons or rolled in hoops. Often a number of planters in a neighborhood joined together to take their crops to market; they could pool their horses and wagons, and the trip was more sociable that way. For Henry's grandfather, the "market" meant the wharves of wealthy planters with land along the James River. These men oversaw the loading of their neighbors' crops onto merchant ships and dealt with the agents of British merchant firms. They acted as middlemen, selling English and European imports to smaller planters, sometimes extending credit, often making substantial fortunes from their role as merchants.[32]

In the 1730s, the Virginia legislature passed "inspection" laws meant to upgrade the quality of exports, requiring that all tobacco pass the scrutiny of appointed inspectors. The government set up official tobacco warehouses, and over the years towns grew up around many of them. By Henry Saunders's time, the main market and county seat in Isle of Wight was Smithfield, on the banks of Pagan Creek, where small vessels could sail down from the James. Most of those who lived in Smithfield were involved in trade: representatives

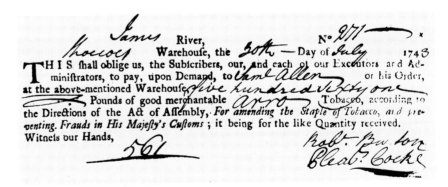

This tobacco note attests that James Allen owned 561 pounds of "merchantable" tobacco at a James River warehouse.

THE AMBITIONS OF A TIDEWATER PLANTER

A high-style, tilt-top tea table, crafted in Philadelphia in 1760–1770, was an excellent prop for anyone in pursuit of the social ideal of genteel living.

of Scots tobacco firms, independent merchants, and sea captains bought up lots in town, where they arranged for the collection and shipment of local tobacco and other products and the importation of English and European goods for local use. They built wharves and warehouses along the river edge and houses and shops above. Henry could take his crop to Smithfield and, if his tobacco passed muster, receive a "tobacco note" from the inspectors. The note functioned as money: Henry could use it to buy imported goods from the merchants in town. Some years Henry probably marketed closer to home, in Suffolk, the county seat of nearby Nansemond County. The River Nansemond was navigable just as far south as Suffolk, and boat traffic made the village the scene of "a pretty brisk trade." In either town, merchants carried much the same sort of goods. Some stocked imported fabrics: calico, Indian cottons, Persian cottons, and others, along with shirt buttons, thimbles, and felt hats. Some brought in West Indian goods, such as coffee, molasses, sugar, rum, salt, and allspice. Some carried imported tablewares and teawares from Britain.[33]

On trips to town Henry could see what the market had to offer, yet

In this 1754 drawing, South Carolina planters enjoy the good life, drinking and making toasts late into the night, while a slave boy nods off by the window.

The English mirror below from the 1780s is indicative of America's economic and aesthetic links with Europe.

it was not at stores but at other planters' houses that he learned the significance of imported goods. Fine fabrics, silver, teacups, and clothing were desirable not in themselves, but for the uses Virginians put them to, the meanings society assigned them. Before midcentury, some well-to-do Virginians began to use imported goods to shape a distinctive way of life. Thomas Pierce, for example, a merchant planter in Smithfield, owned a backgammon table and box, china punch bowls, teacups and saucers, a tea table, silver teaspoons, large and small looking glasses, and eight tablecloths—one of fine damask with matching napkins. All these goods spoke of the importance their owner placed on entertaining other gentlemen and ladies of the county in the proper style. Contemporaries called this style "gentility." More than just the possession of tasteful and expensive goods, gentility implied personal attributes: polished manners; graceful bearing; skill at conversation, dancing, cardplaying, and other games. When they entertained guests in well-appointed parlors, gentlemen like Thomas Pierce exhibited their own refined accomplishments and demonstrated their generosity to others. For Pierce and other such gentlemen, tea-

THE AMBITIONS OF A TIDEWATER PLANTER

cups, punch bowls, and silver spoons were accouterments, necessary props in pursuit of a social ideal.[34]

Far from all white Virginians embraced that ideal, and only the most elite could afford to live in the style of Thomas Pierce. While the rich studied etiquette, practiced deportment, and built spacious houses, the majority lived quite a different life. In the 1770s, Thomas Jefferson considered the houses of laborers and small farmers and concluded that it was "impossible to devise things more ugly, uncomfortable, and happily more perishable." Jefferson may have had unduly high standards, and many middling farmers, like the Saunders family, fared better. Still, few enjoyed the opulent existence of the society's most well-to-do, with neither time, money, nor opportunity to develop genteel graces, travel to Europe for education, or spend long hours conversing in parlors and dining rooms.[35]

But if gentility was not easily accessible, its pursuit was not confined to the elite either. As the century wore on, imported tea sets, silver spoons, and other appurtenances of gentility became more widely owned, and greater numbers of Virginians proved willing to go into debt to get them. In 1761 Henry Saunders's father's best goods included "a parcell of pewter," "a parcel of table knives & forks," a "looking glass," and "a parcel of Table Linnen" worth seven shillings. He could hardly entertain in the style of Thomas Pierce, but genteel living may still have been important to him. Like their social betters, ordinary white Virginians could aspire to excel at horsemanship, dancing, and cardplaying. As the ideal of gentility caught the imaginations of middling and lesser planters, it became a measure of social standing in white society. In a variety of public settings where planters of different classes mixed together, gentility became associated with the authority of the elite. Aspiring young planters like Henry Saunders could spare little time from work to spend entertaining, but they could hardly fail to learn their society's ideals for social authority. Young Henry knew that if he worked hard himself, and if he forced work out of his slaves, he could amass wealth and its trappings. He could aspire to a more genteel way of life—and more social eminence— than his father had enjoyed. He spent most of the 1770s single and working, finding his feet in Isle of Wight society.[36]

Above: Chinese porcelain bowl, 1780s.

Wealthy Virginia planters might enjoy an evening's violin music at home, or else join their social inferiors to hear fiddling in taverns or more humble households.

Local society was dominated by a select group of well-to-do white men, most of them born to the genteel style that young Henry had to work to attain. Most important among the elite were those who sat as justices of the peace on the Isle of Wight county court. The law required that justices be among the most "honest, judicious, and able" men of the county. In practice, in Isle of Wight as elsewhere in Virginia, family connections were at least as essential as integrity and ability. While Henry Saunders was a young man, the court included several members of locally influential and prestigious families: Michael Eley and Benjamin Eley, James Bridger and Joseph Bridger, Daniel Herring, Sr., and Daniel Herring, Jr. were all justices. The dominance of a very few families reflected the undemocratic basis of the courts: the royal governor appointed judges, and he chose them according to the recommendations of those already on the bench. The prestigious men of the county picked their brothers, sons, and in-laws to join them in power, and many served for twenty or even thirty years. There was little room for anyone who was not born into an influential family or who did not marry into one.[37]

Not surprisingly, men with the social standing needed to become justices usually enjoyed substantial wealth as well: Brewer Godwin owned thirty slaves; Richard Hardy owned 1,075 acres of land, twenty one slaves, and even seven pounds' worth of silver plate. Not all were primarily planters. The Scots merchant George Purdie also served for many years; with thirty-two slaves he was the second largest slaveholder living in Smithfield. Benjamin Eley owned seventeen slaves, and John Scarsbrook Wills owned forty-two—all substantial numbers in a county where over 40 percent of all white householders owned no slaves and less than 3 percent owned more than twenty. These were the men who had decided Mage's case, and they were the men who shaped Henry Saunders's ambitions.[38]

The first Thursday of every month these wealthy and well-connected men met to hold county court in Smithfield, and the little town became crowded as planters from throughout the county gathered to conduct business and socialize with one another. Bewigged and dignified, the "gentlemen justices" ruled with ceremony over the many transactions of rural society. The county court heard criminal cases, probated wills, appointed men to make inventories of estates, ruled on actions for debt, and kept records of sales and indentures. It was here that Martha brought Tom, Joan, Mage, and Jubilee when she wanted to hire out their labor, and here that Henry traveled to record his purchases of land. In the courthouse, Virginians made contracts and commitments publicly, under the eyes of the powerful justices. In turn, the "gentlemen justices" had an audience who would appreciate the knowledge, dignity, and lenience or severity with which they ruled. Outside the courthouse was a long, open arcade, where planters could meet and converse about events inside. By showing due respect for the justices, Henry Saunders and other ordinary planters could hope to gain their recognition and patronage. Court days could reinforce both the hierarchy and the unity of white society.[39]

Even when he had no official business with the court, Henry could enjoy the day. Conveniently located next to the courthouse was Richard Taylor's tavern, where planters met to discuss the weather, the crop, and their hopes for the price their tobacco would

An evening at the tavern, depicted at left by Benjamin Latrobe in Hanover Town, Virginia, in 1797, combined distinctions of class and skill with camaraderie.

Early American tavern signs were often highly decorative, like the one above.

Familiar faces at the tavern and at card tables in private houses.

bring. Here Henry might pick up news from London or Richmond or discuss more local affairs over a glass of rum. He might also try his hand with other planters in a variety of contests of luck and skill—games of cards, dice, and wrestling—which all took place in or near the tavern. Early in the 1770s, Taylor added to the attraction of his tavern by transforming the "counting house and storehouse" next-door into a billiard room. Betting on such contests was by no means limited to the disreputable members of the society; the county's most respected men risked their coin and tobacco. In 1778, for example, the Isle of Wight grand jury indicted fourteen men for gaming. (They had not broken any law, but gambling struck many as unseemly during wartime.) The list of the indicted was impressive: Nathaniel Burwell, Josiah Parker, James Bridger, Sr., Harrison Whitfield, Thomas Goodson, Jr., Francis Wren, John Scarsbrook Wills, Willis Wills, Emanuel Wills, Henry Lightfoot, William Bridger, Jr., James Wills, William Orr, and John Sinclair. Henry Saunders and other middling planters would have been happy to be gambling—and even to be indicted—with men such as these. Henry undoubtedly sometimes socialized in their company and drank at their expense, for such well-to-do planters showed their liberality and good will by treating their social inferiors to a round or two of drinks.[40]

Indeed, in the tavern, elite men adhered less strictly to the rules of gentility than they did in private parlors. Mingling not with upper class ladies, but with men from the middle and lower classes, county leaders shed some of the finer points of etiquette in the more rough-and-tumble atmosphere of an all-male gathering. By doing so, they created bonds of camaraderie with ordinary planters. Such familiarity was a means toward ensuring the racial unity essential to a society based on racial slavery. Yet white unity grew not only from a sense of familiarity: it grew as well from a shared sense of hierarchy, a common awareness of the lines of rank and social order. Gentility played a role at the tavern too. By treating their social inferiors to drink, the great planters demonstrated their wealth and generosity. And by their dress, demeanor, and conversational style, they could make distinctions of rank clearly felt. Far from abandoning claims of pre-eminence and authority, by participating in tavern life elite men made their social power more secure.

Henry had other opportunities to drink, gamble, or rub elbows with the elite. One such occasion was the horse race, a popular entertainment throughout Virginia. A race could be an informal quarter-mile match carried out on back roads or a formal event posted in the Petersburg newspaper and run on tracks laid out for the purpose. Lots of men (even slaves) gathered to take part and enjoy the excitement, but it was the wealthy who owned the top horses. Some even imported thoroughbreds to match against the horses of their richest neighbors. John Scarsbrook Wills brought over "Hero," a noted English horse, to Isle of Wight in the mid-1760s, and Henry Saunders might well have had the chance to see Hero run. At races, as at taverns, Henry was introduced to a competitive culture full of activities designed to determine publicly which of the county's white men were better, richer, faster, or stronger.[41]

Even elections to the Virginia legislature took the form of public competition. Candidates, always members of the county's powerful families, sat at tables at the county court on Election Day. Ordinary voters like Henry stepped forward one by one to announce their choice and receive public thanks from the candidate himself. The ritual expressed the upper-class candidates' superiority, but also underscored the importance of the small planters who chose between them. When Henry cast his vote for John Scarsbrook Wills, it expressed his respect for that gentleman while also making clear Henry's own political importance.[42]

Virginia law required young Henry Saunders to participate in another communal social occasion. Anglicanism was the established religion of the colony, so that Henry was required to attend Sunday services, either at the Bay Church five miles from Smithfield or at the chapel of ease closer to home. The quality of Anglican preaching varied through the years. Ministers enjoyed relatively little power and security in Virginia, and few well-trained and able clergymen wanted to leave England to serve in the distant provinces of America. Virginians living south of the James River had particularly dismal experiences with ministers—in part because the government set ministers' salaries in tobacco and, as one southsider pointed out, local tobacco was "much inferior" in kind and value to the stuff grown in the more prosperous counties to the north and west.[43] Henry Saunders's parish had a hard time finding a minister who would simply act respectably, much less shepherd the souls of his parishioners. In the 1720s, "Newport Parish" planters struggled to rid themselves of the Reverend Thomas Bayley, "a most notoriously wicked man" accused of drunkenness, fighting, and "swearing twelve oaths in one day." When Henry Saunders was a young man, the parish worked to dismiss the Reverend John Milner, accused of attempted sodomy. Milner resigned under pressure in 1770, to be replaced by the Reverend Henry John Burges, whose behavior, somewhat remarkably, caused no complaints. Meanwhile, in nearby Nansemond, some of Henry's cousins lived under the pastoral care of Patrick Lunan, a minister "of evil and profligate manners," who spent his time drinking at William Dixon's tavern in Suffolk.[44]

Despite these weaknesses, the Church of England taught important lessons to its parishioners in Virginia. If clergymen did not

always set an example to their congregations, other church officials did. The vestrymen, "twelve of the most able and discrete persons" of the parish, met at least twice a year to levy local taxes, take care of the poor, and oversee the behavior of individual parishioners. In Henry Saunders's parish, for example, vestrymen fined James Garretty to help pay the expenses of Martha Burt, who had delivered an illegitimate child. In 1768 they paid out £1 in Virginia money to Mary Murphy for her expenses in keeping her impoverished sister, spent £4 5s. to keep "Jones's orphans," and reimbursed Ralph Gibbs £7 for expenses incurred keeping Sarah Miles. In these and countless similar acts, the vestry ordered local life, watching over the welfare and morality of the community in which Henry Saunders lived.[45]

In Isle of Wight, as in most other Virginia counties, secular and religious authority rested in the same hands. Men who served on the county court—John Eley, John Scarsbrook Wills, Daniel Herring, James Bridger, Josiah Parker, and Richard Hardy—sat on the vestry too. Henry Saunders did not have to get into trouble (moral or legal) to feel their importance. That was clear from the moment they arrived at church every Sunday, in carriages or astride fine horses. Inside the church, carefully segregated seating reinforced the parish social hierarchy. Special pews were set aside for vestrymen, justices of the peace, and officials of the county. Rich planters purchased the most prominent pews, so that their entrance and attendance could be observed by the rest of the congregation. Whites occupied preferred parts of the church, distinctly apart from their black slaves. Men sat separate from women, and the "wifes of the Justices and vestrymen" sat in "the corner Pew of the chancel" while other women took inferior places. At church, as at other gatherings, Henry encountered the many social distinctions of his society.[46]

This Grice flintlock pistol was an officer's weapon, too expensive to issue to enlisted men.

THE AMBITIONS OF A TIDEWATER PLANTER

During the 1770s, when Henry reached maturity, he felt the power of the county's leading men in another institution: the militia. The local elite served as officers, presiding over the annual musters where the county's white men gathered for military drill and to prove their willingness to turn out to defend the community. In peacetime, the militia served more actively to oppress part of that community: once a month militiamen patrolled the slave quarters and other local meeting places of black Virginians. About the time that Henry began parading as a militiaman, Virginia's attention turned to the colonies' deteriorating relationship with England. Henry followed John Scarsbrook Wills and other county leaders who took up the patriot cause. When war broke out in 1775, he drilled along with the other white men of Isle of Wight. The British occupied Norfolk nearby, and refugees fled to Suffolk and Smithfield, which became a depot for supplies for the patriot army. To subdue the rebels, Governor Dunmore issued a proclamation offering freedom to slaves who took the British side. For several years the Isle of Wight militia's duty was to prevent black "desertions" and protect army supplies. Henry must have faithfully performed his share of that duty. In 1778, he was appointed a second lieutenant in Captain Daniel Herring's company. He might have seen action, since British cavalry passed twice through Isle of Wight, one time burning Suffolk and marching on to Smithfield. Just across the line in Nansemond County, Isle of Wight troops attacked the cavalry; Henry, who lived within a few miles of the spot, might have been among the patriot force driven back from the scene. Whatever his experience in the war, his ranking as an officer was important to Henry: he used his militia title for many years after, when signing land deeds and on other nonmilitary occasions. Official records rarely listed the names of the leading men of the county without adding the title "Gentleman"; Henry lacked that distinction, but after 1778 he could put "Lieutenant" before his name.[47]

During the war, Henry also became head of his own family. In 1779 he married Anne Tallough, daughter of William Tallough, a small planter in the neighborhood. In general the Tallough family resembled the Saunders, owning a slave or two, planting moderate tracts of land with tobacco and corn, raising cattle and sheep, and doing some coopering and carpentry on the side. In economic terms, Anne Tallough married well in marrying Henry; she was not necessarily an impressive match for an aspiring young planter. Within a few years Anne had borne two children, one a daughter named Betsy, the other not identified in the surviving records.[48]

Betsy's name may have reflected Henry's family consciousness: since the seventeenth century, each generation of Saunderses had its Elizabeth—and its Thomas, Robert, Henry, and John. Yet in important ways Henry differed from his relatives. His cousins' lives followed a pattern of small farming. Starting with old John Saunders's seventeenth-century tract near the Blackwater River, each generation had divided its holdings among sons. When any son's share fell below the 100 to 200 acres needed for a family tobacco farm, the Saunders generally patented a little more. No one suffered—but no one made great advances, either. Possibly they lacked the economic resources to expand their holdings, or else they were content to live as their parents had done, keeping a family farm.

Henry Saunders also probably started with an inherited tract, but he aimed at turning it into a great deal more. His side of the family had long done somewhat better than his cousins' side; his father's estate was more substantial than most, and since Henry was the only son, he started off with advantages over his cousins. Those advantages may have whetted his appetite for accumulation, for he followed a different pattern from most of his family. He bought up farmland in the area and then sold off portions of it to finance purchases of slaves and more purchases of land. The year after his marriage he bought 620 acres of land located on the "Blackwater branches" from the Carstephans, his stepfather's kin; 420 acres of the tract were called "Sellaways Quarter," and another 200 acres adjoined, next to "Ned's Old Field." On this land he would later build his house. With it he acquired neighbors: William Eley and Benjamin Eley were the most well-to-do. In 1782 Wright Roberts became a neighbor by purchasing 118 acres of Henry's new land. Apparently

Henry disposed of several hundred acres, and invested the proceeds from these sales in labor. When the tax assessors listed his assets in 1782, he had 297 acres of land left and owned eleven slaves.[49]

At this point Henry was hardly more than thirty years old, yet he already owned more slaves than nine-tenths of the planters in the county and more land than the vast majority of them as well. A good number of free men in Isle of Wight owned no land at all. Of those who did hold title to a tract, three-quarters held less—and most of them substantially less—than Henry's 297 acres. Roughly 58 percent of all householders owned fewer than 200 acres. As young as Henry was, he was doing better than all but the very richest in Isle of Wight and better than all but one or two of his own kinsmen besides. Four of his cousins fell into the largest single category of landholders in the county, the 38 percent who held 100 to 199 acres. One cousin did have landed property comparable to Henry's, and one uncle actually surpassed him for the moment. But Henry had only started to accumulate land. In 1783 he obtained a 57-acre grant. In 1787 he bought 687 acres from the estate of another planter. This gave him 1,041 acres. He was at the height of his holdings, with acreage at least the equal of the Eleys and his other important neighbors.[50]

The record does not reveal how Henry amassed the capital to buy so much land; the fact is, he prospered just when hard times were hitting many Virginia planters. Warfare had disrupted the tobacco economy almost from the moment his career began. The Revolutionary movement cut off tobacco exports in 1775, and for the following eight years the Royal Navy blockaded American ports and the American government restricted exports. During the war some continued an illicit trade with Britain, often dealing with the enemy indirectly through the "foreign" West Indies. Yet many cargoes were lost at sea and tobacco rotted in the warehouse for lack of export. Some planters suffered when the British cavalry invaded Isle of Wight, burning houses and barns, destroying tobacco and carrying away livestock and slaves. Although the tobacco trade with Britain revived quickly after the war, prices remained unstable through the 1780s and early 1790s.[51]

While some objects that Afro-Americans made and used were distinctive, most were similar to the objects used by poor rural whites.

The key to Henry's success may have been flexibility toward the market. He began planting at a time when many southeastern Virginians were reconsidering the amount of land devoted to tobacco as a cash crop. They had always grown some corn and wheat, and the Revolution created a greater demand for those items at home and abroad. During the war, barred from trade with Britain, southerners sold their goods in the French West Indies more than ever before. When Spain became an ally, Cuba became a market for foodstuffs. Demand for wheat in particular continued to be high after the war, in part because both Britain and France suffered years of scarcity, so that growing wheat and Indian corn became a more lucrative endeavor.[52]

Many Virginia planters discovered that they could grow more corn and wheat without reducing the land and labor they devoted to tobacco. Grain required intense but brief periods of fieldwork—sowing in the fall, harvesting in the spring or summer. If a planter could muster his hands for hard labor at those periods, he could still have them tend the tobacco crop during the rest of the season. Planting

THE AMBITIONS OF A TIDEWATER PLANTER

wheat, a farmer would also use many more of his acres. In the short run, tobacco took less land than wheat. Each year a worker could tend two or three acres of tobacco, as compared with thirteen to eighteen acres of wheat. But land that had grown tobacco for three successive years needed as much as twenty years rest before it could be replanted with the same crop, so tobacco farmers always needed to leave large tracts of land fallow. Wheat land required only one fallow year for every two successive years of crop, so that in any one year a wheat farmer could plant two-thirds of his acreage. With wheat prices high, it was hard to leave a lot of tobacco land lying fallow and unused. So, while tobacco production expanded rapidly in the western counties of the state, in the east many cut their tobacco acreage and increased their growth of grain. It may have helped Henry to start farming just at the beginning of the war, when demand for foodstuffs was particularly high. He may have diversified his crop more readily than more established farmers did, gaining social and economic ground in the 1780s and 1790s.[53]

Meanwhile, that ground was shifting in important ways. Even before the Revolution, some Virginians had parted company with the Anglican Church. In Isle of Wight County, a group of dissenters agreed "to joyn together in a gospel church Relation" in 1774. They founded the Mill Swamp Baptist Church, pledging to "watch over one another," "to Encourage and to Reprove if need be . . . and to be admonished and Reproved by one another," and to observe all "mutual

The Saunders family slaves might have ground corn into meal in a standing mortar such as this. Corn was a staple of many black Americans' diet—roasted, boiled into mush, baked into hoecakes, or cooked on a footed griddle like the one below left, placed right over the coals of a fire.

Baptists and Methodists thought that humble surroundings were compatible with a rich inner spirit. Mill Creek (Mauck's) Meeting House in the Shenandoah Valley was probably a Baptist meeting house.

duties toward one another." In effect, they seceded from the oversight of the local vestry and formed a community of their own. They had their own ideas about good living: they disapproved of dancing, gambling, and drinking. They opposed display and competition. They created more equal social relations than those embodied in Anglican doctrine and practice. Some dissenting groups extended fellowship to blacks as well as whites. The Mill Swamp Baptists thought about extending the vote to women in church affairs and debated the morality of making money. In 1778 they discussed whether it was "agreeable to the Spirit of Christianity to buy or sell principally with a view of getting gain."[54]

Questions such as these did not trouble Henry Saunders, bent on acquisition as he was, but they troubled many Virginians, especially among the less well-to-do. Dismayed by the rise of dissent, some leading Virginians worried that their moral authority was eroding, and many whites were uneasy about the loss of unity that religious

THE AMBITIONS OF A TIDEWATER PLANTER

dissent signaled. More was at stake than just continued attendance at the Anglican church, for dissenters flatly rejected the ideal of gentility that helped hold white society together. The Baptists withdrew from taverns, horse races,and other public social places; they prized plainness rather than elegance, sincerity rather than wit, and regarded the acquisition of expensive tea sets as evidence of sinful pride rather than admirable taste. Their challenge to genteel Virginia society was fundamental. So when the pastor of the Mill Swamp Baptists preached in nearby Nansemond, it did not seem too strong a reaction for a crowd of people to interrupt him with jeers and dunk him and his companion in the river. The dunking was a parody of Baptist practice; at the same time it expressed some Virginians' fear of the fragmentation of white society.[55]

American independence struck another blow against the authority of the Church of England, as the outbreak of battle prompted the legislature to loosen legal underpinnings of the religious establishment. From 1776, residents in the county were no longer bound by law to attend the Anglican church nor support its ministers with their taxes. In 1784 the church freed itself of its official ties to England and incorporated as the Protestant Episcopal Church, now with an elected vestry and less control over county affairs. Step by step, the Episcopal church lost its place of eminence in Virginia. In 1786, the Assembly passed "an act for the establishment of religious freedom," releasing Virginians from any remaining obligations to attend church, support the clergy, or submit to the scrutiny of the vestrymen. Episcopal vestries still cared for the parish poor for a few years, then locally elected officials took over that job too. In 1790, Henry's cousin John Saunders signed a petition protesting the remaining privileges held by the Episcopal Church. "The glorious Revolution which some Years ago took place in this Country . . . we honestly confess was the happy means to opening our Eyes to discover the Rights of Mankind," the petitioners wrote. Thinking they would enjoy "equal Freedom" after the war, they found instead that the law left trustees of the Episcopal church in charge of glebe lands, churches, and other buildings, all property paid for and maintained by all taxpayers before the Revolution. They asked the government to let all religious sects use the churches and to sell glebe property to support the county poor or set up seminaries of learning. So the church continued to lose its position of privilege and the allegiance of much of the population.[56]

Equally important, in the same years that they dissolved the dominion of the Episcopal church, Virginians brought slavery, the very basis of the society, under attack. The Revolution's ideals of liberty had led Virginians to ban importations from Africa and, from 1782, to allow individual slaveholders to free their slaves. Isle of Wight residents took advantage of the manumission law. Courtney Hollowell, for example, "being fully persuaded that freedom is the natural right of all mankind and that it is my Duty to do unto others as I should desire to be done by," freed Titus, aged about twenty-four, and Micah, three years old, reserving the right to act as Micah's guardian until he came of age. Later in the 1780s and 1790s, other Hollowells and other Virginians followed Courtney's example. Joseph Hill decided "that no law morral or divine hath given me a just right or property in the persons of any of my fellow Creatures," so he freed eleven slaves in 1783. Antislavery sentiment affected some of the very well-to-do: in his will, Timothy Tynes freed all of his eighty-two slaves and divided much of his land among them. Most slaveholders kept their blacks in bondage, and a good number opposed the manumission law. Yet the ideas of the American Revolution and ideas of evangelical religion helped create a remarkable shift in sentiment among many white Virginians.[57]

Naturally enough, black Virginians' lives changed too. A small population of free blacks emerged in Isle of Wight. Free blacks held few rights in Virginia, but they could learn how to read and write or even make enough money to buy friends and kin out of bondage. The possibility of private manumission gave many slaves hope for the future, encouraging them to press their owners for their freedom. For those willing to leave family and community behind, the abolition of slavery in states to the north opened another road out of bondage. Some runaway blacks relied on relatives and friends on other plantations to hide, feed, and direct them on their journey to freedom. The growing free black population became an important part of the underground network available to slaves. Moreover, as the free black pop-

TO BE SOLD,
A likely ſtrong Negro
Girl, abcut 17 Years of Age ; ſold
by Reaſon that a Boy would ſuit
the Owner better. Enquire at
R. & S. Draper's Printing Office

"In Maryland, it has always been the practice of masters and mistresses, who wished to terrify their slaves to threaten to sell them to South Carolina where it was represented, that their condition would be a hundred fold worse." Charles Ball, Fifty Years in Chains, *1837.*

ulation grew, slaves had a better chance of passing for free, at least long enough to get onto a ship bound for a northern port.[58]

In the closing decades of the century, more and more black Virginians lived in towns at least part of the year. In part this resulted from the increased emphasis on wheat farming. As planters abandoned tobacco, they no longer needed to keep their slaves tending crops all year long. It was more profitable to have a skilled labor force to transport grain, store it, mill it, and load it onto ships for export. More slaves learned these skills and spent the slack season of the year hired out to grain dealers, millers, or others. More escaped the constant surveillance of the home plantation. As towns grew, so did black literacy. "Every year adds to the number of those who can read and write," said a slaveholder in 1800. "This increase of knowledge is the principal agent in evolving the spirit we have to fear."[59]

The spirit he dreaded, he said, was "the love of freedom," ironically the very same spirit prized by whites when they were considering their circumstances. Black Virginians' desire to be free was fed not just by American independence but by even more recent events. In France men and women fought a revolution for liberty, equality, and fraternity, while in the French West Indies, inspired by the upheaval in Europe, thousands of blacks, free and slave, rose up against white masters on the island of Saint-Domingue. Planters from that island fled to the American South, bringing with them what slaves they could. In 1793, these new immigrants entered Portsmouth and Norfolk, causing white Virginians to worry about the contagion of rebel-

Toussaint L'Ouverture, the leading general and statesman of the Haitian Revolution, as pictured in An Historical Account of the Black Empire of Hayti *by Marcus Rainsford, published in London, 1805.*

THE AMBITIONS OF A TIDEWATER PLANTER

lion. Rumors of slave insurrections spread through Petersburg, Richmond, and York, and throughout the 1790s whites watched carefully for any plans for revolt among their workers.[60]

Perhaps most frightening for slaveholders, blacks' participation in the Revolution, their connection with whites through evangelical religion, and the growth of a free black community threatened to undo the racial lines built up for over a century. Might poor whites and blacks forge alliances against slaveowners? Some Virginians thought so. "Fanaticism is spreading fast among the Negroes of this county, and may form in time the connecting link between the black religionists and the white," wrote one. "It certainly would not be a novelty, in the history of the world, if Religion were made to sanctify plots and conspiracies." In Norfolk, an anonymous public poster claimed that a mob of eighty men, thirty-four of them white, the rest black, planned to burn the town. The rebellion that *did* happen involved only blacks: in 1800, slaves in the Richmond area organized behind a small group of slave artisans, led by a man named Gabriel, and marched on the city. A torrential rain and the work of informants cut short the insurrection, but whites remained in terror. In Saint-Domingue, over a decade of bloody warfare culminated in the establishment of the free black republic of Haiti in 1802. Few Virginia slaves or slaveholders could think it insignificant.[61]

Despite this surrounding upheaval, many things stayed the same in Isle of Wight County. After the Revolution, political power remained in the hands of the county's well-to-do planters, and if they had to be more vigilant toward their slaves, they still enjoyed their wealth and leisure. But those planters no longer presided over a white community unified by shared values and shared institutions. Even as Henry Saunders moved up, entering the lower ranks of the county elite, he may have felt that that role counted for less and less to some whites in the community. He and many others could still play out their social roles at church, at the tavern, on militia day, and at horse races, but not everyone in the society attended or even cared about those events. Henry must have known that some Virginians disputed his right to hold slaves, rejected the ideal of gentility, and questioned the moral authority of wealthy planters. Either he ignored the challenge to the conventional social order or, more likely, acted in conscious defiance of it. In the mid-1790s, he followed other leading planters in the area in deciding to build himself an expensive and fashionable house.[62]

*H*enry's near neighbor William Eley set the tone for the neighborhood. About a quarter-mile south of the Saunders plantation, he built a brick-ended frame house with heavy, ornate molding inside the rooms. Keeping up with the Eleys was expensive. Henry Saunders sold off some of his land about the time he began to build, then apparently needed a loan to finance the house too. In 1797, he mortgaged the rest of his acreage, including "the tract on which I now reside," for £295 to Joseph Scott, a Quaker merchant in nearby Suffolk.[63]

The Saunderses' new house was probably smaller than the Eleys', but like it, it had brick ends, an ornate interior, and a basic two-room plan on each floor. Most of the decoration centered in the hall, the larger of the two rooms on the first floor, for it was the scene of formal dining and entertaining and the room that any visitor using the front door entered first. The focal point of the room was the gable wall on the visitor's left, with a fireplace in the center and decorative paneling all around. Over the mantle was an unusual applied panel with carved rosettes at the corners and in the center. To the left of the fireplace was a cupboard, where the family could store and display their finest belongings behind glass panes. At the far end of the same wall was a stairway, decorated with a short balustrade designed in the fashionable Chinese Chippendale manner.[64] The hall provided an elegant setting for genteel living.

The other, smaller ground-floor room also had decoration, but it was a more private space, used for everyday family meals and possibly for Henry and Anne's bedroom as well. A door at the side of the room gave access to the yard and nearby outbuildings, including the kitchen, where Anne, Betsy, and female slaves prepared daily meals, and the cellar, a storage place for cider, beer, vinegar, and other foodstuffs. While the larger hall lent itself to entertaining and impressing visitors, the smaller room, or "parlor," was the scene of day-to-day living, the coming and going of slaves, and ordinary household work.[65]

Finally, the house had more private areas, away from the yard and the visitor. In many similar houses the stairs faced the front door, along the partition between the two ground-floor rooms. By contrast, the upper chambers of the Saunders house were reached by a stairway at the far end of the hall. The upstairs, generally used for storage and sleeping, was less accessible to outsiders. Some historians suggest that, late in the eighteenth century, Virginia families were becoming more private, withdrawing from their neighbors and keeping more to themselves; the arrangement of the Saunders house, with its formal hall for entertaining and its staircase tucked away, may reflect this preference for privacy. If so, the house combined two disparate impulses—an impulse toward genteel social display and an impulse toward withdrawal into the family. Both were appropriate responses to the conflict within late eighteenth-century Virginia society.[66]

The fireplace wall of Henry Saunders's main room, or "hall," had decorative woodwork and a cupboard.

A burst of manufacturing activity in England increased the volume and variety of imported goods available to American consumers in the eighteenth century. Still, in the homes of affluent planters, luxurious imports like this fine glassware and liquor chest lived among such plain, American-made goods as this bed and basin.

There is little evidence besides the organization of the Saunders's house to tell us about the family's private life. In 1806, Anne Saunders signed a deed of gift, turning over title to a variety of goods to her daughter Betsy. The gift included "two fether Beds and furniture, One Cow, Six Seting Chears, two Pewter basons and two pewter Dishes, One Cotton wheel and one lining [linen] wheel, two Chests & two tables and One Pare Cart wheels." It was a handsome gift, possibly on the occasion of Betsy's marriage and her removal to a household of her own. The gift, Anne wrote, expressed the "Natural love and affection" she held for Betsy. The inclusion of cotton and linen spinning wheels reflected some of the shared work that had fostered affection between mother and daughter. We have one glimpse, then, of companionship in the Saunders household.[67]

By contrast, we know almost nothing about Anne and Henry's marriage. In 1808, two years after Anne's gift to Betsy, the Isle of Wight county court charged Henry with the murder of Anne. Henry hired a lawyer and asked for more time to gather witnesses for his defense. The court agreed and duly bound over twenty-one witnesses for the prosecution, a list inlcuding ten women and eleven men— Eleys, Robertses, Saunderses, and others—Henry's neighbors and relatives (excluding, however, daughter Betsy, who might have been a witness for the defense). For an unspecified reason, the court moved the trial to neighboring Nansemond County, and it is there that the case was recorded and the records later burned. So we do not know what those witnesses said. In August, the Isle of Wight court recorded the verdict and sentence in the case: Henry was found guilty and sentenced to spend eighteen years in the state penitentiary at Richmond.[68]

In the absence of those court records, nothing we know is adequate to explain the murder. Newspapers of the time covered larger events—news from Richmond, Washington, or abroad—while local news traveled from person to person at taverns, court sessions, and other gatherings, leaving little trace for historians to find. Still, it is difficult just to dismiss Anne's death, not to seek its meaning somehow or speculate on what little we do know. We cannot know the particular circumstances of the Saunders tragedy; we *can* try to discover something about the place and meaning of such violence in the society where the Saunderses lived.

One colonial Virginian claimed that violence by husbands against wives was relatively rare in his society. We do not have the statistics to know if he was right. But violence against *some* women (and some men) was common, even casual, in Isle of Wight. Surely slaveholding had an effect on the personalities of white Virginians. Thomas Jefferson, a slaveholder himself, thought that control over slaves made whites "despots." Jefferson was generalizing; slaveholders' personalities varied, and there was room in the master-slave relationship for kindness too. Yet Jefferson was right in describing a tendency: however hidden or masked it might be, slavery involved brutality. At times white society was forced to be explicit about it. Virginia law, for example, excused white masters from prosecution for felony when they killed their own slaves in the course of disciplining them. "Murder," after all, required malice, and how could a slaveholder deliberately try to deprive himself or herself of a valuable asset like a slave? The logic of the law recognized that ordinary correction of one's slaves could slip over into brutality without warning, without the master quite knowing that it had occurred. It was possible for the slaveholder to lose control, possible not to know what was happening.[69]

In fact, some kind of blinder was almost necessary for even the kindest slaveowner. How could white people really face the humanity of their slaves and still live with themselves? Those white Virginians who began to recognize blacks as their equals felt pressed to free them. Those who remained unwilling to live only by their own labor—like Henry Saunders—needed to block out knowledge of their slaves' lives and feelings. It was an active sort of ignorance, an ignoring, a refusal to see the pain felt by people when separated from friends and family, when forced to work for someone else's benefit, and when treated without respect. That deliberate blindness was also a form of violence, and if it did not cost lives, still it cost black people dearly. As Jefferson seemed partially to realize, it affected whites as well.[70]

These sorts of violence were central to slavery, but did violence spill over into relationships among whites? Or did white Virginians direct aggression less often at each other just because they could direct it at

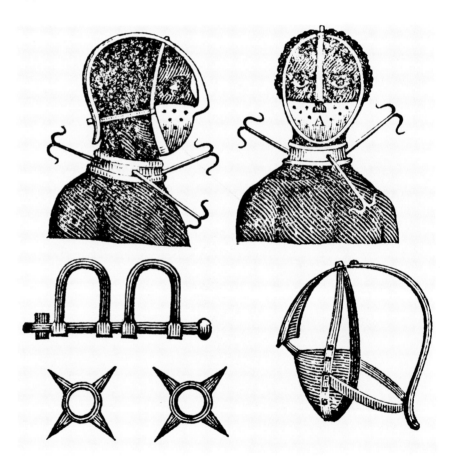

The tools of the slave trade included masks and collars, as well as chains and manacles. Illustrations like these, from the late eighteenth or early nineteenth century, made a convincing case against the importation of Africans.

> **Run-away from the Subscriber,**
> On the 18th of June last,
>
> A NEGRO BOY named JACK, aged about sixteen years.—— Any person taking up said Negro Boy, and delivering him to his Master, shall have one Guinea Reward for his trouble; and also a Reward of Five Guineas for discovering such person or persons, who may have employed, harboured, concealed, or entertained said Negro Boy. JEROMUS LOTT.
>
> King's-County, July 29, 1783.   *

Runaway ads attest to the desire of slaves for freedom and, sometimes, to the willingness of other Americans to help them.

black people? Surely Henry Saunders found it easier to ignore the experience and feelings of his slaves than the experience and feelings of the woman he lived with. Marriage, after all, was not slavery. But if married white women were not slaves, neither were they free by the standards applied to white men in their society. They had a special legal status: "feme covert." They could neither sue in court nor, generally speaking, possess property of their own. The law gave a wife some say in the family's business affairs, but for the most part she was supposed to go along with her husband's wishes. There is no evidence that Anne Saunders resented that sort of inequality, that it made her unhappy, or that she even considered whether or not it was fair. Anne gave property to Betsy knowing that economic resources mitigated a woman's disadvantages. But we do not know whether Anne had learned that the hard way—through her own experience with Henry—or not. If their marriage was unhappy, Anne and Henry would have found it difficult to get a divorce, though couples did sometimes separate, and Anne had family she could have gone to. So far as we know, she lived in Henry's house until her death.[71]

One other aspect of life in Isle of Wight might have related to marital violence. When Baptists Thomas and Elizabeth Tynes had trouble getting along, their Mill Swamp brethren worked to reconcile them, chastising them for "Living at Variance betwixt them selves." Henry and Anne lacked a community of fellows to watch the way they lived together. The vestry of the Anglican Church, which had solemnized their marriage, had become ineffective in overseeing parishioners' morals. Within two years of the murder, suffering from neglect, the Bay Church near Smithfield was torn down.[72]

So there we are. The murder may have had to do with Henry's ambition, his willingness to use other human beings as a means to his own leisure and benefit, his assumption of authority over all the other members of his household, or even the lack of a community of brethren to oversee his married life. But none of these factors explains the murder; after all, most white men of Isle of Wight County assumed their right to rule over blacks and women and many harbored ambitions to get ahead, yet few killed their wives. The inequality Virginia society set between men and women differed from the inequality set between white and black, and Virginia's system of legal justice reflected nothing so strongly as that vital racial line. Henry's white neighbors found the murder of Anne appalling and brought Henry to "justice"; it is harder to understand how they thought that sentencing Mage to death for petty theft was also just, or to accept the equanimity with which so many used threats and violence to force work out of slaves. Still, Virginians were not the only Americans whose vision was blurred on matters of race and class. For some years after the Revolution white Americans from New England to the Chesapeake looked with new eyes at practices and modes of thought they had once taken for granted. Some rejected slavery, along with the definition of justice and tolerance for violence that slavery imposed. Then, with the new century, opposition to slavery waned. It would be many years after the Revolution before most white Americans were willing to take a second look.

*H*enry Saunders was still living in the penitentiary at Richmond in 1811, but that is the last we know of him. He probably died in prison.

The Saunders house as it appeared in Isle of Wight County in 1981.

In 1809 the mortgage on his land was foreclosed and much of his property sold at auction. Ann Scott, Joseph Scott's widow, acquired "the quarter plantation" and "the maner plantation," where the house built to establish Henry Saunders's prominence in the county still stands today.[73]

THE LIMITS OF
LIBERTY

Richard Allen,
Freedman of Philadelphia

$\mathscr{B}$lack Americans were offered little voice in the creation of a new American nation. Africans and their African-American descendents numbered roughly half a million on the eve of the war for independence, comprising one-fifth of the population of the thirteen continental colonies. Most lived in the areas along the Atlantic seaboard from Maryland south to Georgia, but fair numbers lived in northern cities and some worked on northern farms. In every colony the law carefully defined and defended chattel slavery, and in every colony the vast majority of black people were slaves.[1]

To a significant extent, it was their labor that secured American independence, for the tobacco raised by southern slaves provided the colonies' most valuable bargaining chip in the diplomacy by which an ill-prepared revolutionary movement gained vital support from France. Short of arms, ships, gunpowder, and money, the American colonies might well have failed to win independence without an alliance with Britain's longstanding rival empire. Moreover, thousands of black soldiers fought British armies in battle, while behind the lines black laborers drove supply wagons, built fortifications, and maintained military encampments, making incalculable contributions to the war effort. Once political independence had been won and a new government formed, that government still relied on the value of slave-made goods to help establish and maintain its sovereignty. After tobacco came cotton, the great staple of the nineteenth century that, from the mid-1830s to the Civil War, made up more than half the value of all American exports. As one historian has noted, "the position of the United States in the world depended not only in 1776 but during the span of a long lifetime thereafter on slave labor." It is an extraordinary and fundamental fact of late eighteenth-century history that, through black slavery, white America became "free."[2]

It was not slaves, unquestionably the most oppressed class within colonial society, who began America's movement for liberty, nor was that movement pursued on their behalf. Nonetheless, many American blacks did reach freedom during the years of revolutionary change. Republican ideals of liberty, the Enlightenment's optimistic belief in humankind's capacity for improvement and reform, and the antislav-

Yarrow Mamout, an African Muslim who was sold into slavery in Maryland, bought his freedom, acquired property, continued to practice his religion, and eventually settled in Georgetown, now part of Washington, D.C. In 1819, when Charles Willson Peale painted this portrait, Mamout was more than one hundred years old.

ery tenets of early evangelical religion all led many white Americans to reconsider their acceptance of African bondage. Equally important, black Americans seized hold of these same strains of thought to create pathways for their own liberation. It took few eloquent Revolutionary orators or incendiary republican pamphlets to convince African-Americans of the value of being free. "That liberty is a great thing we know from our own feelings," said slave Jupiter Hammon.[3] Once white Americans began to question slavery, blacks took every opportunity to press for their own liberation. Where possible, slaves sued for their freedom in courts of law, petitioned state legislatures for emancipation, and negotiated (or at least argued) with their masters for manumission. It was for their own freedom that some 5,000 blacks enlisted in Washington's Continental Army; pursuing the same goal, thousands of others took the British side. As they won their freedom, American blacks broadened the boundaries of the war for independence, appropriating the Revolutionary era as their own. Although rarely consulted by the white leaders who discussed how to shape a new government and direct a new nation, black Americans indelibly impressed their ideals and aspirations on the emerging American society.[4]

Richard Allen was born a slave in 1760. As a young man, he felt the profound influence of evangelical Methodism, a religion that helped him out of servitude and shaped the rest of his life. Along with other blacks of his generation, he made the journey from slavery to freedom, only to discover that the new nation offered a limited kind of liberty. Like white Americans, he lived in a world economy governed by forces far out of his control; unlike many whites, Allen inherited few resources to help him weather its adversities. As a slave he enjoyed no political rights, economic security, or even the self-assurance given to people who know that their own efforts might improve their lot. When he became free, he found himself near the bottom of a society dominated by people quite unlike himself and, for the most part, unsympathetic with his plight.

There were whites on the bottom of free society too and, in the Revolutionary era, common economic hardship united many poor people across the lines of race to a degree unknown in later years. Yet, unlike propertyless whites, Richard Allen and other free blacks lived with the knowledge that the majority of their race remained in bondage. They knew as well that some whites considered blacks inferior, not merely in social condition, but by their very nature. Far more than the Scots, German, and Irish immigrants who reached the New World in the late eighteenth century, free blacks faced the question of whether there was room for them in American society at all.[5]

When some suggested that free blacks should return to Africa, Richard Allen replied: "This land which we have watered with our tears and our blood is now our mother country." The great majority of free black Americans agreed with him. They had, quite literally, slaved to build America. Against great odds, they had formed family and community ties there. Yet it remained to be seen what place free blacks might fill in the new society. Would it be possible to get off the bottom rungs of the social ladder? Could they actually aspire to full equality? Would it be possible—or even desirable—to remain in white institutions, or should black people set themselves apart? And far from least important, what was their relationship to the great majority of blacks who remained enslaved?[6]

Richard Allen spent his life shaping answers to these questions. He became a significant leader in Philadelphia's free black community and, by the end of his life, was about as successful as a black person of his times could possibly be. Yet Allen lived to see the waning of white America's antislavery efforts, a retrenchment in which those with property and privilege beat a fearful retreat from the ideals of the Revolution and the commitments of early Methodism. He could do little to stem that decline or prevent the growth of racism that accompanied it; yet he negotiated these changes with a tireless zeal for bringing liberty of all kinds to American blacks. His story helps us understand the freedom available to rich and poor, white and black, in early America.

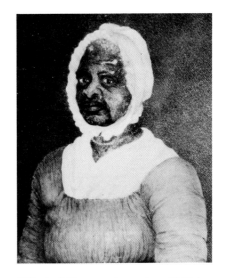

Elizabeth Freeman, born about 1742 in Africa, was sold to the Ashley family in Sheffield, Massachusetts. After a member of the household struck her, she left and refused to return. She told her story to an antislavery lawyer, Theodore Sedgwick, who helped her sue her owner and win her freedom. In 1811, when Freeman was nearly seventy, young Susan Sedgwick painted this portrait.

$\mathscr{P}$hiladelphia was the youngest but nearly the most populous of the major North American cities in 1760, the year of Richard Allen's birth. Founded in 1682 as the capital of William Penn's Quaker

Taverns, inns, and grog shops abounded in the city. They were places to eat and drink, meet friends, swap stories, discuss the news of the day, and argue about politics. This Philadelphia tobacconist's trade card, 1770, shows men smoking pipes in a tavern.

colony, the city lay roughly 100 miles up the Delaware River, at its junction with the waters of the Schuylkill. English Quakers, persecuted in England for dissenting from the established church, flocked to the new colony, and it was not long before Welsh, Scots-Irish, and German immigrants joined them, attracted by Pennsylvania's promise of prosperity and by Penn's policy of religious toleration. Soon Anglican, Lutheran, German Reformed, and Presbyterian churches joined Quaker meeting houses in the city. Shortly after midcentury, Philadelphia surpassed Boston, fifty years its elder, in population, and the town grew rapidly for the rest of the century. In 1760 the "City of Brotherly Love" held roughly 16,000 people.[7]

From early on, settlers clustered near the Delaware, where it was coolest in the summer and where they could set up shops and warehouses convenient to the river traffic. Philadelphians built wharves out into the river—by 1760 there were sixty-six of them along a two-mile stretch fronting the Delaware, on each a merchant's warehouse or two for storing goods. Except in the coldest winter when ice sometimes closed the harbor, numerous vessels lay alongside the wharves, taking on or dispensing cargo, their masts piercing the city skyline. Also on the waterfront were shipyards, where artisans from carpenters to caulkers to ropemakers to carvers applied their skills to the construction of merchant ships. On higher ground lay artisan shops, retail stores, taverns (over 100 of them), churches of many denominations, marketplaces, and nearly 3,000 dwellings. Some Philadelphians lived in houses that were "mean and low and much decayed," but many residences were two or three stories high, made of wood or stone or brick. The city boasted new rowhouses—"Fourteen Chimnies"—on Fifth Street above Sassafras (now Race) Street and a few fine new Georgian townhouses as well. Yet most of the wealthy who desired opulent homes built retreats in the surrounding countryside in order to escape city heat and the occasional epidemic of contagious disease. Visitors to the city noted its prosperity in 1760, but in keeping with the Quakers' commitment to plainness, Philadelphia presented a generally modest aspect.[8]

City streets were flanked by trees: elms, locusts, water beeches, and

City dwellers strolled, conversed, shopped, sold goods, fetched water, did business, and sometimes held political meetings on city streets. William Birch showed city life in "South East Corner of Third and Market Streets," 1798–1800.

This seaman's chest is decorated with carvings, the owner's name, and the date 1799.

lime trees; and whale oil lamps set on posts illumined part of the city at night. On the eve of the Revolution, the city was "the best lit" as well as the second largest (next to sprawling, massive London) in the whole British empire. Visitors often wondered at the noise and commotion. "Here the thundering of Coaches, Chariots, Chaises, Waggons, Drays, and the whole Fraternity of Noise almost constantly assails our Ears," one complained. Much of the street traffic consisted of wagons, "continually going with flour and wheat to the ships" at the wharves. Some well-to-do urbanites traveled the streets in fashionable four-wheeled chaises, but many more city residents rode on horseback when they rode at all. Pedestrians walked the cobblestones, shopping for farm produce at one of the three marketplaces of the city, doing business at artisan shops or merchants' offices, fetching water from one of the many streetside pumps, traveling down to Budd's or Emlen's wharves to buy firewood brought in from the Delaware valley.[9]

The prosperity of the city depended in large measure on the produce of its rich hinterlands. Large and small farms surrounding the city provided it with produce, grain, livestock, and timber, both for consumption by city inhabitants and for export overseas. River shallops linked the city with the farms and towns of the Delaware valley, carrying produce along the waterways to Philadelphia and carrying English and Philadelphia manufactures back. In the other direction, the Great Wagon Road led to Lancaster, 60 miles to the west and market center of the fertile Pennsylvania backcountry. There, Philadelphia merchants owned retail stores and appointed business agents, responsible for gathering marketable farm surplus and supplying countryfolk and southbound immigrants with imports and city manufactures. Conestogas loaded with freight made the journey from Philadelphia to Lancaster and back. Philadelphia merchants dispatched the goods they gathered from the hinterlands to Europe, the West Indies, Portugal, the Mediterranean, as well as to places closer to home. Their ships carried flour, pork, and beef to Boston in return for New England fish. They traded rum and molasses from the West Indies to South Carolinians in exchange for rice and turpentine. Philadelphia ships carried a host of American goods to England in ex-

change for British manufactures. By the middle of the eighteenth century, the city was fast becoming the commercial hub of the continental colonies.[10]

Commerce ordered Philadelphia's social structure as well as its economic life. At the top of city society were the well-to-do merchants who owned the ships, organized and underwrote the voyages, and reaped the bulk of the profits from the city's maritime trade. Sharing their wealth and prestige were a few successful professionals and the proprietary officials appointed by the Penns to run the colonial government. In the middling ranks of city society were small shopkeepers and artisans of varying degrees of skill, ranging from prestigious silversmiths to humble shoemakers. Beneath the artisans, and numbering perhaps one-third of the whole population, were those whose lack of property left them to face the daily need to "work or starve." Free white workers picked up casual work on the docks, found laboring jobs in the construction trades, or hired out as servants. Other whites were bound workers, apprenticed to learn a trade or indentured to serve a number of years, paying off the price of their passage to

The city docks, often bustling, sometimes slow, provided seasonal work for many laborers. The shipyards employed others, including some two dozen different types of craftsmen—carpenters, joiners, caulkers, riggers, blacksmiths, anchor makers, sail and rope makers, among others—constructing the largest and most complex machines of the time. Left: William Birch, "Arch Street Ferry." Below: "The Shipwright," from The Book of Trades, *1807.*

The craftsmen with the highest prestige in the city were those who worked in precious metals, keeping current with foreign fashions and catering to a prosperous clientele. Here are a goldsmith's trade card, and a silver teapot made by John McMullin, Philadelphia, 1790s.

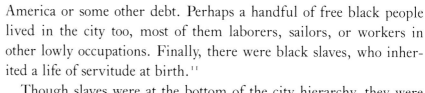

America or some other debt. Perhaps a handful of free black people lived in the city too, most of them laborers, sailors, or workers in other lowly occupations. Finally, there were black slaves, who inherited a life of servitude at birth.[11]

Though slaves were at the bottom of the city hierarchy, they were closely and "extensively woven into the fabric of city life." In 1767 there were somewhere in the vicinity of 1,400 slaves in the city proper, roughly one-twelfth of the total number of inhabitants. Most of them lived and worked in the households of white families, a few doing skilled craftswork, many more serving as domestic workers. Most slaveowners ranked in the top quarter of the wealthholders in the city, but a good number of bakers, ropemakers, and a wide range of other artisans owned a slave or two, as did even some laborers and sailors. No one owned large concentrations of slaves comparable to those in the plantation South; only some wealthy merchants, proprietary officials, and "gentlemen" owned as many as four or more slaves. So while Philadelphia's slave population was fairly small in numbers, slaveholding itself was still widespread. One historian has calculated that an African-American slave lived in one out of every five city households.[12]

As the incidence of slave ownership indicates, most Philadelphians spent little time worrying if slavery might be wrong. True, the Quakers who founded Pennsylvania held strikingly egalitarian beliefs for their day: every individual, they thought, possessed God's guiding "inner light." It followed that women and men of all classes and conditions had direct and equal access to God's word. The Quakers thus dispensed with clerical authorities and, equally important, fiercely resisted even civil officials' demands for deference. In England, members of the Society of Friends had pointedly refrained from removing their hats in the presence of magistrates, and they had refused to take oaths of loyalty to the state. The Quakers' stubborn efforts to live by their belief in "the brotherhood of man" made conservative English people glad to see them emigrate.[13]

In the New World, the commitment of the Quakers to equality made theirs among America's first voices raised against African slavery. In the seventeenth century, the founder of the Society of Friends, George Fox, had reminded West Indian Quakers that Christ had died for "the *Tawnies*" and "the *Blacks*" as well as for white people. In the mid-1700s, New Jersey Quaker John Woolman took the logic of the argument one step further: riding horseback through Virginia and the middle colonies, he urged fellow Friends to free the people they held in bondage. Besides oppressing blacks, he contended, slavery did slaveholders incalculable spiritual harm. "For while the life of one is made grievous by the Rigour of another, it entails Misery on both," he wrote. Philadelphia Friend Anthony Benezet also took up the cause. The Quakers' foremost antislavery pamphleteer, he spent thirty years working to disprove the idea that blacks were inferior to whites. For decades Benezet taught African-American children to read, write, and figure, and in 1770 he set up a school where black students could receive "religious and literary instruction" to prepare them for freedom. Through the years some Quakers continued to regard brotherhood (and sisterhood) as a real and vital goal.[14]

Yet most other Philadelphia Quakers failed to match the commit-

The cordwainer ranked among the more humble craftsmen, but some Philadelphia shoemakers made fine and expensive shoes. "The Shoe-maker," from The Book of Trades, *1807. Below is a size stick, for measuring customers' feet.*

ment shown by Woolman and Benezet. As the Quaker community gained prosperity, and as American-born generations of Friends succeeded the first wave of persecuted immigrants, many became more engrossed in economic and political concerns than in spiritual life. With commercial success, some Friends abandoned their commitment to equality and to plain living. Others left the Society altogether, worshipping instead at Anglican or Presbyterian churches in the city. The messages of Woolman and Benezet stirred some of their fellows to liberate their slaves or refrain from acquiring any, but for the most part those messages fell on deaf ears. In 1758, the Philadelphia Yearly Meeting yielded to Benezet and Woolman to condemn the slave trade, yet in the 1760s Quakers were still as active in slaveholding as any other Philadelphians.[15]

City residents calmly accepted slavery in part because they assumed society inevitably involved many types of inequality. In one sense, of course, slavery was an anomaly. As Woolman pointed out, no one would think of enslaving a white child, no matter how poor that child's parents. Long association between black skin and servitude created race prejudice in many minds. At the same time, Philadelphians were also accustomed to seeing white people in positions of servitude and

Printers' woodcuts, used to highlight newspaper advertisements of slave sales, reflect the frequency and general acceptance of slave importations in the colonies.

Negroes for Sale.

A Cargo of very fine stout Men and Women, in good order and fit for immediate service, just imported from the Windward Coast of Africa, in the Ship Two Brothers.— Conditions are one half Cash or Produce, the other half payable the first of January next, giving Bond and Security if required. The Sale to be opened at 10 o'Clock each Day, in Mr. Bourdeaux's Yard, at No, 48, on the Bay. May 19, 1784. JOHN MITCHELL.

Benjamin Chew helped design Cliveden, his country estate in Germantown, outside Philadelphia.

poverty. Even Quakers believed the commonplace of the age, that it was natural that society include such distinctions as "Prince and People, Master and Servants, Parents and Children." Before the Revolution, many Americans agreed with the Quakers that hierarchy was simply a normal state of affairs. Midcentury Philadelphia was part of an Anglo-American world that simply took many forms of human inequality for granted.[16]

$\mathcal{R}$ichard Allen was born into a family that legally owed its labor and its loyalty to white lawyer Benjamin Chew and his wife, Elizabeth Oswald. Benjamin Chew enjoyed the prestigious position of attorney general of the colony, appointed by the proprietor in England. He worked for many of the city's wealthiest merchants and socialized with the elite in city society. He did very well. In the 1760s, when others suffered from a decline in trade, Chew spent £3,000 to build a luxurious country estate, called "Cliveden," outside the city. Chew em-

"The Accident in Lombard-Street," by Charles Willson Peale, 1787, was captioned: "The pye from Bake-house she had brought / But let it fall for want of thought / And laughing sweeps collect around / The pye that's scatter'd on the ground."

ployed the Allen family to help his wife with the running of the house, the rearing of five children, and with social entertaining. Even as a young boy, Richard Allen probably shared in small ways the round of tasks required to keep the socially active Chew household going. He had an older sister and brother to play with and to keep him out of the way of his parents. He learned early that his parents' time and lives were not entirely their own. The choices open to a slave family had stark limits.[17]

Yet within those limits, most slaves and servants worked to carve out space for themselves. Most tried to find some measure of freedom in their life of bondage, and their resistance shaped the institutions of servitude along with the demands of masters and the dictates of the law. No doubt the Allens managed to share family talk and family times, fitting their own lives into the moments they could snatch from their work for the Chews. An ex-Quaker, Chew himself worshipped at the Anglican Christ's Church, and the Allens might have gone to services there as well. Along with other white churches, Christ's Church opened its doors to city blacks, so at Sunday worship at least some slaves found a spiritual community.[18]

Richard's family also had access to a wider community of slaves, servants, and poor whites within the city. Beginning in midcentury, some upper-class whites complained that blacks, free and slave, met to dance, sing, and socialize at the "potter's field," the burial ground for blacks and paupers, in the southeastern quadrant of the city. At night, in the city marketplace and at some city taverns, there were interracial gatherings. In 1751 one Philadelphian complained in the newspaper that some free blacks had "taken Houses, Rooms, or Cellars, for their Habitations," where they created disorders with "Servants, Slaves, and other idle or vagrant Persons." What the writer in the *Gazette* perceived as disorder, participants no doubt experienced as a brief spell of freedom and relaxation, precious time away from the oppressive presence of their social superiors. Common bondage brought white servants and black slaves together, to socialize at one another's houses, on the streets, or in taverns. How much the Allen family took part in lower-class society we don't know. But when errands took them across town or free time allowed visiting with other blacks, they entered a vibrant community of their fellows.[19]

When Richard Allen was eight, the world outside his family's control intruded abruptly into their lives. Through 1760 the city had enjoyed prosperity, for as frequently happened in the eighteenth century, England's wars with France had spilled over into America. Philadelphia merchants fattened off the traffic supplying armies in the French and Indian Wars, and artisans and laborers found ready employment too. With the end of the wars came a drop in foreign trade that hurt many Philadelphians. The effects began to reach Chew toward the end of the decade; slower business for merchants meant fewer legal transactions for lawyers like Chew. To make matters worse, Chew was sympathetic to the English side of the argument that was developing between England and its American colonies. A well-to-do Anglican and an appointed proprietary official, his loyalties lay with English authority rather than the upstart patriot movement. As a result, many city inhabitants who sided with the growing resistance cause passed over Chew to hire other lawyers more in tune with their own political opinions. To make ends meet, Chew sold his family of slaves. Young Richard, just eight years of age, suddenly learned that he and his family had become the property of a man named Stokeley

Sturgis, a farmer who lived in Little Creek Hundred, near the town of Dover, Delaware.[20]

Years later, Richard Allen remembered Sturgis as "what the world calls a good master," a phrase that expressed Allen's conviction that no such being could ever exist. Sturgis was in any event a kind man, and over time there grew a relationship of sympathy between the white master and his slaves. The social distance between the Sturgises and the Allens was significant, but not so vast as the distance that separated the Allens from the Chews—or that separated elite planters of the southern colonies from their slaves. Sturgis was a middling farmer, typical of central Delaware, where subsistence farming was slowly yielding to specialized grain production for the Philadelphia market.[21]

With the move to Delaware, the Allens left behind a bustling, cosmopolitan world for a more rural and isolated scene. They had to learn new tasks and adapt to life in a less affluent household. The change may well have affected the Allen women less than it affected the men. Most likely, Richard Allen's mother and sister worked at the cooking, gardening, and household production that consumed the time of most eighteenth-century women, black and white, slave and free. Unlike Sturgis's wife, though, at times they may have done farm work in the field, a task from which white women were generally excluded. The male members of the Allen family learned to cultivate

"Seasoned" slaves, those born into or long used to slavery, were preferred by most masters to newly arrived Africans. Many had acquired skills valuable to whites, like the carpenters, cook, and washerwoman mentioned here.

Thirty Seasoned Negroes
To be Sold for Credit, at Private Sale.

AMONGST which is a Carpenter, none of whom are known to be dishonest.

Also, to be sold for Cash, a regular bred young Negroe Man-Cook, born in this Country, who served several Years under an exceeding good French Cook abroad, and his Wife a middle aged Washer-Woman, (both very honest) and their two Children. Likewise, a young Man a Carpenter.

For Terms apply to the Printer.

such crops as wheat and hay and to care for farm animals. The family lived nearly a decade on Sturgis's farm, and Richard Allen grew up learning the skills of rural life. New children were born to Richard's parents there, and new ties created in the community. Then, late in the 1770s, for the second time the world outside their control stepped in and changed the Allens' lives.[22]

Like Chew, Sturgis came upon hard times, and decided to sell some of his slaves. Unlike Chew, however, Sturgis needed to keep some bound laborers if he were ever to recoup his fortunes. He chose to keep three young Allens who were entering their most productive working years: Richard, now about 17, his older brother, and his older sister. The three found themselves suddenly separated from their parents and their younger sisters and brothers.[23]

Years later, Allen was able to recount these events without expressing the pain, rage, and bewilderment that he must have felt at the time. The division of the Allen family must have affected all three young people deeply. Shortly after their parents were sold away from the farm, all three children found solace in a profound personal transformation. In some measure, perhaps, the religious movement called Methodism filled the void left in their lives by the loss of their parents and siblings.[24]

*M*ethodism originated in England as a revival movement within the established Anglican church. Its founders, John and Charles Wesley, dissented less from Anglican doctrine than from the dry and formal nature of Anglican piety. The Methodist version of the faith stressed the emotional experience of conversion and the possibility of reaching earthly perfection. Where many Anglicans kept a largely nominal membership in the church, sincere Methodists turned their lives into constant quests for sinlessness. Indeed, it was the sweeping, methodical nature of the converts' self-discipline that gave Methodism its name. Methodist preachers challenged many established clergymen, attacking their lack of heartfelt faith. Denied access to the pulpits of the offended establishment, they took to the homes and workshops of the towns and preached in fields and graveyards across the country-

In "Bunn, the blacksmith, at a Campmeeting near Georgetown," 1809, Benjamin Latrobe captured some of the emotional power of evangelical religion as well as its openness to plain, unlettered preachers.

side, affecting a broad audience of ordinary English women and men.[25]

A few Methodist preachers traveled to the colonies in the 1760s, and in the next decade the Wesleys officially delegated more. In 1771 they appointed Francis Asbury their emissary, and through the 1770s Asbury and other English itinerants made converts throughout the American South. They traveled almost constantly to serve the scattered rural population. They touched the lives of many Americans, some of whom became preachers in turn. As a critic of the movement lamented, "any layman, or mechanic, if he finds a motion within him from the spirit, may leap from the anvil or plough, and in a few minutes go forth a preacher of the word of God." Of its preachers Methodism required no Latin or other book learning, just a converted heart and a readiness to speak of God.[26]

Such "spiritual egalitarianism" appealed much more strongly to the ordinary people, black and white, than to the sophisticated and privileged. Methodist preaching was fiery and emotional, in contrast to the dry, learned sermons given by Anglican ministers in the churches preferred by the elite. Anglican ministers tended settled congregations, delivered uninspired conservative sermons and, for the most part, cut their morality to please well-to-do white planters. By contrast, Methodist preachers rode the circuit from place to place, lived simple, austere lives, and preached to humble people with zeal and conviction. They found responsive listeners in the poor and plain folk of much of the South. Like the Baptists, Methodists criticized the gentry's high living and appealed across lines of race. To many in the planter class, the dissenters' success seemed threatening to the social order.[27]

In the middle colonies, where Richard Allen lived, the population was bound by no established church. In Maryland and Delaware, fair numbers of middle-class and elite Americans warmed to the Methodist faith. But in Delaware also, it was plainer folk and slaves who responded most fervently to the message of Methodist preaching. There too, members of the upper class or Anglican rectors might view the revival as a threat. Said one, "The enthusiastic notions of ignorant Methodists" might "overturn all order and decency in the church." One preacher's account of a Methodist meeting helps to illustrate that concern:

I had gone through about two-thirds of my discourse, and was bringing the words home to the present—Now, when such power descended, that hundreds fell to the ground, and the house seemed to shake with the presence of God. The chapel was full of white and black, and many were without that could not get in. Look wherever we would, we saw nothing but . . . faces bathed in tears . . . My voice was drowned amidst the groans and prayers of the congregation. . . . This mighty effusion of the Spirit continued for above an hour; in which time many were awakened.[28]

The power of such events worried conservative onlookers and unsettled people committed to cosmopolitan and genteel standards of living. Methodist worship embodied alternative values—a new brotherhood and sisterhood, new emotionalism and zeal.

Either at a similar revival meeting, or at a smaller gathering led by a Methodist preacher, Richard Allen became converted. Many years later he recalled the power of that experience. At first, he remembered, he had felt great joy. "I went rejoicing for several days and was happy in the Lord, in conversing with many old experienced Christians." Yet shortly after, a sense of doubt, of his own sinfulness, replaced his happiness. "I went with my head bowed down for many days. My sins were a heavy burden. I was tempted to believe there was no mercy for me. I cried to the Lord both night and day. One night I thought hell would be my portion. I cried unto Him who delighteth to hear the prayers of a poor sinner, and all of a sudden my dungeon shook, my chains flew off, and glory to God, I cried. My soul was filled."[29]

Across the upper South, other new adherents gave similar accounts of powerful experiences of conversion. There was something in Methodism that seemed to free people from their "chains," to give them a sense of liberation. In some measure, that liberation stemmed from Methodism's explicit teachings. Along with other Protestant Americans, Methodists believed that people were sinful by nature. Unlike most others, however, Methodists believed that salvation was not simply in the hands of God. Instead, each person had the power to choose God and salvation. Allen might not be able to keep his family together, pick a master to work for, or control many aspects of his daily life. Yet Methodism taught him that he was far from helpless. In his

Lemuel Haynes, the first black preacher in the American Congregational Church, was depicted on this early nineteenth-century tray by an unknown artist.

THE LIMITS OF LIBERTY

spiritual life, he found a form of "liberty" that no master could take away.[30]

Yet the Methodist faith was in no way permissive. By choosing Methodism, Allen committed himself to making profound changes in his daily life. Methodist preachers called on the converted to improve and even perfect themselves. Believers should work hard, lead sober, industrious lives, and give up such earthly pleasures as drinking and gambling, and such frivolities as singing and dancing. Anglicans saw little reason for such strictness: "I am sure there is no harm in civil mirth, in going to balls and taking a civil dance; enjoying one's self among young people, hearing the fiddle; it revives ones spirits." But the Methodists' fear of backsliding kept even the converted in a state of constant vigilance against sin. For Methodists, religion was not just a matter of going to church; it shaped an entire life.[31]

Living out their faith, Richard Allen and his brother worked hard for Sturgis, always finishing their farm work before going to a religious meeting, even skipping meetings if they had to bring in the corn. Yet many of Sturgis's neighbors urged him to stop his slaves from attending Methodist classes and hearing Methodist preachers. Most white Americans probably considered themselves Christians of one denomination or another, but many worried that their religion might give dangerous ideas to their slaves. Slavery necessarily implied inequality and put a vast social distance between white owners and black slaves. Whites opposed black conversion, as one put it, feeling it "shameful, to have a spiritual brother or sister among so despicable a people; partly by thinking that they should not be able to keep their negroes so meanly afterwards; and partly through fear of the negroes growing too proud, on seeing themselves upon a level with their masters in religious matters."[32] Of course, Christianity could be used to defend and reinforce social distances. Wealthy whites favored preachers who told poorer people, white and black, that God had created them unequal and given them the job of working contentedly for others. But when Christianity was out of the control of the upper classes, it might carry revolutionary implications. It rested on the dangerous idea that all people stood as equals in the sight of God.[33]

Even without religion, many slaves refused to accept white people's claims that blacks owed them labor and loyalty. Like other exploited workers, slaves devised ways of witholding their work from their masters. They could pretend to be sick, cooperate with one another in working slowly, or do their work poorly. Slaves could run away at harvest or other times when their labor was most needed. Using these means, they sometimes managed to gain concessions from their masters, like shorter work hours or permission to spend spare time growing vegetables in their own garden plots. In response to black efforts to limit white control, slaveholders charged their slaves with being lazy and disloyal. But slaves were loyal to one another, and they worked hard when given the opportunity to work for their own benefit. Choosing to work poorly meant refusing to collaborate with slaveowners, dissenting from white people's claim that blacks owed labor to their masters. Working poorly expressed blacks' belief in the injustice of slavery. If this was the way many slaves acted without religion, what would happen when they became as good (or better) Christians than their masters? How could whites expect obedience from the converted?[34]

On the surface, none of these fears seemed justified in the case of the Allen brothers. They worked harder than ever before, and convinced Sturgis that religion actually made slaves better workers. But Sturgis's neighbors were right in seeing that Methodism gave a new power to the Allens, and that that power posed a threat to the institution of slavery. Richard Allen's hard work was as much a rebellion against slavery as was other slaves' refusal to work. Allen might act as Sturgis wanted him to act, but he did not do it to please Sturgis. He did it to please God. He did it for himself. Allen's work was not an admission that he owed obedience to Sturgis. That it pleased his white master was largely incidental. Methodism helped Richard Allen transform his work and his servitude so that it took on new meaning for him.[35]

Yet there was a contradiction in that experience: whatever it seemed like to Richard Allen, wasn't the practical result of his conversion that he became a better slave? Wasn't Methodism's God merely a better overseer than Sturgis could ever be? The same contradiction existed in the lives of other slaves and working whites who, embracing Methodism, internalized a work ethic that lined the pockets of their masters and bosses. The Methodist prescription for constant toil would help to discipline workers to the new and ceaseless drudgery of nineteenth-century factory labor. For slaves like Richard Allen, there were other ironies too. Allen recorded later that, in Delaware, slaves worked in their garden patches late into the night, then gave much of their own produce and earnings to the white preachers who traveled through the area and spoke to slave gatherings. The slaves' donations reflected the value that they placed on the respect and brotherhood so rarely offered them by whites. Yet didn't blacks toil all day to feed and support white people? What sort of "liberation" would have them serve whites even more?[36]

These questions have no simple answer, yet eighteenth-century Methodism undeniably brought liberty to some slaves in two fundamental ways. First, in Methodism many found a new religious community. The conversion experienced by Richard Allen and others was intense, inner, and personal. But it was not a private experience. It was common for "sinners" to see the light not in solitude but at meeting, where a host of believers gathered around the penitent, praying together for God's grace. His conversion to Methodism linked Allen to other people in a new way. After revival meetings, said one preacher, "Those who were happy in God themselves were for bringing all their friends to him in their arms." Methodism grew because those who heard the preaching went home to "spread the flame through their respective neighborhoods, which ran from family to family."[37]

Richard Allen reacted to his experience of conversion as many others did. Separated from his parents and younger brothers and sisters, he found a new community among Methodists. He went "from house to house . . . telling to all around what a dear Saviour I had found." He worked to bring his "old companions" into fellowship with him. Both his brother and sister became converts too. If his faith began to waver, he could turn to newfound brethren for help. With his brother, Richard attended preachings in the forest every two weeks, and every week he went to Benjamin Wells's farm for a "class meeting," a gathering where members prayed together, recounted religious experiences, shared doubts, and admonished one another for backsliding. Richard Allen had discovered that, as a slave, he was powerless to keep his family together. It made enslavement "a bitter pill," no matter how "humane" the master. Through Methodism, Allen could be sure that, whatever might happen to separate him from those he depended upon and loved, he would still find a community of fellows.[38]

Equally important, Methodism worked for Richard Allen, and for many other blacks of his generation, as it never worked for white laborers. For in the revolutionary ferment of the eighteenth century it proved possible for some slaves to escape their state of bondage. Early Methodism did not retreat into spirituality, leaving aside the struggle for practical social change. "Liberty is the Right of every human creature," wrote John Wesley in 1774, and Methodist preachers in the New World took him literally, as they spoke out directly against the holding of slaves. Wesley's disciples taught that everyone—white as well as black—should lead sober, industrious lives. It followed that slaveholders, especially those who aspired to live a life of leisure off the work of others, were sinful. Early Methodism was evenhanded: it applied its standards for good living to people of all colors and all classes, and in the 1770s, it was implacably opposed to slavery.[39]

Sturgis's neighbors, then, were right to have their suspicions of slave religion; at the same time, attacks on inequality could be found in those ideas central to the American Revolution as well. Americans were beginning to reject the easy assumption that either God or Nature had established such distinctions as that between "Prince and People." Pamphleteer Tom Paine caught the imagination of readers and listeners when he pointed out how nature itself ridiculed hereditary privilege and monarchy by so often "giving mankind an ass for an lion." And if monarchy were not so natural or justifiable then perhaps one could doubt the justice and inevitability of other traditional distinctions as well. Ordinary white men, accustomed to leaving the world of politics to their social superiors, were beginning to seek greater liberty for themselves. White Americans could not easily deny the efforts of blacks to claim liberty too. As early as 1774, Abigail Adams wrote to her husband John, that, "It always appeared a most iniquitous scheme to me to fight ourselves for what we are daily robbing and plundering from those who have as good a right to freedom as we have."⁴⁰

Other whites, north and south, agreed. When slaves took up arms for the British in return for their freedom, patriot whites deplored it, but they understood it very well. In the northern and middle colonies, many slaves sought to make the Revolution their own by fighting on the patriot side. At the outset, General Horatio Gates had ordered the exclusion of "any stroller, negro, or vagabond." from the Continental

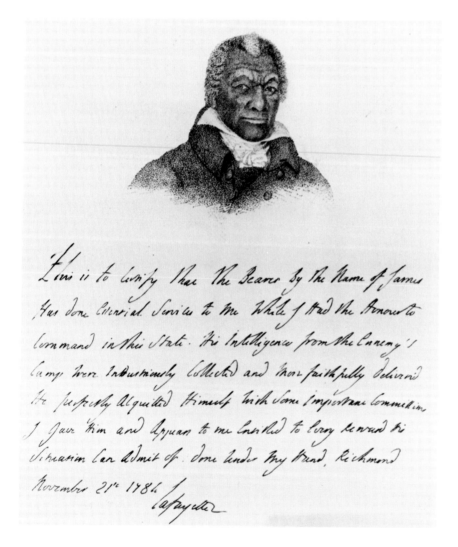

During the Revolution, James, a Virginia slave, pressed his master for permission to enlist under the French general, Lafayette. In 1784, the general wrote this testimonial to James's valuable service as a spy. Two years later, James Armistead Lafayette received his freedom from the Virginia General Assembly.

Army. Yet soon the difficulty of recruiting led the struggling states to welcome black participation. In some states, slaves were given or promised freedom when they enlisted. Despite the initial intentions of white patriots, blacks began to broaden the Revolution into a movement to liberate their own people.[41]

Although the ideals of the Revolution and the teachings of Methodism coincided in their opposition to slavery, the two movements were never in easy alliance. Methodists, after all, remained tied to the Church of England, and Wesley himself publicly opposed the colonies' bid for independence. Some Methodists in the colonies were pacifists who refused to fight, others were sympathetic to British authority. Patriot suspicion of his loyalties caused Francis Asbury to spend much of the war in semiretirement, avoiding popular ill will. Other intrepid preachers faced down mobs to preach through the war years, and many sincere Methodists were also sincere patriots. Tensions between the two movements declined as the war progressed and Asbury's support for the American cause became known. During the war years, in uneasy truce, itinerant ministers and patriot committees worked in Little Creek Hundred. Camp meetings of the one brought Methodism, while the pamphlets, orators, and patriotic gatherings of the other brought republican ideas.[42]

Influenced by these currents of thought, the Allens' master was slowly won over to the cause of his slaves. As he grew "old and infirm," Allen remembered, Sturgis grew concerned about his own spiritual state. He let the Allens hold prayer meetings in the kitchen of his house, and after a while he and his wife began to attend. The prayer meetings moved to the parlor, and religion came to play a central role in the household. As his own piety grew, Sturgis became increasingly willing to accommodate his slaves' spiritual lives. "We had our stated times to hold our prayer meetings and give exhortations etc. in the neighborhood," remembered Allen. The slave convinced his master to allow a preacher to come to the farm to hold services. For several months circuit riders made stops at the farm to preach on Sunday. The most significant of these, from Richard Allen's point of view, was Freeborn Garrettson who, born to a prosperous and slaveholding Maryland family, had freed his own slaves shortly after his

English antislavery sentiment fueled the American movement for emancipation. This medallion, made at Josiah Wedgwood's factory in Staffordshire, England, late in the eighteenth century, reads "AM I NOT A MAN AND A BROTHER?"

own conversion. At the Sturgis home, Garrettson spoke on the Biblical text, "Ye have been weighed in the balance and found wanting," stressing that the sin of slaveholding lay among the heaviest of earthly offenses. Deeply moved by Garrettson's message, Sturgis resolved to reform his life. He told Richard Allen and his brother that they could buy their freedom. The price would be £60 gold and silver, or $2000 continental paper money.[43]

This was a formidable amount to accumulate by hiring out on Sundays or making profits from little garden patches, but Sturgis was more generous than many masters who offered their slaves a chance to buy freedom: he gave the Allen brothers time to go out and work to accumulate the price. In January of 1780, Stokeley Sturgis signed an agreement with "Richard Negro." The slave would purchase his freedom in five annual installments, with payment due on the second of February every year. If Richard decided to pay in the depreciating continental money, the agreement stipulated, then he had also to work two full days in harvest time, "wages free," on the Sturgis farm. Otherwise, Sturgis decided, he would "fully trust and Impower" Allen to "Hire Deal and Transact for himself with any person Whatsoever."[44]

"Richard Negro" took to the road looking for a job. He started out cutting wood and soon became skillful enough to cut a cord and a half to two cords each day. He worked for a brickyard for $50 a month. In the late years of the Revolution, he found employment with the Delaware government, driving a wagon delivering salt from Rehoboth to army suppliers throughout the state. All along he was haunted by his master's ill health, afraid that Sturgis would die and his slaves be sold to pay off his debts. Allen relied on his faith for comfort. He preached wherever he found himself, making stops along the road as he delivered salt, telling of his conversion and experience of God. The hard work Methodism had inspired now became doubly meaningful, since it opened the way out of slavery. Aided by the sharp inflation of the time, Allen succeeded in raising the money before five years had passed. August of 1783 found him back in Little Creek Hundred, perhaps working his two days of harvest, certainly making his final cash payment to his master. Sturgis provided freedom papers, so that Richard could prove to anyone who asked that he was indeed "a Free Negro Man," adding that he had "Beheaved himself Soberly and Honestly when he wrought about this place." With his freedom "Richard Negro" apparently acquired a surname in the eyes of the whole world, for in 1783 Sturgis included it in writing: "Richard Allen."[45]

Freedom brought Allen greater control over his own future, but also a new insecurity. Though he had mastered a variety of skills of value in rural society, he owned nothing. He had to make his way in the free market, armed only with his health and ability to work. He made money picking up odd jobs. What mattered to him most was preaching the gospel, a vocation that committed him to near constant traveling. He spent his first years of freedom on the road, exhorting others to religion and reform. Like other Methodist itinerants, Allen accepted accommodations from believers in the towns and villages where he preached but worked to pay for his own clothing and other

Printers issued numerous religious tracts, stories, and illustrations like this woodcut of an established clergyman, from a book called The Life of the Holy Jesus.

needs. In the early 1780s he saw a great deal of the country. He traveled the circuit to Wilmington, Delaware, and preached in Lancaster, Pennsylvania, where a fellow Methodist gave him a horse to speed his travels. In West Jersey he made money by cutting wood for one Captain Cruenkleton, while preaching the gospel nights and Sundays. At times he traveled along with white ministers, like Richard Whatcoat on the Baltimore circuit. In his travels he was testing his ability to preach to other people, learning to trust his own powers. He became recognized in Methodist circles as a talented lay exhorter, a position just below that of preacher.[46]

In the Revolutionary era the Methodist church lauded such black men for their ability and dedication. Methodists were convinced that blacks were as capable of profound religious experience and moral discipline as were whites. Such egalitarianism was consistent with Methodism's support for manumission. In 1784, when the Methodist Conference at Baltimore officially separated from the Episcopal church, delegates also declared themselves in opposition to slavery, vowing to expel any church member who bought or sold slaves unless for the purpose of freeing them. Lay members of Methodist societies in the mid-Atlantic states also showed themselves to be willing to accept a black man as their spiritual equal and even guide. Throughout his travels Allen met with widespread acceptance by white believers. In 1784 Allen found responsive listeners in Radnor, Pennsylvania, where he stayed for several weeks. There were "but a few colored people in the neighborhood," he later recorded. "The most of my congregation was white." Allen held "comfortable meetings with the Germans" in Lancaster and Little York as well. Allen's account of his travels often leaves unclear whether his hosts and audiences were white or black. For a few years, for a few Americans, race did not seem particularly to matter.[47]

Yet Richard Allen recognized that there were sharp limits to this tolerance. In 1784 Bishop Francis Asbury urged Allen to accompany him on a tour of the South. Allen could preach with the bishop, but he could not preach to slaves, and he would have to sleep in the coach in deference to southern white opinion. Despite the compliment implied in the bishop's offer, Allen could not imagine being cut off from

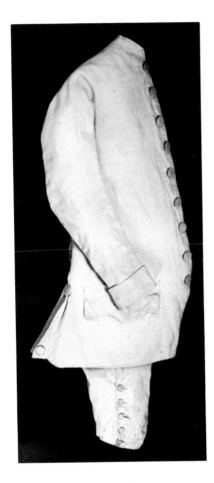

Skilled workers learned the art and mystery of a craft through apprenticeships with established master craftsmen. On finishing training, some received a new set of clothes, or "freedom suit," like this coat and breeches given to Jonathan Sheldon, who became a journeyman cabinetmaker in 1775.

southern slaves. "I told him if I was taken sick, who was to support me?" Allen needed the black community, to whom he could turn for fellowship and mutual care. Though he rode circuit with white ministers, and preached to white and black alike, his primary concern lay with those of his own race. This was a matter of loyalty, of course, but also one of personal security. Like most free blacks and many whites, Allen was *merely* free, without valuable skills, education, or property. To combat the limits of merely legal liberty, Allen could only turn to solidarity with his own community. Instead of going south, Allen accepted an invitation to preach from the white Methodist elders of St. George's Church, Philadelphia. In 1786 Allen returned to the city of his birth.[48]

$\mathcal{P}$hiladelphia, he discovered, had grown and changed. After the Revolution, immigrants from Ireland and France poured into the port. Many went on to the countryside in search of land, while others stayed to pick up jobs on the docks, learn a craft, or work as domestics. Immigrants from rural America arrived in the city too, landless people in search of opportunities. Where city residents had numbered 30,000 on the eve of the Revolution, by 1790 there were more than 42,000.[49]

A growing number of Philadelphians were legally free. Those who had been indentured servants before the Revolution had served their time by the end of the war, and the war had cut off much new immigration from Europe. Some postwar immigrants entered as bound laborers, but increasingly urban employers showed a preference for free workers. Subject to the starts and stops of world commerce, merchants and master artisans turned more and more to "free" labor, labor that could be hired for a short time, then let go when there was no work available. Both indentures and the practice of apprenticeship declined in the closing decades of the century.[50]

Most important to Richard Allen, black slavery was also in decline in Philadelphia. After the Revolution, the northern and mid-Atlantic states, where slaves comprised a relatively small proportion of the population, acted to put slavery on the road to extinction. Pennsylvania

Samuel Jennings, an expatriate Philadel-phian living in London, sent "Liberty Displaying the Arts and Sciences" to the Library Company of Philadelphia in 1792. Liberty promises enlightenment and progress in this antislavery painting.

was particularly active in extending the bounds of Revolutionary lib-erty. Through the years of the war, citizens inside and outside the Society of Friends widely echoed Woolman's and Benezet's injunctions against slaveholding. In the 1770s and 1780s, influenced by republi-canism and the optimism of Enlightenment thought, a growing num-ber of Philadelphians organized to oppose slavery. In 1775 the Pennsylvania Abolition Society convened, made up of middle-class shopkeepers and mechanics. They pressed for an end to slavery and for legal protection for free blacks kidnapped and sold south as slaves. Partly as a result of their efforts, the state enacted a plan for gradual emancipation in 1780. The law had its drawbacks: it freed no slaves living at the time of its passage and the liberation it offered those yet to be born was agonizingly slow. All children born to slaves after passage of the act would be freed when they reached the age of twenty-eight. Still, the law did doom chattel slavery in Pennsylvania, and its passage reflected the valuable alliance that city blacks were forging with Philadelphia's artisan class.[51]

Artisans' tools. From left to right on this page: a cooper's cresset, to hold fires to make wood staves pliable; a silversmith's bellying hammer; a blacksmith's anvil; a seamstress's box iron; a shoemaker's mallet and block. From top to bottom, opposite: a cabinetmaker's plane; wing dividers; a line reel used by house carpenters.

That class had grown more powerful and self-confident through the course of the Revolution. For the most part artisans were proponents of a radical, egalitarian republicanism. They held to the idea that "virtue"—self-reliance, hard work, economy, and austere living—formed the necessary basis of republican government. The mainstay of American society was its virtuous citizens, working people and mechanics such as themselves. Their hostility to privilege and aristocracy, and their belief in equality, made many republican artisans oppose slavery. Tom Paine, the irreverent pamphleteer who had attacked monarchy and other hereditary privilege in *Common Sense*, was one of their spokesmen. Enlightened upper-class reformers also extended their support to the city's blacks, but for the most part it was the artisans and their representatives who opposed hierarchy and inequality in their society.[52]

Indeed, it was Pennsylvania's artisans, as much as its upper-class reformers, who moved to give substance to merely legal freedom. In

1776 artisans and their allies succeeded in enacting an egalitarian state constitution. It established a single house legislature, designed to be responsive to public desires, with no aristocratic upper house. The constitution also broadened the suffrage to include all free men who paid any taxes at all—so that even among the poor, many men could vote. Even some free black men probably voted, since the state constitution did not explicitly exclude them. The radical republicans who supported the 1776 state constitution could not simply eliminate inequality, but they favored a broad distribution of property and worried about the growing gulf between rich and poor.[53]

These changes conspired to make Philadelphia a more hospitable city for blacks than it had been when Richard Allen left. The free black community had grown in numbers, since many had won freedom in the war or gained manumission like Allen. When census takers counted the population in 1790, they found 1,630 blacks in the city, 1,420 of them legally free. Like Allen, however, most enjoyed legal freedom while limited by material poverty and lack of opportunities. Most blacks remained near the bottom of city society. In 1795 the Pennsylvania Abolition Society reported on the jobs open to free blacks: "Some of the men follow Mechanick trades, and a number of them are mariners, but the greatest part are employed as Day labourers. The Women generally, both married and single, wash clothes for a livelihood." Women also worked as seamstresses, cooks, and dressmakers. Men worked as servants, waiters, barbers, coachmen, bootblacks, porters, secondhand clothing dealers, and hod carriers. People in all of these occupations enjoyed some kind of freedom, but most lived in poverty or on its edges.[54]

Many blacks still worshipped in the city's Anglican churches, and during the Revolution some Quakers had redoubled their efforts to bring blacks into fellowship. Yet most city blacks, according to Allen, were unchurched and untaught. "I soon saw a large field open in seeking and instructing my African brethren, who had been a long forgotten people and few of them attended public worship." Allen set about reaching the city's free and enslaved black population and bringing them into the fellowship that had brought him both spiritual and material liberty. He traveled to different parts of the city to reach as

Coopers made both small, common house-hold vessels and large barrels for transporting commercial products ranging from rum to tobacco to dried fish. Right: a cooper, from The Encyclopedia of Early American Trades, *1837.*

Few women were apprenticed into skilled trades, though they often managed a shop after a husband or father died. The 1800 Philadelphia city directory listed 73 seamstresses, 31 dressmakers, and 156 female boardinghouse keepers, but only 11 women bakers, and one blacksmith, cooper, coachmaker, and printer. Below: a dressmaker, from The Book of Trades, *1807.*

many as possible. He preached as many as four or five times a day, starting at five o'clock in the morning and often finishing his last meetings late in the evening. He set up prayer meetings that attracted a regular group of forty-two participants, and he held adult classes in the evenings at St. George's. The message he gave them was undoubtedly much like the one he had received himself. He told his listeners about their power to liberate themselves spiritually and, perhaps, materially as well. He told them of their ability to take control of their lives through hard work and self-discipline. And he told them of the particular love that God held for the weary and the oppressed of the world. It was an appropriate message for those who remained in bondage, looking for ways to make their lives their own. And it was appropriate for the newly freed as well, those at the bottom of society in need of a larger vision to give meaning to lives of deprivation and hard labor.[55]

Allen also found allies who agreed with his goals, most notably Absalom Jones, an ex-slave who was sixteen years his senior and who shared Allen's commitment to the black community. Jones, too, had been a slave in Delaware, where his small size exempted him from field work and placed him as household servant. In the house of his white master, Jones had learned to read and write, and when his master moved to Philadelphia to set up a store, Jones proved a valuable worker there. Slowly he earned enough money to help purchase his wife's freedom—since their mother's legal status determined whether children were born slave or free, it made sense to some couples to devote their earnings to the woman's manumission. By 1784 the Joneses managed to save enough to buy Absalom's freedom as well. When he met Richard Allen, Jones was working as a free man at his ex-master's store. The two men differed—Allen was the more able preacher, Jones more moderate and reserved. They became close allies. Together, they worked to organize the city's black community.[56]

Almost from the first Allen and Jones considered establishing a house of worship solely for the city's blacks. So long as blacks remained in churches run by whites, their freedom was limited by white prejudice. White preachers, Allen recorded later, "would act to please their own fancy, without discipline, till some of them became such tyrants, and more especially to the colored people. They would turn them out of the society, giving them no trial, for the smallest offence, perhaps only hearsay." It would be better for blacks to control their own churches. Other blacks—according to Allen, the "most respectable people of color" in the city—opposed the idea of a separate black church, however. So did white elders, one of whom "used very degrading and insulting language to us, to try to prevent us from going on." Despite the opposition, Allen, Jones, and a handful of compatriots continued thinking about the advantages of a separate black church, and continued trying to reach and help fellow blacks in the city. When a white elder told Allen and Jones to stop holding meetings for prayer and exhortation, they refused, seeing the "forlorn state of our colored brethren, and that they were destitute of a place of worship."[57]

Looking back many years later, Allen described his own aspirations for a separate black church as rooted in the prejudices and sentiments of St. George's white Methodists. Black members, remembered Allen, were increasingly "considered as a nuisance" by their white breth-

American craftsmen—"mechanics" in eighteenth-century parlance—enjoyed high esteem. "The People have a saying, that God Almighty is himself a Mechanic, the greatest in the Universe; and he is respected and admired more for the Variety, Ingenuity, and Utility of his Handiworks, than from the Antiquity of his Family." Benjamin Franklin, 1788.

Benjamin Banneker, a free black, was a farmer, mathematician, and astronomer whose finely calculated almanacs, published in the 1790s, challenged some whites' doubts about the mental abilities of Afro-Americans.

ren. Surely if whites had welcomed them into full and equal participation in church decisions and leadership, blacks would have had less reason to consider setting out on their own. Yet there was another side to Allen's desire for a separate black church. His people, he realized, had needs and aspirations that set them apart from whites. It was not just that they were poor—there were poor white Methodists too. But every free Philadelphia black lived with the knowledge that he or she was connected with people who were slaves. In Virginia and the rest of the South, some whites acknowledged the evils of African bondage, but nowhere in the South was a plan for emancipation under way. Allen surely recognized that Philadelphia blacks had a vital stake in the liberation of others of their race, a stake not shared so deeply by white Methodists. More immediately, Philadelphia blacks shared common problems with one another that drew them together and separated them from white parishioners at St. George's. Even those who were free were just up from slavery, after all. Many were illiterate; some had trouble deciding what they would—or could—do with their lives; all faced prejudice every day. To counter these problems, they needed more than equal treatment from their white brethren at St. George's. They needed their own community. Black parishioners' history of enslavement and their encounters with white racism outside the church made injuries and insults suffered at St. George's all the more difficult to tolerate.[58]

Despite the opposition to their plan for a black church, Allen, Jones, and a handful of others nonetheless decided to establish an institution that would help unify and sustain the black community. In 1787 they formed "The Free African Society," open to all orderly and sober blacks without regard to their particular religious beliefs. The Society concerned itself with both the material and moral well-being of city blacks. It was a mutual aid society, its members paying dues to a fund for support of those in sickness, and to benefit members' widows and fatherless children. At the same time, the Society also provided its members with moral discipline along the lines of Methodist and Quaker practice. Members could be admonished or expelled for immoral behavior, as when one member was expelled for taking up with a "common woman." Through such self-discipline, Richard

Allen believed, free blacks were expressing solidarity with those still enslaved. The free community had to act responsibly, in order to promote white antislavery opinion and disprove whites' claims that blacks were unfit for freedom. And by underscoring their commitment to slaves, the city's free blacks bound themselves to one another all the more strongly. Within a few months, the group extended its range of disciplinary oversight by adopting the Quaker practice of sending visiting committees to meet with Society members in their homes. The group met at Allen's house until May of 1788, then grew too numerous and rented room elsewhere.[59]

Though not a church, the Free African Society embodied religious as well as secular aims, and it laid the foundation for a separate black religious organization. Yet over issues of religion Richard Allen and his fellows dissented. Many still worshipped on Sundays at St. George's or at other churches around the city. In 1789 the Society began meeting in the Quaker African School House and decided to open meetings with fifteen minutes of silence. Allen objected to including this element of Quaker worship; it was too great a deviation from the faith that had liberated him. Allen stopped attending and, when he proved unresponsive to the organization's efforts toward reconciliation, the Society chided him for "attempting to sow divisions among us" and finally announced his expulsion.

Nothing could be more uncharacteristic of Richard Allen than sowing divisions among blacks. Yet his preference for Methodism represented loyalty to a faith that, Allen remained convinced, promised to be meaningful to more African-Americans than Quakerism or any other religion. "The plain and simple gospel suits best for every people," he insisted, "for the unlearned can understand, and the learned are sure to understand; and the reason that the Methodist is so successful in the awakening and conversion of the colored people [is] the plain doctrine and having a good discipline." Methodism's insistence on the liberating experience of conversion, its emotional qualities, and its doctrine all seemed essential to Allen.[60]

A group of Society members followed Allen out of the organization and joined his efforts toward setting up a black Methodist church. Absalom Jones assumed leadership of the Free African Society and continued to work in the same direction from within the old ranks. With the bulk of established churches against them, and with little money in their coffers, the two projects proceeded slowly. Both groups appealed to upper-class white benefactors, men like Doctor Benjamin Rush, staunch opponent of slavery, and Presbyterian merchant Richard Ralston. With their help, Jones and the Free African Society launched a subscription campaign to raise funds for an "African Church of Philadelphia." It was an ecumenical appeal, and soon Richard Allen offered his energies to the project too. The rift between Allen and Jones did not seem to create strong personal animosity. In 1792, moreover, the behavior of whites of St. George's helped to unify the black community all the more.[61]

The crisis at St. George's took place around the issue of separate seating. When the church had only a few black members, they had sat wherever they wished among the white congregation. As Allen's streetcorner preaching attracted more blacks to Sunday services, the white congregation confined them to inferior seats "around the wall"—a practice common among white congregations of other denominations. When the church built a new gallery, whites decided that blacks must sit in segregated parts of it. The day the gallery opened, a white sexton met black worshippers as they arrived at the door to direct them to their allotted seats. Black parishioners had probably anticipated the challenge, for they responded as a group, complying with white officials just halfway. They climbed the stairs to the gallery as required, but they did not take seats around the sides, where whites had intended them to sit. Instead they sat in the middle, just above their old seats on the floor below. The service began, and at the front of the church the presiding elder opened prayer. Allen recorded what happened next: "We had not been long on our knees before I heard considerable scuffling and low talking." A white trustee took hold of Absalom Jones, saying "You must get up—you must not kneel here." Jones asked the trustee to wait until the end of the prayer, but to no avail. A second trustee arrived to pull another black member up to his feet. The prayer ended, and St. George's blacks marched out of the church "in a body."[62]

William Birch, in "Gaol, in Walnut Street, Philadelphia," showed men moving a two-story building in the foreground. It may have been the black-smith shop that became a meeting place for Allen's Methodist church.

The walkout was a stirring moment that expressed and reinforced the unity of St. George's black members. Yet it left them vulnerable. White elders threatened to read them out of the Methodist church entirely, and they still lacked sufficient funds to establish their own place of worship. Within the year, however, they got substantial loans from a well-to-do white citizen. The church building completed, its members asked Allen to become their preacher. But the majority, fed up with Methodism, wanted to establish an Episcopal church, and nothing could shake Richard Allen from the religion that had freed him or reconcile him to the pomp of Episcopalian worship. When he declined, Absalom Jones agreed to serve, despite his own preference for Methodism as well. Jones became pastor of St. Thomas African Episcopal Church, a two-story brick church.[63]

Allen now stood in a minority of city blacks persisting in Methodist worship. He bought a blacksmith shop and moved it onto his own lot, hiring carpenters to make it over into a house of worship. In July of 1794 Bishop Asbury opened the Bethel African Methodist Episcopal Church, with some 100 members and Richard Allen pastor.[64]

The pattern of events that unfolded in Philadelphia was followed in other towns as well. Shortly after the black walkout from St. George's, blacks in Baltimore began to set up their own place of worship. The development of separate black churches marked blacks' efforts toward greater self-determination. Yet everywhere free blacks remained a minority, in need of allies from the white community. The celebration that accompanied the building of St. Thomas's church boded well for black-white relations. Benjamin Rush described the event: "About 100 white persons, chiefly carpenters, dined at 1 table, who were waited upon by Africans. Afterward about 50 black people sat down at the same table, who were waited upon by white people. Never did I see a people more happy." He himself offered a toast at the occasion: "May African Churches everywhere soon succeed African bondage." Philadelphia blacks, at least, enjoyed the good will of some white artisans and some among the enlightened upper classes of the city.[65]

Yet more and more whites were coming to agree with those members of St. George's who felt hostile to the city's blacks. The tide was turning away from liberty in the new United States. In the 1790s whites saw the principles of their recent revolution put into practice by Haitian blacks, who rose up to overthrow French plantation masters and establish an independent black state. In response, southerners' support for slavery hardened. Virginia, long expected by some to join states to the north in abolishing slavery, failed to do so. South Carolina even reopened the slave trade, which had been banned during the Revolution. In the north as well, many whites were reaching the limits of their antislavery energies. In many respects the founding of the new federal government in 1787 represented a retreat from the commitment to end slavery. The Constitution defined black people as three-fifths human for purposes of apportioning taxes and representation throughout the states. It tacitly accepted slavery, and explicitly prevented the new Congress from outlawing the slave trade for a span of twenty years. The Constitution represented the decision by white Americans that union among the new states was more important than pressing divisive issues like the liberty of black people.[66]

Indeed, the retreat from antislavery was part of a larger retreat from some of the broadest ideals of the American Revolution. In Pennsylvania, conservative merchants mounted an attack on the egalitarian constitution of 1776. In other states, too, well-to-do Americans acted to stem the more radical and egalitarian elements of the Revolution. Even such figures as Benjamin Rush worried about what seemed to be an "excess" of liberty. There had been many Americans who supported the Revolution, seeking a separation from England but not a change in their own society. In the late 1780s and the 1790s, these more conservative Americans were in ascendence, aided by the federal Constitution of 1787, which moved power away from the state legislatures responsive to the desires of local voters.[67]

In Philadelphia, white hostility to free blacks was related to a growing concern about the numbers of poor within the city. As free labor gradually replaced bound labor, and as propertyless immigrants poured into the city, there were increasing numbers of poor who were not controlled by masters. Even the staunchest of republicans had reservations about the place of poor people in American society. If a

Three large buildings represented some Philadelphians' efforts to reform and control the poor: the Almshouse, the House of Employment, and the Prison. "A View of The House of Employment, Alms-house, Pennsylvania Hospital, and Part of the City of Philadelphia," by Nicholas Garrison, engraving by J. Hulett, c. 1767.

Treatments for yellow fever varied. The "modern" treatment called for inducing extensive bleeding to remove poisoned blood. More traditional doctors used a variety of barks, roots, herbs, and stimulants. Regardless of the treatment, most patients died. Shown here are a medical chest, with natural roots, herbs, and manufactured concoctions, and, below, a fleam, a knife used for bleeding.

republic depended on independent, industrious, virtuous citizens, then the poor had little place. People without property had little reason to acquire the virtues of economy and hard work. And since they depended on working for others, they even posed a threat to republican government. Weren't they susceptible to being bought off by wealthy men with tyrannical ambitions? These ideas led many republicans to favor a broad distribution of property, but in the absence of such equality, they also led to an intense distrust of the poor. In the last two decades of the century, Philadelphians increased their efforts to control the poor, confining many to poorhouses and workhouses where hard work and economy were compulsory. For many, locking up the poor who were free took precedence over freeing the poor who were enslaved.[68]

Social and political theorists justified the retreat from the commitment to liberty. Increasingly, commentators stressed that the idle poor were "vicious" in character, naturally degenerate and, in fact, hardly human. They used similar characterizations to justify denying liberty to black people. Thomas Jefferson, who had fought a revolution out of the conviction that "all men are created equal," drew back from the implication that his notion applied to people who were black. In his *Notes on the State of Virginia*, written early in the 1780s, Jefferson expressed the suspicion that blacks were inferior to whites. The Revolution had challenged so many longstanding forms of social inequality that defenders of slavery had to find new ways to make slaveholding appear legitimate. They therefore turned more and more to arguments based explicitly on race to justify keeping blacks enslaved.[69]

In the very same year that they celebrated the construction of St.

Most physicians performed simple surgery and also dispensed drugs. This surgical kit, made in France and used during the Revolutionary era in America, includes amputation saws, knives, tissue scissors, forceps, lancet, tourniquets, and a set of suture needles.

Thomas's, a city-wide catastrophe dramatized the extent of the difficulties facing blacks. In 1793 the city suffered from a devastating epidemic of yellow fever that swept through the town in summer and fall. The fever brought terror and death, driving thousands of inhabitants away from Philadelphia, leaving all who could not go to suffer the miseries of disease, bereavement, and horror. Like most poor whites, the city's blacks could do nothing but remain there throughout the long, hot months of suffering. In September, Richard Allen and Absalom Jones went to the mayor to offer the services of the city's blacks for the taxing and terrifying jobs needed to hold the society together. Blacks nursed the dying, gathered dead bodies, and dug graves. Under Benjamin Rush's instructions, Jones and Allen treated patients by bleeding and purging them, and by so doing, the doctor believed, saved many. Yet when the epidemic finally waned in early winter, it had claimed the lives of almost 4,000 Philadelphians.[70]

Despite white assurances that blacks were immune to yellow fever, the affliction claimed hundreds of black residents. To make it worse, in the aftermath of the crisis, the city's African-Americans found themselves attacked in the public press. Publisher Matthew Carey made his case in a pamphlet, recounting the epidemic with little reference to black services and charging black nurses with extorting money from their patients. Together Allen and Jones wrote a response to Carey's version of events, noting numerous instances of generous black assistance to suffering whites, reporting black deaths, and noting that Carey himself had no way to know what had happened in his absence from the city. The publisher later retracted his accusations, but the incident proved the disadvantages under which blacks lived. As racism grew, they became all the more vulnerable to such unsubstantiated attacks. Increasingly, black Americans found they had to defend themselves against the prejudice of whites.[71]

*I*n the face of shifting white attitudes, Richard Allen struggled to keep alive the liberating movement he knew as Methodism. In the South, white planters began to deny all Methodist preachers access to their workers, fearful of the message of freedom that they carried.

Methodists responded to the changing tide of thought. In the early 1780s Bishop Asbury had been willing to refuse Allen access to slaves in deference to southern white opinion. Now even white preachers were denied the chance to preach to slaves because of their antislavery views. As Asbury saw it:

We are defrauded of great numbers (of converts) by the pains that are taken to keep the blacks from us; their masters are afraid of the influence of our principles. Would not an *amelioration* in the condition and treatment of slaves have produced more practical good to the poor Africans, than any attempt at their *emancipation*? The state of society, unhappily, does not admit of this: besides, the blacks are deprived of the means of instruction; who will take the pains to lead them into the way of salvation, and watch over them that they may not stray, but the Methodists? Well; now their masters will not let them come to hear us. What is the personal liberty of the African which he may abuse, to the salvation of his soul; how may it be compared?[72]

Methodism's white leadership, then, felt compelled to separate spiritual from material liberty and to choose between the two. They decided on behalf of blacks which goal mattered most, sacrificing their commitment to actual freedom in order to offer slaves spiritual liberty. They set about creating a Methodism that accepted slavery and, in time, a Methodism that could actively justify and defend it. They created a Methodism willing to work within the "state of society" rather than a movement implacably committed to changing it. Richard Allen and black Methodists rejected these changes, holding fast to Methodism's original vision, insisting on the unity of spiritual and material liberty.[73]

Within the city, Allen and his congregation struggled to gain fuller control over their own religious lives. For over a decade after the walkout, Bethel members had to combat efforts of the city's white Methodist hierarchy to take control of their church property. Allen recorded that they suffered "much persecution" from white Methodists. St. George's elders sought to gain title over Bethel Church property, and claimed the right to preach at Bethel, asking payment of a substantial fee. Only in 1799 did Bishop Asbury ordain Richard Allen a deacon, and only in 1800 did the General Conference of Methodism

After the 1798 yellow-fever epidemic, Benjamin Rush, one of the few doctors to stay in the city throughout the various plagues, was presented with a silver tray from the city hospital association for his work.

Richard Allen, painted by an unknown artist in 1784.

officially endorse Bethel's separation from St. George's church. As white opposition to black liberties mounted, it became more and more urgent for blacks to achieve autonomy in religious matters. In 1816 black Methodists from Baltimore, Wilmington, Salem, New Jersey, and Attleborough, Pennsylvania, gathered in Philadelphia to establish the National African Methodist Episcopal Church. They elected Richard Allen their first bishop.[74]

THE LIMITS OF LIBERTY

Under Allen's leadership, Bethel Church continued to be an important center of black community life in Philadelphia and a focus of black politics through the early nineteenth century. Bethel was the scene of resistance to the American Colonization Society, formed in 1816. The Society promoted the voluntary emigration of American blacks to Africa. Colonizationists argued that white racism prevented blacks from finding meaningful freedom in America. Wouldn't blacks be better off with more substantial freedom in their own country? But, as Richard Allen objected, Africa was hardly the home continent of most American blacks. The Colonization movement actually rested on the whites' desire to rid America of blacks as well as on benevolence. Equally important, as Allen recognized, the Society directed its energies only to the emigration of free blacks, leaving slaves in bondage. Colonization could work as a defense of slavery, removing the discordant element, the group whose very existence upset the simple equation between blackness and slavery. A month after the American Colonization Society was formed, some 3,000 free blacks crowded into Bethel Church to oppose it. Richard Allen used the occasion to reassert one of his most basic beliefs: free blacks should stay in America, because they had obligations to their enslaved brethren.[75]

For the rest of his life, Allen sounded these themes whenever he addressed American readers or listeners. To slaveholders and other defenders of black bondage he insisted on blacks' capacity for freedom. He combatted the racist argument that slaves were happy, pointing to rebellions as evidence that black Americans shared white Americans' love of liberty. To enslaved blacks, Allen counseled both patience and awareness of their own inner spiritual power. Slaves, he said, should feel "an affectionate regard" toward the white families who owned them. "This will be seen by them, and tend to promote your liberty." And if whites proved unyielding, at least slaves would know that they had the "favor and love of God . . . which you will value more than anything else, which will be a consolation in the worst condition you can be in, and no master can deprive you of it." To free blacks, Allen counseled continued commitment to their enslaved fellows. By their example, and their political efforts, it was free blacks' role to combat slavery, "to help forward the cause of freedom." Allen did his best to maintain the connection between spiritual and material liberty, and the link between blacks who remained enslaved and those who were free.[76]

It was a hard row to hoe. In 1831, at the end of Allen's life, a Philadelphia Quaker described the situation of free blacks:

The policy and power of the national and state governments, are against them. The popular feeling is against them—the interests of our citizens are against them. The small degree of compassion once cherished toward them in the common wealths which got rid of slavery, or which never were disfigured by it, appears to be exhausted. Their prospects either as free, or bond men, are dreary, and comfortless.

This unhappy prognosis proved all too correct. In the decade that followed, Pennsylvania—and other northern states—extended the vote to all white males, but disenfranchised blacks at the same time. The Jacksonian "age of the common man" explicitly reserved liberty for men who were white.[77]

Richard Allen died in 1831 at the age of seventy-two. Perhaps his closing years were indeed "dreary and comfortless." In his youth he had gained freedom and seen other members of his race liberated by the forces of evangelical religion and the Revolution. He lived to see racism and fear of the poor enervate white Americans' commitment to freedom. Yet it is hard to imagine that Allen's faith and commitment ever allowed him to despair. He and his community had carried the belief in liberty for many decades after the birth of Methodism and the American Revolution. Building black churches, they had created institutions that stood as powerful symbols of black Americans' version of Christianity, a faith dedicated to liberation here on earth as well as to spiritual freedom. At Bethel and in meeting houses elsewhere, black Americans carried forward their "cause of freedom" in the decades that followed.[78]

Notes

I have relied on two comprehensive research reports by Edward F. Zimmer, "A Study of the Origins of the Connecticut Valley Parlor in the National Museum of American History, or Ignorance Is Bliss," September 1981, and "Report on Selected Topics Pertaining to Samuel Colton (1727–1784), Merchant of Longmeadow, Massachusetts: House; Household; Furnishings; Business Methods; 1776 Raids; or Five Easy Pieces," August 1982. In particular, Zimmer's care in collecting and transcribing copies of numerous primary documents has saved me hours of labor.

1. Diary of Rev. Stephen Williams, July 23, 24, 1776, bk. 9, pp. 117, 121–22, typescript copy, Richard Salter Storrs Library, Longmeadow (hereafter cited as RSS).

2. Colton wrote two accounts of the raid in remonstrances to the General Court. The first was Samuel Colton's Reply to the General Court, c. February 1, 1781, Massachusetts Archives, 231: 142–44, Massachusetts State House, Boston; the second, dated May 30, 1781, survives only in excerpted form in "The Merchant Samuel Colton Documents," appendix in *The Longmeadow Centennial: Proceedings at the Centennial Celebration of the Incorporation of the Town of Longmeadow, 1883* (Longmeadow, 1884), pp. 213–20.

   The account here is from "Merchant Samuel Colton Documents," p. 217, and Samuel Colton's Reply, p. 144. Accounts by raiders and their sympathizers are: Petition of Nathaniel Ely, Festus Colton, and Azariah Woolworth, December 15, 1780, Massachusetts Archives, 231: 136–39; Depositions of Jonathan Burt II and Gideon Burt, February 28, 1781, ibid., pp. 133–34a. Stephen Williams was sympathetic to Colton, but his account mentions no destruction of property or looting. Diary of Stephen Williams, July 23, 24, 1776, bk. 9,

pp. 117, 121–22. Other goods in the store appear in "Boston Purchases Book," 1756; in "Goods in the Shop," Inventory of Samuel Colton Estate, 1785, pp. 9–15; and in Samuel Colton's daybooks and ledgers, all at the Longmeadow Historical Society (hereafter cited as LHS).

3. "Old Days in Longmeadow, *Springfield Weekly Republican*, October 13, 1905, based on a paper presented by Mrs. George E. Brewer before the LHS. Ely's offers of the sales money to Colton, and the eventual delivery of the money, appear in "Merchant Samuel Colton Documents," pp. 218–19, Petition of Nathaniel Ely et al., pp. 137–38, and Depositions of Jonathan Burt II and Gideon Burt.

4. One hundred twenty-six supporters of the raiders signed the Petition of Nathaniel Ely et al., pp. 140–41. Ely, Woolworth, and Festus Colton were all from prominent, property-owning families: Ely and Woolworth both served on the Longmeadow precinct committee, as did their fathers; Festus Colton's father, Simon, was the richest man in Longmeadow in 1750. Zimmer, "Samuel Colton," pp. 115, 166–68. The Springfield tax list of 1771 shows Ely (0819), Simon Colton (1532), and Azariah Woolworth's father, Richard (1432), to be solid citizens. Bettye Hobbs Pruitt, ed., *The Massachusetts Tax Valuation List of 1771* (Boston, 1978), pp. 426–27, 432–33.

   No evidence establishes the identity of the other raiders. Samuel Colton claimed that some of the 126 who supported the raiders' petition were "Parties and as much Concern'd in the original Trespass and Violence as the Petitioners Themselves." "Merchant Samuel Colton Documents," p. 220. Approximately 42 (or 33%) of the petition signers appear in Springfield in the tax valuation of 1771, and another 15 (or 12%) appear in nearby Wilbraham that same year. Of the Springfield petitioners located, 86% owned real estate, as compared with only 77% of the rateable polls in Springfield as a whole. All the petitioners located in Wilbraham held property in 1771. Zimmer notes that about 45% of the petitioners dealt with Samuel Colton at his store, and that 14 of the 21 men who served on the Longmeadow precinct committee between 1770 and 1781 signed. Zimmer, "Samuel Colton," pp. 166–68.

5. "Merchant Samuel Colton Documents," p. 217; "Old

Days in Longmeadow." "Fixing Prices in 1775—The Story of Samuel Colton," *Magazine of History* 25 (1917): 85, takes the legend one step further, claiming that Colton never spoke aloud again. Both versions seem unlikely, since Colton continued to run his store, but the merchant's remonstrances to the General Court leave no doubt of his sense of injury.

6. Petition of Nathaniel Ely et al., pp. 137–38; Samuel Colton's Reply, p. 145.

7. E. P. Thompson, "The Moral Economy of the English Crowd in the Eighteenth Century," *Past and Present* 51 (1971): 76–131; Gary B. Nash, *The Urban Crucible: Social Change, Political Consciousness, and the Origins of the American Revolution* (Cambridge, Mass., 1979), pp. 77–80.

8. On crowd actions in the patriot movement, see Pauline Maier, *From Resistance to Revolution: Colonial Radicals and the Development of American Opposition to Britain, 1765–1776* (New York, 1974). Maier recounts the Tea Party on pp. 276–77.

9. Linda M. Rodger and Mary S. Rogeness, eds., *Reflections of Longmeadow, 1783/1983* (Canaan, N.H., 1983), pp. 3–4; Stephen C. Innes, *Labor in a New Land: Economy and Society in Seventeenth-Century Springfield* (Princeton, N.J., 1983), pp. 5–6; Mason A. Green, *Springfield, 1636–1886: History of Town and City* (Springfield, Mass., 1888), pp. 1–16. The quotation is from Henry M. Burt, *The First Century of the History of Springfield: The Official Records from 1636 to 1736*, 2 vols. (Springfield, 1898–99), 1: 17–18. On white-Indian relations see Gary B. Nash, *Red, White, and Black: The Peoples of Early America* (Englewood Cliffs, N.J., 1974), pp. 78–87.

10. Innes, *Labor in a New Land*, pp. 5–11, 30–34; "William Pynchon," *Papers and Proceedings of the Connecticut Valley Historical Society*, vol. 2 (Springfield, Mass., 1904), pp. 20–39. For trade in the eighteenth century, see Margaret E. Martin, *Merchants and Traders of the Connecticut River Valley, 1750–1820*, Smith College Studies in History, vol. 24, nos. 1–4 (Northampton, Mass., October 1938–July 1939).

11. Innes, *Labor in a New Land*, pp. 7–11, 20, 30–34, 72; Martin, *Merchants and Traders*, pp. 4–6; Lee Nathaniel Newcomer, *The Embattled Farmers: A Massachusetts Countryside in the American Revolution* (New York, 1953), chap. 1; Robert J. Taylor, *Western Massachusetts in the Revolution* (Providence, R.I., 1954), pp. 5–10.

12. "Genealogical Appendix," *Longmeadow Centennial*, pp. 30, 35; Vera Colton Halstead, Colton Genealogy in RSS; "First Generation," xerox in RSS. George Colton appears in Green, *Springfield*, pp. 79, 95–96. 125, 130, 209–10; Innes, *Labor in a New Land*, pp. 47, 63. In 1688, Pynchon recorded that there were 20 men in Longmeadow, compared with 28 on the west side of the river and about 60 in Springfield center. Innes, *Labor in a New Land*, 125–26.

13. Burt, *First Century*, 2: 360–61, 364; Green, *Springfield*, p. 209.

14. Green, *Springfield*, pp. 210, 268; Burt, *First Century*, 2: 367, 369–70, 399; Rodger and Rogeness, eds., *Reflections of Longmeadow*, pp. 14, 26. Innes, *Labor in a New Land*, pp. 125–27, underscores Longmeadow residents' sense of being separate from Springfield. For local affairs, see the *"Longmeadow Precinct Book of Records: Meetings of the Inhabitants of the Precinct From February 10th, 1713 To March 13th, 1783,"* typescript in RSS.

15. Burt, *First Century*, 2: 333, 373 on hiring schoolmasters; "Springfield in Olden Times," *Papers and Proceedings, Connecticut Valley Historical Society*, 2: 115–19, 122–23. On women's preference for doing work with neighbors, see Laurel Thatcher Ulrich, *Good Wives: Image and Reality in the Lives of Women in Northern New England, 1650–1750*, (New York, 1982), chap. 3. On the importance of community in Connecticut valley towns, see Gregory H. Nobles, *Divisions Throughout the Whole: Politics and Society in Hampshire County, Massachusetts, 1740–1775* (New York, 1983), pp. 12–14.

In *Labor in a New Land*, Innes interprets seventeenth-century Springfield as an important exception to the rule that New Englanders highly valued community. Focusing on the overwhelming importance of the Pynchons in the area, Innes portrays Springfield settlers as materialistic and individualistic and Springfield society as pointedly unequal. My disagreement with Innes's view reflects in part a difference in focus (eighteenth-century Longmeadow instead of seventeenth-century Springfield) and in part a difference in interpretation.

My sense is that early New Englanders assumed both social inequality and a degree of individual self-seeking, which is why they clung to an ideal of communal harmony and enforced regulations to attain it. Innes shows that there was conflict in early Longmeadow, but I take some of his evidence (such as the practice of drawing jury members only from the precinct) to illustrate the vitality of many community ideals: see pp. 127–28 and passim.

16. Christopher Clark, "The Household Economy, Market Exchange and the Rise of Capitalism in the Connecticut Valley, 1800–1860," *Journal of Social History* 13 (1979): 172–75; Robert E. Mutch, "Yeoman and Merchant in Pre-Industrial America: Eighteenth-Century Massachusetts as a Case Study," *Societas* 7 (1977): 279–87; David P. Szatmary, *Shays' Rebellion: The Making of an Agrarian Insurrection* (Amherst, Mass., 1980), pp. 1–4. See also Michael Merrill, "Cash Is Good to Eat: Self-Sufficiency and Exchange in the Rural Economy of the United States," *Radical History Review* 14 (1977): 42–71; James A. Henretta, "Families and Farms: *Mentalité* in Pre-Industrial America," *William and Mary Quarterly*, 3rd ser., 35 (1978): 3–32; cf. Winifred B. Rothenberg, "The Market and Massachusetts Farmers, 1750–1855," *Journal of Economic History* 41 (1981): 288–314.

17. Clark, "Household Economy," pp. 173–75; Merrill, "Cash Is Good to Eat," pp. 53–54, 56, 58, 61. On debts and their meaning, see Christopher Clark, "Economies as Cultural Systems: Rural America in the Eighteenth and Nineteenth Centuries," paper presented at the Annual Meeting of the British Association for American Studies, Reading, April 13, 1984; Szatmary, *Shays' Rebellion*, pp. 19–36.

18. Michael Zuckerman, *Peaceable Kingdoms: New England Towns in the Eighteenth Century* (New York, 1970), pp. 70–72.

19. Ibid., pp. 94–106, 132–35; Zuckerman, "The Social Context of Democracy in Massachusetts," *William and Mary Quarterly*, 3rd ser., 25 (1968): 523–44; Burt, *First Century*, 2: 281, 383; Green, *Springfield*, pp. 209–10.

20. Burt, *First Century*, 1: 247, 300–1; Jonathan French, *A Practical Discourse Against Extortion* (Boston, 1777),

p. 11. Longmeadow minister Stephen Williams agreed that in times of hardship, "takeing advantage of peoples necessity" was unjust. Diary of Stephen Williams, bk 9, p. 25.

21. Burt, *First Century*, 1: 164, 166, 169, 171, 186, 202–5, for regulation of sales and wages; 2: 366, 369, 375, 413, for election of town officials to regulate exchange. For regulation of James Osborne's transactions, ibid., 1:359. On the historical background of regulatory ideas and practices, see Richard B. Morris, *Government and Labor in Early America* (New York, 1975), pp. 55–84; Morris and Jonathan Grossman, "The Regulation of Wages in Early Massachusetts," *New England Quarterly* 11 (1933): 470–500; Jon C. Teaford, *The Municipal Revolution in America: Origins of Modern Urban Government 1650–1825* (Chicago, 1975), chaps. 1–3.

22. On the importance of reputation, see Ulrich, *Good Wives*, chap. 3. On Boston marketing, see G. B. Warden, *Boston 1692–1776* (Boston, 1970), pp. 53–56, 74–77, 105. On church discipline and the preference for informal admonitions over recourse to formal action or to courts of law, see Emil Oberholzer, Jr., *Delinquent Saints: Disciplinary Action in Early Congregational Churches of Massachusetts* (New York, 1956), pp. 30–33, 36–39, 173–82; Seldon Daskon Bacon, "The Early Development of American Municipal Police: A Study of the Evolution of Formal Controls in a Changing Society," Ph.D., diss., Yale University, 1939; Richard Bushman, *From Puritan to Yankee: Character and the Social Order in Connecticut, 1690–1765* (New York, 1970), chap. 1; Zuckerman, *Peaceable Kingdoms*, pp. 61–65, 117–18, 147, and passim. Philip J. Greven, *Four Generations: Population, Land and Family in Colonial Andover, Massachusetts* (Ithaca, N.Y., 1970), stresses the importance of kinship connections in communities: pp. 15–16, 138–41, 171–72, 175–76, 215–21.

23. "Genealogical Appendix," *Longmeadow Centennial*, pp. 30, 35; Halstead, Colton Genealogy in RSS.

24. "The Frost Family," xerox in RSS.

25. Taylor, *Western Massachusetts*, pp. 11–26; Nobles, *Divisions Throughout the Whole*, pp. 17–20; Innes, *Labor in a New Land*, pp. 20–22, stresses the importance of the Pynchons' connections outside Springfield.

26. "Bell Rate," valuation list for Longmeadow, February 18, 1743/44, in LHS Scrapbook 7, p. 3; Inventory of Samuel Colton, Sr., Hampshire Probates, 6: 222–26; Ephraim Colton's Account of His Guardianship of Samuel Colton, 1744–1748, LHS Document Cases. All are cited in Zimmer, "Samuel Colton," pp. 113–14; see also pp. 33–34.

27. Greven, *Four Generations*, chaps. 6–8; Kenneth Lockridge, "Land, Population, and the Evolution of New England Society, 1630–1790," *Past and Present* 39 (1968): 62–80; Lockridge, *A New England Town, The First Hundred Years: Dedham, Massachusetts, 1636–1737* (New York, 1970), chap. 8; Robert A. Gross, *The Minutemen and Their World* (New York, 1976), chap. 4; Patricia J. Tracy, *Jonathan Edwards, Pastor: Religion and Society in Eighteenth-Century Northampton* (New York, 1980), pp. 39–43, 87.

28. See Tracy, *Jonathan Edwards*, pp. 40, 87, 92–106; Greven, *Four Generations*, chaps. 6–8.

29. Ephraim Colton's Account of His Guardianship of Samuel Colton, 1744–1748, LHS Document Cases, cited in Zimmer, "Samuel Colton," pp. 33, 41. Colton's business records at LHS include daybooks, ledgers, and other records, catalogued as BV1 through BV24. When I have relied on the excerpts or citations in Zimmer, "Samuel Colton," I have so noted. Otherwise, citations refer to my own notes from research at LHS. Colton's hirings appear in BV9, vols. 2 and 3, and BV17, p. 13, both cited in Zimmer, "Samuel Colton," p. 34. His trip to Boston and early sales are in BV9, vols. 1, 2, and 3, cited in ibid., pp. 114–15.

30. Martin, *Merchants and Traders*, pp. 1, 16; Taylor, *Western Massachusetts*, pp. 5–9; Tracy, *Jonathan Edwards*, p. 40; *Longmeadow Sesquicentennial, 1783–1933, Official Souvenir* (Springfield, n.d.), n.p. Colton's entrance into the West Indies trade in the 1750s appears in BV9 and BV17, cited in Zimmer, "Samuel Colton," pp. 116, 122.

31. A description of the house appears in "Old Days in Longmeadow." More information is in a series of agreements between Colton and the builders: July 20, 1754 agreement with P. King; February 1, 1755 agreement with Henry Chandler; February 12 and April 25, 1755 agreements with Solomon Chandler; all abstracted in Zimmer, "Samuel Colton," pp. 6–8. The progress of the work can be followed in the daybooks and ledgers. The quotation is from BV18a, p. 34, cited in Zimmer, "Samuel Colton," p. 6. On the housebuilders, see Zimmer, pp. 14–15. "Old Days in Longmeadow" notes the stepstones in front. The Colton door is now in the Boston Museum of Fine Arts.

32. Colton's substantial landholdings appear in Pruitt, *Tax Valuation List*, pp. 432–33 (no. 1530). Rentals are in BV5, p. 221; BV16, pp. 228, 278, 288; BV21, p. 246: all cited in Zimmer, "Samuel Colton," pp. 113–16, 128–29; see also p. 133. The shop is described in June 5, 1756 agreement between Colton and Parmenus King, BV5: 322, abstracted in Zimmer, p. 9, and in "Old Days in Longmeadow."

33. Samuel Colton m. Flavia Colton, Marriages and Church Records, bk. 1, 1716–1844, p. 8–C, in RSS; Diary of Stephen Williams, bk. 5, p. 240, records burial of the baby, February 4, 1760; "Register of Sam'l Colton's Family," in LHS; "Genealogical Appendix," *Longmeadow Centennial*, p. 35. I am indebted to Michael Zuckerman for the point about New Englanders' average ages at marriage. On the acceptance of premarital sex, see Innes, *Labor in a New Land*, p. 135; Mary Beth Norton, *Liberty's Daughters: The Revolutionary Experience of American Women, 1750–1800* (Boston, 1980), pp. 52–56; cf. Greven, *Four Generations*, pp. 112–16, on earlier New England attitudes.

34. On woman's role as household mistress, see Nancy F. Cott, *The Bonds of Womanhood: "Woman's Sphere" in New England, 1780–1835* (New Haven, Conn., 1977), pp. 20–23. "Register of Sam'l Colton's Family." Besides Tom, inherited from Samuel Colton, Sr., Samuel junior bought "Jack" from George Cooley of Somers in 1769 for £60 ("Old Days in Longmeadow"). Pruitt, *Tax Valuation List*, pp. 432–433 (no. 1530), cites Colton as owning two "Servants for Life" in 1771. In 1775, Colton bought "Timothy," for £60. BV16, p. 15; BV21, p. 117; cited in Zimmer, "Samuel Colton," pp. 40–42.

Other artisans in the household are in BV16, pp. 211, 238, 247, 56, 208, 177; BV21, pp. 88, 246. The live-in relatives are in BV16, pp. 235, 237. All are cited in Zimmer, "Samuel Colton," pp. 40–42, 45–46, 36.

35. These examples are from "Old Days in Longmeadow." The Colton Business Records, LHS, record similar transactions, as does Zimmer, "Samuel Colton," pp. 107–40.

36. "Old Days in Longmeadow"; Zimmer, "Samuel Colton," pp. 131–34; Martin, *Merchants and Traders*, on the general practice of trading for farm goods, pp. 143–44, 149–56; Merrill, "Cash Is Good to Eat"; Clark, "Household Economy," pp. 172–75. Some examples of Colton's use of store goods to pay for labor in August 1762 are in the back of his "Boston Purchases Book," 1754.

37. Christopher Clark describes merchants' need to fit local standards of exchange as well as to transform them in "Taking Stock of the Nineteenth-Century Country Store," paper presented at the 78th Annual Convention of the Organization of American Historians, Minneapolis, April 18–21, 1985, esp. pp. 3–6.

38. Colton's Boston contacts appear in his "Boston Purchases Book," 1754. The building of the *Friendship* can be followed in Colton's records, BV11, pp. 362–63; BV12, pp. 14–17; BV20, pp. 14, 21; all cited in Zimmer, "Samuel Colton," pp. 137–39. See also Martin, *Merchants and Traders*, pp. 23–24, 94; *Longmeadow Centennial*, pp. 44–45.

39. Martin, *Merchants and Traders*, p. 137; "The Springfield Homestead," n.d., xerox in RSS, says that Colton's brother-in-law, Captain Frost, was the ship's master of the *Friendship* for many years. Three Boston merchants who were Colton's chief creditors are listed in his probate. Hampshire Probates, 18: 225, cited in Zimmer, "Samuel Colton," pp. 127–28. On local merchants' behavior toward their customers, see Szatmary, *Shays' Rebellion*, pp. 8–9, 12; Clark, "Economies as Cultural Systems," n.p.

40. "Old Days in Longmeadow"; Martin, *Merchants and Traders*, p. 158. Martin, p. 94, describes Springfield merchant Josiah Dwight's similar use of interest.

41. Clark, "Taking Stock of the Country Store," pp. 9–15; see also Mutch, "Yeoman and Merchant," pp. 295–98.

42. Richard Bushman, "Massachusetts Farmers and the Revolution," in Richard M. Jellison, ed., *Society, Freedom, and Conscience: The American Revolution in Virginia, Massachusetts, and New York* (New York, 1976), pp. 77–124; Tracy, *Jonathan Edwards*, pp. 38–43, 92–106; Douglas L. Jones, "The Strolling Poor: Transiency in Eighteenth Century Massachusetts," *Journal of Social History* 9 (1975): 28–54; Nobles, *Divisions Throughout the Whole*, chap. 5.

43. On New Englanders' general suspicion of commerce, see Edmund S. Morgan, "The Puritan Ethic and the American Revolution," *The Challenge of the American Revolution* (New York, 1976), pp. 90–92.

44. Richard D. Brown, *Revolutionary Politics in Massachusetts: The Boston Committee of Correspondence and the Towns, 1772–1774* (Cambridge, Mass., 1970), pp. 94–102; Taylor, *Western Massachusetts*, pp. 62–63.

45. Edmund S. and Helen M. Morgan, *The Stamp Act Crisis: Prologue to Revolution*, rev. ed. (London, 1962), chaps. 3–5.

46. Ibid., pp. 43–58, 86–87, 109–19; Bernard Bailyn, *The Ideological Origins of the American Revolution* (Cambridge, Mass., 1967), pp. 160–75.

47. Stephen Hopkins, "The Rights of the Colonies Examined," in Merrill Jensen, ed., *Tracts of the American Revolution, 1763–1776* (Indianapolis, 1977), p. 43.

48. On Americans' view of constitutionalism, see Maier, *Resistance to Revolution*, chap. 2; Bailyn, *Ideological Origins*, pp. 67–77, 175–98.

49. Morgan, "The Puritan Ethic," pp. 95–108; Bailyn, *Ideological Origins*, pp. 46–53, 59–60, 83–93, and passim, on American concern about British and colonial "corruption."

50. Morgan, "The Puritan Ethic," pp. 95–108.

51. Trade boycotts and crowd actions against dissenters are recounted in Morgan and Morgan, *Stamp Act Crisis*, esp. chaps. 8–10; Maier, *Resistance to Revolution*, chaps. 3–5; Arthur M. Schlesinger, *The Colonial Merchants and the American Revolution. 1763–1776* (New York, 1968), chaps. 2–5.

52. David Ammerman, *In the Common Cause: American Response to the Coercive Acts of 1774* (New York, 1974), chaps. 1–2; Green, *Springfield*, pp. 275–77.

53. Ammerman, *Common Cause*, chap. 6. The Continental Association appears in Samuel Eliot Morison, ed., *Sources and Documents Illustrating the American Revolution, 1764–1788*, 2nd ed. (New York, 1965; reprint 1977), pp. 122–25.

54. Henry A. Booth, "Springfield During the Revolution," *Papers and Proceedings, Connecticut Valley Historical Society*, 2: 287–92; Green, *Springfield*, pp. 275–83.

55. "Longmeadow Precinct Book of Records," pp. 71, 78–81, 83; Green, *Springfield*, p. 277; Taylor, *Western Massachusetts*, pp. 11, 19, 21; Nobles, *Divisions Throughout the*

Whole, pp. 178–79, 181–84; Newcomer, *Embattled Farmers,* p. 60.

56. Catherine S. Crary, *The Price of Loyalty: Tory Writings from the Revolutionary Era* (New York, 1973), pp. 29–30; *Boston Gazette,* November 28, 1774; ibid., January 2, 1775. Colton spoke of the "Mobs and popular Tumults," Samuel Colton's Reply, p. 144. On enforcement of the Association across Massachusetts, see Ammerman, *Common Cause,* chap. 8, and Barbara Clark Smith, "The Politics of Price Control in Revolutionary Massachusetts, 1774–1780," Ph.D. diss., Yale University, 1983, chap. 2.

57. Diary of Stephen Williams, July 20, 1774, bk. 8, p. 294; Petition of Nathaniel Ely et al., p. 137; "Merchant Samuel Colton Documents," pp. 215–16.

58. Green, *Springfield,* p. 279. Colton pointed out that he had sold to the army in both his Reply, p. 143, and his May Remonstrance, "Merchant Samuel Colton Documents," pp. 215–16.

59. Petition of Nathaniel Ely et al., p. 138; Statements of Edward Chapin and Nathaniel Brewer, December 1780, Massachusetts Archives, 231: 135; Deposition of Jonathan Burt II.

60. Colton underscored the fact that other traders had raised prices in his Reply, p. 143, and his May Remonstrance, "Merchant Samuel Colton Documents," p. 215. On the change in the committee, see Remonstrance, pp. 216–17, and Reply, pp. 144–45. On financing of the war with paper money, see E. James Ferguson, *The Power of the Purse: A History of American Public Finance, 1776–1790* (Chapel Hill, N.C., 1977), pp. 26, 35–44. See also Oscar and Mary Flug Handlin, "Revolutionary Economic Policy in Massachusetts," *William and Mary Quarterly,* 3rd ser., 4 (1947): 3–26; Ralph V. Harlow, "Economic Conditions in Massachusetts During the American Revolution," *Publications of the Colonial Society of Massachusetts* 20 (1917–1919): 163–90; Harlow, "Aspects of Revolutionary Finance, 1775–1783," *American Historical Review* 35 (1929): 46–68.

61. Diary of Stephen Williams, July 11, 1776, bk. 9, p. 117; *Centennial Celebration Proceedings,* pp. 271–72.

62. "The Springfield Homestead," RSS; Samuel Colton's Reply, p. 144; Diary of Stephen Williams, July 18, 1776, bk. 9, p. 119.

63. Petition of Nathaniel Ely et al., p. 137.

64. Diary of Stephen Williams, July 30, 1776, bk. 9, p. 124; Booth, "Springfield During the Revolution," p. 289; Samuel Colton's Reply, p. 145; "Merchant Samuel Colton Documents," p. 218.

65. "Journal of the Proceedings of the Convention at Dracut in November, 1776," *Collections of the New Hampshire Historical Society,* vol. 2 (Concord, N.H., 1927): 64–65. A convention of Middlesex County towns met in Concord in August 1776 and agreed to disarm and confine those who discouraged others from accepting the money at face value. *Boston Gazette,* September 9, 1776. The Massachusetts price control law is in *Acts and Resolves, Public and Private, of the Province of the Massachusetts Bay,* 21 vols. (Boston, 1869–1922), 5: 583–89. Josiah Gilbert Holland, *History of Western Massachusetts,* 2 vols. (Springfield, Mass., 1855), 1: 216–17.

66. On the decline of price controls, see Kenneth Scott, "Price Control in New England During the Revolution," *New England Quarterly* 19 (1946): 453–73; Smith, "Politics of Price Controls," pp. 511–28. On the rise of conservatives in Massachusetts, see Stephen Patterson, *Political Parties in Revolutionary Massachusetts* (Madison, Wis., 1973).

67. Samuel Colton's Reply, p. 144; "Merchant Samuel Colton Documents," p. 216.

68. Petition of Nathaniel Ely et al., p. 137.

69. Ibid.

70. Samuel Colton's Reply, pp. 142–45; "Merchant Samuel Colton Documents," p. 215.

71. Statements of Edward Chapin and Nathaniel Brewer; Petition of Nathaniel Ely et al., pp. 140–41; chap. 83, "Resolve on the Petition of Nathaniel Ely and others, Indemnifying Them Against All Claims of Samuel Colton," February 7, 1781, *Acts and Laws of the Commonwealth of Massachusetts* (Boston, 1890), p. 263. See also chap. 38, "An Act of Pardon and Indemnification" for Berkshire County, *Acts and Resolves,* 5: 932.

72. "Old Days In Longmeadow"; Zimmer, "Connecticut Valley Parlor," pp. E6–E7, E16. The merchant's substantial wealth at his death appears in Inventory of Samuel Colton Estate, 1785.

73. On growing conservatism and continued conflict in

Massachusetts, see Patterson, *Political Parties*, pp. 216–49; Taylor, *Western Massachusetts*, chaps. 6–8; Szatmary, *Shays' Rebellion*.

THE FARM AND THE MARKETPLACE: THE SPRINGER HOUSEHOLD OF MILL CREEK, DELAWARE

I have relied on two unpublished reports as guides to research on the Springers: William S. Pretzer, "The Delaware Log House: A Social and Economic Report," December 30, 1982, and Dell Upton, "Architectural Survey of the Delaware Log House," June 1, 1982, both for the National Museum of American History, Smithsonian Institution. Manuscript references are to New Castle County records in the Delaware Hall of Records (DHR), Dover, unless otherwise noted.

1. Jeannette Eckman, *Crane Hook on the Delaware: An Early Swedish Lutheran Church and Community, with the Historical Background of the Delaware River Valley* (Newark, Del., 1958), pp. 109–12. The quotation is on p. 106.
2. Ibid., p. 106.
3. Ibid., chaps. 1–3. Benjamin Ferris, *A History of the Original Settlements on the Delaware: From Its Discovery by Hudson to the Colonization Under William Penn* (Wilmington, 1846), p. 136.
4. Eckman, *Crane Hook on the Delaware*, pp. 107, 122–33. He also acquired 100 acres in New Jersey and an additional 400 acres in Christiana Hundred, Delaware, for his sons. Ibid., pp. 114–15.
5. Ibid., pp. 82–85, 88, 94, 107, 122–33.
6. Ibid., pp. 71–74, 75. According to Dr. Richard Hulan, the "good ould fashions in meate and drink" probably included Swedish breads and ale.
7. Eckman, *Crane Hook on the Delaware*, pp. 126–28; Ferris, *History of the Original Settlements*, pp. 180–81; James Henretta, "Families and Farms: *Mentalité* in Pre-Industrial America," *William and Mary Quarterly*, 3rd ser., 35 (1978): 3–5. Carl Springer's continued involvement in Old Swedes' can be seen in "Communicant Records, 1713–1756: Holy Trinity (Old Swedes')

Church," pt. 5, 1727–1748, trans. and ed. Courtland B. Springer and Ruth L. Springer, *Delaware History* 6 (1954–55): 307–32.
8. Pretzer, "Delaware Log House," p. 4 and appendix 2: Genealogy Prepared by Mrs. Ann Lee Bugbee, Curator of Holy Trinity (Old Swedes') Church, Wilmington. Jesse Evelyn Springer, *Charles Springer of Cranhook-on-the-Delaware* (Edwardsville, Ill., 1959), pp. 16–18, gives the Springer genealogy, as does Eckman, *Crane Hook on the Delaware*, pp. 135–36. The quotation about providing for daughters is from the will of Evan Rice, Esq. (whose widow Charles Springer later married), October 15, 1783, New Castle County Probate Records. Deed of John Twiggs, John Reece, and wife Rebecca to Charles Springer, February 19, 1762, New Castle County Recorder of Deeds, Deed Book, U-1: 361–63 (hereafter cited as Deed Book); Deed of J. Twiggs and wife Susanna to Charles Springer, June 4, 1762, Deed Book, U-1: 613. Charles Springer bought 33 more acres of Twiggs's land when it was sold for debt the next year. Deed Book, U-1: 404–6.
9. The suggestion that Thomas may have built a "log tenement" prior to building a proper house appears in the deed by which Charles Springer later conveyed the tract to his son. That 1792 deed mentions a "messuage tenement and other improvements" without referring to a house. Deed of Charles Springer and wife Elizabeth to Thomas Springer, April 1, 1792, Deed Book, O-2: 55–57.
10. Henretta, "Families and Farms," pp. 6–8. In a New England town, the age at which sons could expect to inherit changed in the course of the eighteenth century; see Philip J. Greven, Jr., *Four Generations: Population, Land, and Family in Colonial Andover, Massachusetts* (Ithaca, N.Y., 1970).
11. Pretzer, "Delaware Log House," p. 4. Charles Springer married Anne Ogle, April 9, 1752, at Old Swedes'; he married Elizabeth Graham Rice about December 7, 1787. See New Castle County Marriage Index, the Bugbee genealogy, and Springer, *Charles Springer*, p. 17. Evan Rice's taxable property was valued above that of 96% of the taxpayers of Mill Creek Hundred in 1780. Mill Creek Hundred Assessment, 1780.
12. Deed of John Giffin to Thomas Springer, January 25,

1788, Deed Book, N-2: 125–26; Deed of Robert Giffin to Thomas Springer, December 27, 1788, Deed Book, N-2: 126–27. Architectural evidence confirms that the log house was probably built about the last decade of the century. Dell Upton, "Architectural Survey," pp. 8–9.

The evidence is not conclusive that Thomas's wife's first name was Elizabeth. Thomas's will is the source for his daughters' names, but by the time Thomas wrote that will his first wife had died and he had remarried. (He married Margaret Wells in 1802; she had been born in 1777 [New Castle County Birth Index] and was too young to be the mother of Thomas's daughters.) His daughters were Mary and Ann, and the approximate years of their births can be roughly figured from their marriages, in 1809 and 1814 respectively. A Thomas and Elizabeth Springer baptized their daughter Ann at Immanuel Church in 1796—the same church in which Thomas later remarried. That child could easily be the same "Ann Springer" who married in 1814, and so I have taken "Elizabeth" as Thomas Springer's first wife. Will of Thomas Springer, October 4, 1804; Thomas Springer m. Margaret Wells, December 7, 1802, New Castle County Marriage Index; Mary Springer m. Robert McMurphy, September 4, 1809, ibid.; Ann Springer m. Richard Craddock, December 21, 1814, ibid.; New Castle County Baptism Index, 1796.

13. Deed of Charles Springer and wife Elizabeth to Thomas Springer, April 1, 1792, Deed Book, O-2: 55–57. The deed describes the land being sold to Thomas as "now in his actual possession." At about the same time, Charles Springer sold part of the original tract to Samuel Stroud. He charged Stroud £9 local currency per acre (about $25) and charged his son £3 local currency per acre (about $8). Deed of Charles Springer to Samuel Stroud, April 1, 1790, Deed Book, M-2: 169–70. Pretzer, "Delaware Log House," p. 7. At the time of his death, Thomas still owed Charles Springer £270, which might have represented debt on the land, and "one years Interest on land" of $43.20. Account of James Stroud and Jeremiah Springer, executors of the testament and last will of Thomas Springer, 1826, filed with Thomas Springer will and inventory, December 8, 1804.

14. Mill Creek Hundred Assessment, 1798. In Mill Creek, only 30 people—6.5% of the taxpayers in the hundred—owned slaves at all, and only 4 people owned more than four slaves. Twelve owned only one.

15. Ibid. The names of the slaves appear in Thomas Springer's will, October 4, 1804; Inventory of Thomas Springer, December 8, 1804; Inventory of Evan Rice, March 11, 1772 (filed November 17, 1784).

16. Ellen Stanley Rogers and Louise E. Easter, transcribers and eds., 1800 Census of New Castle County, Delaware (Bladensburg, Md., 1960). Thomas Springer's household is listed: 1 male aged 26–45 (Thomas), 1 female aged 26–45 (Elizabeth?), 1 female and 2 males aged 16–25 (?), 2 females under 10 (Mary and Ann), 4 slaves (Will, Ace, Amelia, Sara).

17. On housewifery, see Laurel Thatcher Ulrich, Good Wives: Image and Reality in the Lives of Women in Northern New England, 1650–1750 (New York, 1982). Ulrich, chap. 2, discusses the role of "deputy husband," in which wives took over husbands' duties. On black women's work, see Mary Beth Norton, Liberty's Daughters: The Revolutionary Experience of American Women, 1750–1800 (Boston, 1980), pp. 29–31.

18. Elizabeth Fox-Genovese, "Antebellum Southern Households: A New Perspective on a Familiar Question, "Review—Journal of the Fernand Braudel Center for the Study of Economies, Historical Systems, and Civilizations, at SUNY [Stony Brook], 7 (1983): 222–23. Inventory of Thomas Springer, December 8, 1804; Mark A. Calvert, "The Abolition Society of Delaware, 1801–1807," Delaware History 10 (1963): 295–320. There were 2,562 slaves in New Castle County in 1790, 1,888 in 1800, and 1,047 in 1800. Pretzer, "Delaware Log House," p. 10. Contemporaries of the Springers did debate women's capacity for education, politics, and contributing to the Republic. See Linda K. Kerber, Women of the Republic: Intellect and Ideology in Revolutionary America (Chapel Hill, N.C., 1980).

19. On farming practices in northern Delaware, see R. O. Bausman and J. A. Monroe, eds., "James Tilton's Notes on the Agriculture of Delaware in 1788," Agricultural History 20 (1946): 176–87; Israel Acrelius, A History of New Sweden; or, The Settlements on the River Delaware (first published in Swedish, 1759), Memoirs of the Historical Society of Pennsylvania, vol. 11, (Philadel-

phia, 1874), pp. 147–55. See also James T. Lemon, *"The Best Poor Man's Country": A Geographical Study of Early Southeastern Pennsylvania* (Baltimore, 1972), chaps. 6 and 7. Farmers' livestock holdings are from the Mill Creek Assessment of 1798, eliminating millers, estates, artisans who owned just a few acres, and the landless. The average holding of farmers who owned from 100 to 150 acres of land was about $128 worth of animals. Contemporary inventories from New Castle County give a rough idea of the number and variety of animals that that sum represented; and see Lemon, *Best Poor Man's Country*, pp. 153, 160–67.

Inventory of Thomas Springer, December 8, 1804, lists the quantities of different crops on hand. I computed the acreage devoted to each crop based on Bausman and Monroe, "Tilton's Notes," p. 183: "An acre of ground will produce of Timothy from one to two tons of dry forage—of red clover from 2 to 3 tons—of indian corn, from 15 to 50 bushels—of wheat from 6 to 20 Bushels—of barley and rye, from 10 to 35 bushels—of oats and buckwheat, from 15 to 30 bushels—of irish potatoes, from 100 to 300 bushels." This yields, for 1803–4, between 13 and 26 acres devoted to oats, 7 to 19½ acres to corn, 5 to 16 acres to wheat, and about 1 acre each to rye and potatoes. Ibid., p. 185, gives the number of fields best to devote to various crops. Compare with southeastern Pennsylvania farming as described in Lemon, *Best Poor Man's Country*, pp. 152–53.

20. The New Castle County Assessment, 1798, lists unimproved acreage. Bausman and Monroe, "Tilton's Notes," p. 185, describes woodlands in Delaware. The marsh land is sold to Thomas in Deed of Charles Springer and wife Elizabeth to Thomas Springer, April 1, 1792, Deed Book, O-2: 55–57. Evidence that the Springers owned an orchard appears in the estate inventory, which lists "9 Barrels Cider" and "9 do. [Barrels] apples." Inventory of Thomas Springer, December 8, 1804.

21. The inventory of Springer's crops, and Tilton's account of acreage needed for that produce, suggest that Springer planted somewhere between 27 and 63½ acres that year; the mean of those figures is 45¼ acres, just about half of Springer's 90 improved acres. Inventory of

Thomas Springer, December 8, 1804. On the quality of the soil, manuring, and leaving fallow, see Bausman and Monroe, "Tilton's Notes," p. 180.

22. Inventory of Thomas Springer, December 8, 1804, lists ricks and stacks of timothy and other grasses. Acrelius, *History of New Sweden*, pp. 153–55 on pasturage. Lemon, *Best Poor Man's Country*, describes "general mixed farming" in southeastern Pennsylvania (chap. 6), but ties extensive use of the land to particular emphasis on wheat and notes the connection between livestock specialization and strict rotation schemes, pp. 171, 179–83, 197–98. On English agricultural practices, see Eric Kerridge, *The Agricultural Revolution* (New York, 1968), p. 40, chap. 3, chap. 7, and passim. On "progressive" American farmers in the 1790s, Joyce O. Appleby, "The Changing Prospect of the Family Farm in the Early National Period," *Working Papers from the Regional Economic History Research Center* 4, no. 3 (1981): 1–25.

23. Bausman and Monroe, "Tilton's Notes," p. 179; Acrelius, *History of New Sweden*, pp. 148–51, describes the seasonal round of work. On New Castle and Wilmington, see Sara Guertler Farris, "Wilmington's Maritime Commerce, 1775–1807," *Delaware History* 14 (April 1970): 22–51. Francis Dunlap, Wilmington Tavernkeeper and Ferryman, Account Book 1796–1801, DHR, shows the patronage of John[?] Springer and Samuel Stroud from Thomas's area, and George Peirce (who later married Thomas's widow, see below) in 1800–1801. The three men paid for "stabling," "½ gill gin and sundries," and "wharfage," respectively, pp. 191, 151, 200.

24. Bausman and Monroe, "Tilton's Notes," p. 181.

25. Ibid.

26. Ibid., pp. 182–84. Inventory of Thomas Springer, December 8, 1804, lists "a lot of old sickles."

27. Bausman and Monroe, "Tilton's Notes," p. 183.

28. Ibid., pp. 186, 183, 181. The "9 Barrels Cider" listed in the Thomas Springer inventory of 1804 gives evidence of cider making. John Spurrier, *The Practical Farmer: Being a New and Compendious System of Husbandry* (Wilmington, 1793), gave detailed instructions for cider making. One subscriber to the book was Springer's neighbor Joshua Stroud.

29. Account of Charles Springer Estate, Mill Creek Hundred, 1796; Mill Creek Hundred Assessment, 1798. Tilton said it took two or three horses to pull a plow. Bausman and Monroe, "Tilton's Notes," p. 184. Inventory of John Ball, August 25, 1804.

30. Inventory of Thomas Springer, December 8, 1804; Acrelius, *History of New Sweden*, p. 155; Elinor F. Oakes, "A Ticklish Business: Dairying in New England and Pennsylvania, 1750–1800," *Pennsylvania History* 47 (1980): 198–99.

31. Bausman and Monroe, "Tilton's Notes," pp. 185–86; Federal Writers Project, *New Castle on the Delaware* (Newark, Del., 1973), p. 40; see also Lemon, *Best Poor Man's Country*, p. 197.

32. Norton, *Liberty's Daughters*, pp. 45–51 and chap. 2. The quotation is on p. 42.

33. Acrelius, *History of New Sweden*, p. 151, describes gardens. Oakes, "A Ticklish Business," p. 202; Joan M. Jensen, "Churns and Buttermaking in the Mid-Atlantic Farm Economy," *Working Papers from the Regional Economic History Research Center* 5, nos. 2–3 (1982): 78. See also Arthur Young, *Rural Oeconomy; or, Essays on the Practical Parts of Husbandry*, 2nd ed. (London and Philadelphia, 1776), pp. 44, 48.

34. Oakes, "A Ticklish Business," pp. 202–4. Jensen, "Churns and Buttermaking," p. 80, notes that when milk pans were not placed in running water in springhouses it took from 48 to 60 hours for cream to rise. Jensen describes springhouses and the importance of controlling temperature in dairying on pp. 83–87. Mill Creek Hundred Assessment, 1798, lists no springhouse or milkhouse on the Springer property; indeed, it mentions only one springhouse in the hundred and that one made of stone. However, Orphans Court records suggest that small outbuildings on New Castle County farms often escaped listing by the tax assessors. Rebecca Siders and Bernard L. Herman, transcribers and eds., New Castle County, Delaware, Orphans Court Valuation, 1760–1830. Center for Historic Architecture and Engineering, University of Delaware.

35. Oakes, "A Ticklish Business," pp. 201–4; Jensen, "Churns and Buttermaking," pp. 87, 70–76. Cf. Lemon, *Best Poor Man's Country*, pp. 161–63, who says that cows gave from 1 to 4 quarts of milk a day.

36. Oakes, "A Ticklish Business," pp. 197, 201, 204, 209–11; Jensen, "Churns and Buttermaking," pp. 75–76 on the barrel churn, pp. 89–93 on marketing of butter; Lemon, *Best Poor Man's Country*, pp. 194, 196, 199; Inventory of John Ball, August 25, 1804. The value of neighbors' livestock holdings appears in the Mill Creek Hundred Assessment, 1798.

37. Jensen, "Churns and Buttermaking," pp. 80, 85; Ulrich, *Good Wives*, pp. 10–11; Oakes, "A Ticklish Business," p. 201.

38. Grace Rogers Cooper, "Textile Manufacture in America in the Eighteenth Century," in *The Copp Family Textiles* (Washington, D.C., 1971). esp. pp. 51–53; George H. Gibson, "Fullers, Carders, and Manufacturers of Woolen Goods in Delaware," *Delaware History* 12 (April 1966): 25–29, 33–34, and Gibson, "The Delaware Woolen Industry," *Delaware History* 12 (October 1966): 94–102.; Bausman and Monroe, "Tilton's Notes," p. 186. John Robinson, weaver, appears in the New Castle County Assessment, 1798. We know that Elizabeth's neighbor Nancy Ball sent homespun cloth to the fulling mill; her husband's inventory notes that "17 yards of Blanketing . . . was at the fulling mil at the time of the appraisement." Inventory of John Ball, August 25, 1804. There were other fulling mills in Mill Creek Hundred and in other parts of the county. The Springers' later dealings with the Johnsons (see below) have led to the conclusion that they patronized the Johnson fulling mill.

39. Cooper, "Textile Manufacture," p. 53; Bausman and Monroe, "Tilton's Notes," p. 185.

40. Among the clothes and textiles in the Springer house were those listed in the inventory of 1804: Thomas Springer's clothes—"8 coats, 7 jackets, 5 shirts, 8 pr. trousers, 2 pr. drawers, 2 hats"; a variety of sheets, blankets, pillowcases, and bed curtains; "window curtains," "towills," "a quantity of table linen," "2 coverlids," "3 bed quilts," and "1 cradle quilt." Writing in 1759, Acrelius, *History of New Sweden*, p. 157, said that country people made their own clothes while city people bought theirs from merchants' shops.

41. Bausman and Monroe, "Tilton's Notes," p. 186. On Mordecai McKinney, see Gibson, "Fullers, Carders, and Manufacturers," pp. 33–34; Gibson, "Delaware Woolen Industry," pp. 87, 90–91, 102, 106, 109–10, 115–16. The spinning house appears in Benjamin

Blackiston's estate, 1807, Siders and Herman, Orphans Court Valuation. Lemon, *Best Poor Man's Country*, pp. 166–67, 213–14. The listing in the inventory suggests that the two spinning wheels may well have been kept in the log kitchen. Inventory of Thomas Springer, December 8, 1804.

42. Bausman and Monroe, "Tilton's Notes," p. 186; Acrelius, *History of New Sweden*, pp. 158–59.

43. Norton, *Liberty's Daughters*, chap. 3, esp. pp. 71–84. On ideas of republican motherhood, see Kerber, *Women of the Republic*, chap. 9.

44. On preindustrial patterns of life; see E. P. Thompson, "Time, Work-Discipline, and Industrial Capitalism," *Past and Present* 38 (1967): 56–97.

45. Mill Creek Hundred Assessment, 1798.

46. Ibid. On tenants' payment of rent in produce or livestock, see Bausman and Monroe, "Tilton's Notes," p. 184. Lemon, *Best Poor Man's Country*, pp. 10–11, 94–96, discusses artisans, tenants, and others without land.

47. Mill Creek Hundred Assessment, 1798. On distribution of wealth, see also Lemon, *Best Poor Man's Country*, pp. 10–12, 223–25, and Henretta, "Families and Farms," pp. 8–9.

48. Mill Creek Hundred Assessment, 1798.

49. Ibid.; Pretzer, "Delaware Log House," p. 14.

50. Deed of James Stroud and Jeremiah Springer, Executors of Thomas Springer, April 9, 1805, Deed Book, C-3: 311–14.

51. The Strouds and Harlans were neighbors throughout the Springers' tenure on the tract. They appear in Mill Creek Hundred Assessment Records of the 1790s and early 1800s, New Castle County Assessment Records, reels 1–5; Deed of Charles Springer to Samuel Stroud, April 1, 1790, Deed Book, M-2: 169–70, for 33 acres (saving that Thomas Springer have water rights) and a strip of land "opposite the mouth of Caleb Harlan's mill tail." On the Harlans, see Will of Caleb Harlan "of Mill Town," 1816.

52. Ferris, *History of the Original Settlements*, pp. 184–5, notes the decline in use of the Swedish language and the end of a Swedish ministry at Holy Trinity. See Lemon, *Best Poor Man's Country*, pp. 24, 43–49, and 221–24, on immigration into southeastern Pennsylvania. Frank N. Zebley, *The Churches of Delaware* (Wilmington, 1947), p. 144, gives the dates of William McKennon's ministry at Red Clay Presbyterian Church as 1755–1809. J. Thomas Scharf, *History of Delaware, 1609–1888*, 2 vols. (Philadelphia, 1888), 2: 923, mentions that the Harlans were Quakers. The Springers baptized daughter Ann at Immanuel Church (note 11 above), and Thomas remarried there in 1802 (New Castle County Marriage Index). Charles and Jeremiah Springer appear nearby in the Mill Creek Hundred, New Castle County Assessment, 1798. Also, Thomas's father's cousin Charles Springer owned land nearby—a tract next to the land of Amelia Ball, which in turn adjoined the land of William McKennon, John Ball, and "the Mill Branch." Amelia Ball's children, John and Robert Giffin, sold the acreage they inherited from her to Thomas Springer in 1788. May term 1794, Court of Common Pleas. Marriages involving local families include: John Ball m. Darkeys Springer, 1759; James Stroud m. Hannah Springer, 1806; James Stroud m. Ann Ball, 1815; all in New Castle County Marriage Index. Neighbors acted as witnesses for one another's legal transactions—deeds and wills—and as referees in one another's disputes.

53. On childbirth, see Norton, *Liberty's Daughters*, pp. 78–79. The women's community in the Mill Creek area can be reconstructed from marriage records and wills: Will of Caleb Harlan, 1815 (probate 1816); Will of John Ball, Sr., August 25, 1804; William McKennon m. Elizabeth Thompson, before May 11, 1792; Will of William McKennon, January 21, 1807 (probate May 16, 1809); Jeremiah Springer m. Mary Reece, March 1788, New Castle County Marriage Index.

54. Ulrich, *Good Wives*, pp. 41–43; Bausman and Monroe, "Tilton's Notes," p. 116. Inventory of Thomas Springer, December 8, 1804, lists "tea cups, coffee, sugar dishes."

55. On Dunlap's tavern, see note 12 above; Mill Creek Hundred Assessment, 1798.

56. Andrew Giffin v. John Ball, ex'r of John Ball, deceased, January 1804, New Castle County Court of Chancery Records, 1806–1807, Case G-4.

57. Ibid.

58. Ibid.

59. Ibid. On the meaning of local exchange, see Christopher Clark, "Household Economy, Market Exchange and the Rise of Capitalism in the Connecticut Valley,

1800–1860," *Journal of Social History* 13 (Winter 1979): 169–89; Michael Merrill, "Cash Is Good to Eat: Self-Sufficiency and Exchange in the Rural Economy of the United States," *Radical History Review* (Winter 1977): 12–71.

60. Giffin v. Ball.

61. Account of James Stroud and Jeremiah Springer, Executors of the Testament and Last Will of Thomas Springer, 1826, filed with Thomas Springer will and inventory, October 4, 1804; Inventory of John Ball, August 25, 1804.

62. On neighbors' knowledge of one another's disputes, see Ulrich, *Good Wives*, chap. 3.

63. Inventory of Thomas Springer, December 8, 1804. Acrelius, *History of New Sweden*, describes country houses and their furnishings as he saw them in 1759, pp. 156–57. I have adopted Bernard Herman and Jack Michel's conclusions about the Springers' furnishing plans, based on their inventory. On the effects of one-room and multiroom houses on neighbor relationships, see James Deetz, *In Small Things Forgotten: The Archeology of Early Life* (Garden City, N.Y., 1977), pp. 115–17.

64. Pretzer, "Delaware Log House," p. 6.

65. Andrew Burnaby, 1760, and Ambrose Serle, 1777, quoted in Christopher L. Ward, *The Delaware Continentals, 1776–1783* (Wilmington, 1941), pp. 523–24, 522–23; Federal Writers Project, *New Castle on the Delaware*, p. 40; Lemon, *Best Poor Man's Country*, pp. 45–46, 120–21, 130, 145.

66. Carol E. Hoffecker, *Wilmington, Delaware: Portrait of an Industrial City, 1830–1930* (n.p., 1974), pp. 3–6; Farris, "Wilmington's Maritime Commerce," pp. 25–27; James T. Lemon, "Urbanization and the Development of Eighteenth-Century Southeastern Pennsylvania and Adjacent Delaware," *William and Mary Quarterly*, 3rd ser., 24 (1967): 501–42; Lemon, *Best Poor Man's Country*, chap. 2; David E. Dauer, "Colonial Philadelphia's Intraregional Transportation System: An Overview," *Working Papers from the Regional Economic History Research Center* 2, no. 3 (1979): 1–16.

67. Farris, "Wilmington's Maritime Commerce," esp. pp. 25–27; Peter C. Welsh, "Merchants, Millers, and Ocean Ships: The Components of an Early Industrial Town," *Delaware History* 7 (1957): 319–36; Acrelius, *History of New Sweden*, pp. 144–46. The quotation is

Dr. Robert Honyman, 1775, cited in Ward, *Delaware Continentals*, p. 524.

68. Peter C. Welsh, "The Brandywine Mills: A Chronicle of an Industry, 1762–1816," *Delaware History* 7 (1957): 17–36; Farris, "Wilmington's Maritime Commerce," pp. 25–27; Bausman and Monroe, "Tilton's Notes," pp. 184–85.

69. Welsh, "Brandywine Mills," pp. 19, 24; Farris, "Wilmington's Martime Commerce," pp. 39–44; Welsh, "Merchants, Millers, and Ocean Ships," p. 334; Bausman and Monroe, "Tilton's Notes," p. 185.

70. Welsh, "Brandywine Mills," pp. 24, 26, 29–30, for the travelers' quotations; Bausman and Monroe, "Tilton's Notes," pp. 184–85; Welsh, "Merchants, Millers, and Ocean Ships," pp. 331, 333–36.

71. Petition of divers Inhabitants of Brandywine and Christiana Hundreds, New Castle County, January 2, 1783, Legislative Papers.

72. Ibid.; "An act for the Regulation of certain Water Grist Mills in New Castle County," January 5, 1785, Legislative Papers; "A Supplement to an Act intitled 'An Act for the Regulation of certain Water Grist Mills in New Castle County,' " January 27, 1790, ibid. On quasi-public businesses and activities, see Richard B. Morris, *Government and Labor in Early America* (New York, 1946), pp. 18–21.

73. Mill Creek Hundred Assessment, 1798; Welsh, "Brandywine Mills," p. 29. Joshua Stroud's mill appears in Samuel Bush v. James Stroud, ex'r of the estate of Edward Stroud, New Castle County Court of Chancery Records, 1791, Case B-29. William Stroud's flour dealing appears in Giffin v. Ball. On the new mill machinery, see Bausman and Monroe, "Tilton's Notes," pp. 184–85; Granville Bathe and Dorothy Bathe, *Oliver Evans: A Chronicle of Early American Engineering* (1935; reprint ed., New York, 1972). That similar machinery was in the Stroud mill appears in "An Act Granting Oliver Evans . . . [Patent]," November 10, 1787, manuscript, pp. 452–53, Legislative Acts of Delaware, DHR.

74. Mill Creek Hundred Assessment, 1798. Over 56% of the houses in the hundred were of log, over 18% of stone, and just 11% of brick. There were also frame houses (13%) and a few "mudwall" houses. Acrelius, *History of New Sweden*, pp. 156–57, noted in 1759 that

urban houses were brick while country houses were generally of stone or "oakplanks." I am indebted to Jack Michel for noting the connection between brick houses and a cosmopolitan frame of mind.

75. Elizabeth must have died between 1800, when she appears in the Census of 1800, and 1802, when Thomas remarried. Thomas Springer m. Margaret Wells, December 7, 1802, New Castle County Marriage Index; Margaret's inheritance appears in Will and Inventory of Hannah Wells, June 12, 1801, and Inventory of Harrison Wells, February 12, 1795; Will of Thomas Springer, October 4, 1804.

76. Account of James Stroud and Jeremiah Springer, Executors of the Testament and Last Will of Thomas Springer, 1826, filed with Thomas Springer will and inventory, December 8, 1804; Margaret Springer m. George Peirce, Esq., January 8, 1807, New Castle County Marriage Index. Stroud and Springer's accounting of Thomas Springer's estate shows that Margaret had become Margaret Peirce by the 1820s. A Margaret Springer married a Jesse Peirce about 1814, but she is identified as the daughter of Charles Springer in his will, 1817. That our Margaret married *George* Peirce is confirmed by his dealings with the Wells family (in his estate, 1826) and by death and tombstone records (DHR), which indicate that George Peirce's wife died in 1826, the same year that the Thomas Springer estate records that Thomas's widow Margaret died. George Peirce paid Francis Dunlap for "wharfage" in 1800, which suggests that he was involved in trade. Francis Dunlap Account Book. Probate records list Peirce's occupation as "Esquire." Will of George Peirce, March 9, 1826. Peirce is listed as the owner of three lots and three houses in New Castle in the New Castle Hundred Assessment, 1803–1804.

77. Mary's and Ann's changes of surname appear in the account of Stroud and Springer of Thomas Springer's estate, which confirms marriages listed in the New Castle County Marriage Index; Mary Springer m. Robert McMurphy, September 4, 1809. Evidence of the McMurphys' running the tavern is in Inventory of Robert McMurphy, January 7, 1818, probated August 31, 1821, ("1 Tavern sign"), and Siders and Herman, Orphans Court Valuation, p. 68, from which the quotation is taken. McMurphy's estate's disbursements include $4

to George Peirce, indicating some continued connection with Margaret Wells Springer Peirce. Ann Springer m. Richard Craddock, *Delaware Gazette*, December 21 or 27, 1814. Deed of James Stroud and Jeremiah Springer, April 9, 1805; Property Tax Book 1816 mentions the tenant, in Upton, "Architectural Survey," appendix.

THE AMBITIONS OF
A TIDEWATER PLANTER:
HENRY SAUNDERS OF
ISLE OF WIGHT COUNTY, VIRGINIA

I have relied on the unpublished research report of Dell Upton, "The Virginia Parlor, National Museum of American History, Smithsonian Institution: A Report on the Henry Saunders House and Its Occupants," July 1, 1981, as a guide to my research on the Saunders family.

1. "Isle of Wight County Records," *William and Mary Quarterly*, 1st ser., 7 (1899): 205–7; John Bennett Boddie, *Seventeenth Century Isle of Wight County, Virginia* (Baltimore, 1973), pp. 1–4. Compare this account of Smith's dealings in Isle of Wight with Joseph B. Dunn's account of Smith's dealings with Native Virginians in neighboring Nansemond County, *History of Nansemond County, Virginia* (n.p., 107), p. 13.

2. Gary B. Nash, *Red, White, and Black: The Peoples of Early America* (Englewood Cliffs, N.J., 1974), pp. 61–64.

3. Ibid., pp. 51–54; Edmund S. Morgan, *American Slavery, American Freedom: The Ordeal of Colonial Virginia* (New York, 1976), pp. 158–63, 108–10. The quotation is in Winthrop D. Jordan, *White over Black: American Attitudes Toward the Negro, 1550–1812* (Baltimore, 1969), p. 71.

4. Morgan, *American Slavery, American Freedom*, pp. 126–30, 215–34; Nash, *Red, White, and Black*, pp. 53–54.

5. William Waller Hening, *The Statutes at Large; being a collection of all the laws of Virginia, from the first session*

of the Legislature in the year 1619, 13 vols. (Charlottes-ville, 1969), 2: 548, cited in Dell Upton, "The Virginia Parlor," p. 2.

6. Morgan, *American Slavery, American Freedom*, pp. 250–270; Nash, *Red, White, and Black*, pp. 127–34; Boddie, *Seventeenth Century Isle of Wight*, pp. 144–66.

7. Hening, *Statutes at Large*, 2: 548; Virginia State Land Office, Patents, no. 7, p. 72, microfilm, Virginia State Library, Richmond (hereafter cited as VSL), cited in Upton, "The Virginia Parlor," p. 2.

8. "Virginia Quit Rent Rolls, 1704," *Virginia Magazine of History and Biography* 29 (1921), 337–43. The small-farming pattern appears in the Saunders inventories: John Saunders Will and Appraisal, 1772, Isle of Wight County Will Book 8, pp. 136–38, 152–55, VSL (here-after cited as Will Book); Thomas Saunders Will and Appraisal, 1783, Will Book 9, pp. 222–23, Will Book 10, pp. 64–65; Henry Saunders Appraisal (a different Henry Saunders), 1792, Will Book 10, p. 257; Eliza-beth Saunders Will, 1779, and Accounts, 1794 and 1796, Will Book 10, pp. 302, 361–62, 380. Boddie, *Seventeenth Century Isle of Wight*, p. 696, notes land grants given to John Saunders (1681) and Henry Saun-ders (1698) for transporting persons to the colony.

9. On Pennsylvania, see James T. Lemon, *The Best Poor Man's Country: A Geographical Study of Early Southeast-ern Pennsylvania* (Baltimore, 1972); Morgan, *American Slavery, American Freedom*, pp. 299–308.

10. Morgan, *American Slavery, American Freedom*, pp. 299–315.

11. Ibid., pp. 304–5; Allan Kulikoff, "Tobacco and Slaves: Population, Economy and Society in Eighteenth-Cen-tury Prince George's County, Maryland," Ph.D. diss., Brandeis University, 1976, pp. 84, 171–72.

12. Virginia State Land Office, Patents, no. 9, p. 148, cited in Upton, "The Virginia Parlor," p. 4.

13. Quotation in Morgan, *American Slavery, American Free-dom*, p. 304.

14. Rhys Isaac, *The Transformation of Virginia, 1740–1790* (Chapel Hill, N.C., 1982), compares the lives of gen-tlefolk and plain folk.

15. Morgan, *American Slavery, American Freedom*, pp. 311, 330–36; Jordan, *White over Black*, pp. 75–82; Ira Ber-lin, "Time, Space, and the Evolution of Afro-American Society on British Mainland North America," *American Historical Review* 85 (1980): 68–69.

16. Berlin, "Time, Space, and the Evolution of Afro-Amer-ican Society," p. 71; Kulikoff, "Tobacco and Slaves," pp. 84, 175–78, 190, 195–98; Kulikoff, "The Origins of Afro-American Society in Tidewater Maryland and Virginia, 1700 to 1790," *William and Mary Quarterly*, 3rd ser., 35 (1978): 226–59; Morgan, *American Slav-ery, American Freedom*, pp. 318–19.

17. Will Book 7, pp. 103–5. On slave prices, see Kulikoff, "Tobacco and Slaves," pp. 252–53.

18. Kulikoff, "Tobacco and Slaves," pp. 199, 208–9; Kuli-koff, "Origins of Afro-American Society," esp. pp. 240–49. Brewer Godwin's slaveholdings appear in "As-sessors Book for 1778 From Isle of Wight County," *William and Mary Quarterly*, 1st ser., 25 (1916–1917): 169. Benjamin Eley's slaveholdings appear in *Heads of Families at the First Census of the United States, Taken in the year 1790; records of the State enumerations: 1782–1785, Virginia* (Baltimore, 1966), p. 30. Eley's dwelling and other buildings are listed in ibid., p. 92.

19. Kulikoff, "Origins of Afro-American Society," pp. 242, 250, 256. On slaves' naming practices, see Herbert G. Gutman, *The Black Family in Slavery and Freedom, 1750–1925* (New York, 1976), chaps. 3–5, 8.

20. Kulikoff, "Tobacco and Slaves," pp. 277–78; Kulikoff, "Origins of Afro-American Society," p. 227. On white family life, see Michael Zuckerman, "William Byrd's Family," *Perspectives in American History* 12 (1979): 253–311; Zuckerman, "Penmanship Exercises for Saucy Sons: Thoughts on the Colonial Southern Family," *South Carolina Historical Magazine* 84 (1983): 252–66.

21. Account current of the estate of Henry Saunders in ac'd with Mary Saunders, administratrix, July 6, 1769, Will Book 7, pp. 546–47; Isle of Wight County Guard-ians' Accounts 1767–1782, p. 99, VSL.

22. The hire of the Saunders estate slaves is mentioned at Isle of Wight County Guardians' Accounts 1767–1782, p. 99. On general slave-hiring practices, see Sarah S. Hughes, "Slaves for Hire: The Allocation of Black La-bor in Elizabeth City County, Virginia, 1782 to 1810," *William and Mary Quarterly*, 3rd ser., 35 (1978): 260–86.

23. Kulikoff, "Tobacco and Slaves," pp. 208–9, 223–25;

Berlin, "Time, Space, and Afro-American Society," p. 73.

24. Suit of Martha Saunders and Sarah Saunders v. Henry Saunders, 1771, Will Book 8, p. 78; Marriage of John Carstephan and Mrs. Martha Saunders, 1773, ibid., p. 278, listed in Blanche Adams Chapman, *Marriages of Isle of Wight County, Virginia, 1628–1800* (Baltimore, 1976), p. 53.

25. Isle of Wight County Order Book 1772–1780, p. 127 (May 19, 1773), p. 132 (June 3, 1773), VSL (hereafter cited as Order Book).

26. Ibid. The importance of slaveholders' self-image as humane masters, and the slaves' ability to take advantage of that, are described for nineteenth-century slavery in Eugene D. Genovese, *Roll, Jordan, Roll: The World the Slaves Made* (New York, 1974), pp. 70–86, 97–112.

27. Kulikoff, "Tobacco and Slaves," pp. 216–18, 207; Genovese, *Roll, Jordan, Roll*, pp. 3–7, 305, 306, 620–21, 649–57, and passim.

28. No record of Henry Saunders's birth has come to light. I have concluded that he was born about 1750 from two documents: first, mother Martha Saunders's Guardian Account, 1771, Guardian Accounts 1767–1782, p. 106, claiming reimbursement for expenses in educating Henry, which suggests that he was still a minor in 1771 or (since people sometimes filed accounts late) that he had only recently left that status; and Martha and Sarah's suit for settlement of the estate of Henry Saunders, Sr., also 1771, which names Henry junior as the defendant without naming a "next friend" as would be expected if Henry were still a minor. The suit is in Will Book 8, p. 78; Martha's expenditures on the children and their education appear in Isle of Wight County Guardians' Accounts 1767–1782, pp. 98, 99, and 106. The Saunders estate paid quitrents on 250 acres of land, which presumably became Henry's when he reached his majority. Account current of the estate of Henry Saunders in ac't with Mary Saunders, administratrix, July 6, 1769, Will Book 7, pp. 546–547.

29. William Tatham, "An Historical and Practical Essay on the Culture and Commerce of Tobacco," facsimile of 1800 edition, London, England, in G. Melvin Herndon, ed., *William Tatham and the Culture of Tobacco* (Coral Gables, Fla., 1969), pp. 9–18. The quotation is from pp. 17–18.

30. Ibid., pp. 18–27.

31. Lewis Cecil Gray, *History of Agriculture in the Southern United States to 1860*, 2 vols. (Washington, D.C., 1933), 1: 151–59, 161–76, 200–12; Peter V. Bergstrom, "Markets and Merchants: Economic Diversification in Colonial Virginia, 1700–1775," Ph.D. diss., University of New Hampshire, 1980. On the efforts of great planters to achieve self-sufficiency, see Berlin, "Time, Space, and Afro-American Society," p. 73.

32. Tatham, "The Culture of Tobacco," pp. 55–60; Aubrey C. Land, "Economic Behavior in a Planting Society: The Eighteenth-Century Chesapeake," *Journal of Southern History*, 38 (1967): 469–85.

33. On the workings of tobacco inspection laws, see Tatham, "The Culture of Tobacco," pp. 69–87; Segar Cofer Dashiell, *Smithfield, A Pictoral History* (Norfolk, Va., 1977), pp. 9, 35; Dunn, *History of Nansemond*, pp. 7, 32. On planters' growing consumption of store goods in the eighteenth century, see Lois Green Carr and Lorena S. Walsh, "Changing Life Styles in Colonial St. Mary's County," *Working Papers from the Regional Economic History Research Center* 1, no. 3 (1978): 73–119.

34. Dashiell, *Smithfield*, p. 35, gives the list of belongings of Thomas Peirce, Gentleman, d. 1740. Richard Bushman, "Society and Gentility in Early America," lecture at Winterthur Museum, January 1985; Bushman, "American High-Style and Vernacular Cultures," in Jack P. Greene and J. R. Pole, eds., *Colonial British America: Essays in the New History of the Early Modern Era* (Baltimore, 1984), pp. 345–83.

35. Jefferson is quoted in Gregory M. Stiverson, *Poverty in a Land of Plenty: Tenancy in Eighteenth-Century Maryland* (Baltimore, 1977), p. 56.

36. Henry senior's household goods are listed in the Inventory of Henry Saunders, Sr., Will Book 7, pp. 103–4. Bushman, "Society and Gentility."

37. The quotation is from Dunn, *History of Nansemond*, p. 38.; see also Charles S. Sydnor, *American Revolutionaries in the Making: Political Practices in Washington's Virginia* (New York, 1952), chap. 6. The Isle of Wight county court justices are listed in Boddie, *Seventeenth Century Isle of Wight*, pp. 704–6.

38. "Assessors Book for 1778," pp. 168–69, gives landhold-ings, slaveholdings, and ownership of carriages and sil-ver plate for some of the county's most prosperous men. George Purdie's holdings appear in Dashiell, *Smith-field*, pp. 31–32. Boddie, *Seventeenth Century Isle of Wight*, offers information on the families of county court members: Brewers, pp. 403–8; Bridgers, pp. 177, 409–33; Hardys, pp. 225–27; Parkers, pp. 238–41; Willses, pp. 263–64. John Scarsbrook Wills also ap-pears as John "Scarborough" Wills or John "Scasbrook" Wills in various records.

39. Sydnor, *American Revolutionaries*, pp. 83–85; Isaac, *Transformation of Virginia*, pp. 88–94. On the outside arcade and its importance as a place of socializing on court days, see Upton, "The Virginia Parlor," p. 90.

40. Dashiell, *Smithfield*, pp. 18–19; Isaac, *Transformation of Virginia*, pp. 94–98. On treating, see Sydnor, *American Revolutionaries*, chap. 4.

41. Isaac, *Transformation of Virginia*, pp. 98–101; T. H. Breen, "Horses and Gentlemen: The Cultural Signifi-cance of Gambling Among the Gentry of Virginia," *William and Mary Quarterly*, 3rd ser., 34 (1977): 239–57; "The Equine F.F.V.s: A Study of the Evidence for the English Horses Imported into Virginia Before the Revolution," *Virginia Magazine of History and Bi-ography* 35 (1927): 369.

42. Sydnor, *American Revolutionaries*, chaps. 2, 3, 5; Isaac, *Transformation of Virginia*, pp. 110–14. Henry's vote for Wills appears in Deed Book 16, pp. 37–40. He also voted for John Lawrence and Francis Boykin for bur-gesses, ibid., pp. 40–44. For Wills's economic stand-ing, see his probate records, Will Book 20, p. 291.

43. Upton, "The Virginia Parlor," pp. 89–90. The quota-tion is from Alexander Forbes, quoted in Wilmer L. Hall, ed., *Vestry Book of Upper Parish, Nansemond County, 1743–93* (Richmond, Va., 1949), p. xxx; p. xvii describes the activities and responsibilities of vestries. Isle of Wight vestrymen are listed in Boddie, *Seven-teenth Century Isle of Wight*, pp. 179–80, and in New-port Parish, Isle of Wight County, Vestry Book, pp. 84, 107–9, VSL.

44. Hall, *Vestry Book*, pp. xxxi, xxxix–xlii; Newport Parish Vestry Book, pp. 108–9.

45. Hall, *Vestry Book*, p. xx; Newport Parish Vestry Book, pp. 69, 104.

46. Newport Parish Vestry Book, pp. 84, 107–9; Isaac, *Transformation of Virginia*, p. 350; "Isle of Wight County Records," p. 269.

47. On the militia generally, see Isaac, *Transformation of Virginia*, pp. 105–10. Henry's commission is in Order Book 1772–1780, p. 417. Action in Isle of Wight and Nansemond is described in *Hardesty's Historical and Geographical Encyclopedia, Illustrated* (Chicago and To-ledo, 1883), p. 413, and Dunn, *History of Nansemond*, pp. 43–45. Upton, "The Virginia Parlor," p. 7, notes Henry's use of his militia title in later years.

48. Unrecorded Marriage Bond, Isle of Wight County Clerk's Office. Anne and Henry's marriage bond was located by Alvin Reynolds and brought to my attention by Mr. Reynolds and Helen Haverty King. On the Tallough family, see: Land Grants to James Tullaugh, 1684 and 1688, in Boddie, *Seventeenth Century Isle of Wight*, p. 697; James's Tulladgh's Estate, 1698, in "Isle of Wight County Records," p. 250; Will of James Tal-lough, June 25, 1744, Will Book 4, pp. 494–95; Will of William Tallough, 1788, Southampton Wills, p. 84, VSL; Will of James Tallough, Will Book 11 (1803–6), p. 101; Will and Appraisal of James Tallow, Sr., 1804, Will Book 12, pp. 67, 141–42. The state enumeration of 1782 lists three Henry Saunderses in the county (*Heads of Families*, p. 31). Luckily, the Henry we are after listed himself as "Lieutenant Henry Saunders." On the other Henry Saunders, see Upton, "The Virginia Parlor," pp. 103–4. On Henry and Anne's household: *Heads of Families* lists four whites in the family, which suggests two children. That one was named Betsy ap-pears in a deed of gift from Anne Saunders to Betsy in 1806, Isle of Wight County Deed Book 20, p. 306, VSL (hereafter cited as Deed Book).

49. Upton, "The Virginia Parlor," pp. 6–7, 13, 15–20, compares Henry's career with those of his cousins (al-though I have departed from much of that interpretation here). For Henry's inherited advantages, see Henry Saunders's grandfather's inventory, 1735, Will Book 3, p. 349; Henry's father's will and inventory, 1761, Will Book 7, pp. 103–5, Will Book 8, p. 278. For other Saunders family members' lives see note 8 above. On Henry's accumulation of land: the purchase from Car-stephans is in Deed Book 15, p. 205, cited in Upton, "The Virginia Parlor," p. 7. The sale of land to Wright

Roberts is in Deed Book 16, p. 25, and the sale to John Turner in ibid., p. 289.

50. Isle of Wight Land Tax Book, 1782, VSL; Virginia State Land Office Grants, no. 28, p. 93, microfilm, VSL; Land Tax 1787A, cited in Upton, "The Virginia Parlor," p. 8. The changes in Saunders's holdings and the pattern of neighbors' holdings can be traced in Isle of Wight County Land Tax Books, 1782, 1787, 1788, 1790, 1791 et al., and in Nansemond County Land Tax Books, VSL. In 1783, Benjamin Eley owned 830 acres and many Eleys owned less. Nansemond County Land Tax Book, 1783.

51. Gray, *History of Agriculture,* 2: 571–92, 595–96, 602–6.

52. Ibid, pp. 606–13; Winifred J. Losse, "The Foreign Trade of Virginia, 1789–1809," *William and Mary Quarterly,* 3rd ser., 1 (1944): 161–78, esp. pp. 167–70. On grain exports from eastern Virginia in the years before the Revolution, see David Klingaman, "The Significance of Grain in the Development of the Tobacco Colonies," *Journal of Economic History* 29 (1969): 268–78.

53. Paul G. E. Clemens, *The Atlantic Economy and Colonial Maryland's Eastern Shore* (Ithaca, N.Y., 1980), pp. 168, 173–98; Stiverson, *Poverty in a Land of Plenty,* pp. 96–103, 109–10.

54. Records of the Mill Swamp Baptist Church, pp. 1, 3 [?illeg.], 8, VSL; Another example of the meeting's oversight in matters of economic morality is the excommunication of John Davis for "Indolence in discharging his Creditors" and other sins, pp. 16–17. The challenge of dissenting religion to the authority of the established Virginia gentry is described in Isaac, *Transformation of Virginia,* pp. 143–77, and Isaac, "Preachers and Patriots: Popular Culture and the Revolution in Virginia," in Alfred F. Young, ed., *The American Revolution: Explorations in the History of American Radicalism* (DeKalb, Ill., 1976), pp. 125–56.

55. Dunn, *History of Nansemond,* p. 45.

56. Hall, *Vestry Book of the Upper Parish,* pp. lxiv–lxxiv; Richard Beeman, *Patrick Henry: A Biography* (New York, 1974), pp. 111–14. Isle of Wight Petitions, Nov. 15, 1790, VSL

57. Jordan, *White over Black,* pp. 551–60. Courtney Hollowell's manumissions are in Deed Book 15, p. 118;

those by other Hollowells, pp. 119–21; those by other slaveholders, pp. 122–32. The will of Timothy Tynes, April 5, 1802, is in Will Book 11, pp. 587–88.

58. Robert McColley, *Slavery and Jeffersonian Virginia* (Urbana, Ill., 1964), pp. 71–75; Jordan, *White over Black,* pp. 406–14; Gerald W. Mullin, *Flight and Rebellion: Slave Resistance in Eighteenth-Century Virginia* (New York, 1972), chap. 5. An example of free and slave blacks in Isle of Wight cooperating in running away is in Order Book 1806–1809, p. 455. See also Ira Berlin, "The Revolution in Black Life," in Young, *American Revolution,* pp. 349–82.

59. Berlin, "Time, Space, and Afro-American Society," pp. 75–76. The quotation is from St. George Tucker, cited in Mullin, *Flight and Rebellion,* p. viii.

60. St. George Tucker, cited in Mullin, *Flight and Rebellion,* p. viii; Jordan, *White over Black,* pp. 375–91; *Virginia Calendar of State Papers and other Manuscripts, 1652–1781,* 11 vols., ed. William P. Palmer (vols. 1–5), Sherman McRae (vol. 6), Sherman McRae and Raleigh Colston (vol. 7), and under the direction of H. W. Flournoy (vols. 8–11) (Richmond, 1875–1893), 6: 489–90, 494, 470.

61. Mullin, *Flight and Rebellion,* p. viii; *Calendar of State Papers,* 6: 571–72. On fears of insurrection, see Jordan, *White over Black,* pp. 376–78. On Gabriel's Rebellion, see ibid., pp. 393–99, and Mullin, *Flight and Rebellion,* pp. 136–39 and chap. 5.

62. Daniel P. Jordan, *Political Leadership in Jeffersonian Virginia* (Charlottesville, 1983); Isaac, *Transformation of Virginia,* pp. 299–322. Dell Upton dates both the Eley house and the Henry Saunders house as mid-1790s, based on architectural evidence. "The Virginia Parlor," pp. 41–58. On the significance of planters' decisions to build new and permanent houses, see Cary Carson, et al., "Impermanent Architecture in the Southern American Colonies," *Winterthur Portfolio* 16 (1981): 135–96, esp. pp. 176–78.

63. Upton, "The Virginia Parlor," pp. 41–58. William Eley's style of life was not much more genteel than the Saunderses', as reflected in his inventory, Will Book 12, pp. 488–91. Henry Saunders's sale of land to William Gay, 1795, is in Order Book 1795–1797, p. 250. Saunders's mortgage to the Joseph Scott estate, 1797, is in Deed Book 18, p. 241, cited in Upton, "The Virginia

Parlor," p. 9. Upton, pp. 104–5, discusses Quaker merchant Joseph Scott.

64. Upton, "The Virginia Parlor," pp. 35–40; Helen Haverty King, *Historic Isle of Wight* (n.p., 1983), pp. 75–76.

65. Upton, "The Virginia Parlor," pp. 40–41.

66. Ibid.; Isaac, *Transformation of Virginia*, pp. 302–5; Daniel Blake Smith, *Inside the Great House: Planter Family Life in Eighteenth-Century Chesapeake Society* (Ithaca, N.Y., 1980), pp. 21–24, 281–99, and chap. 5; Jan Lewis, *The Pursuit of Happiness: Family and Values in Jefferson's Virginia* (New York, 1983).

67. Deed Book 20, p. 306.

68. Order Book 1806–1809, pp. 348–52, 377.

69. For the statement on violence against wives, see William Fitzhugh to Mr. Kenline Chiseldine, June 8, 1681, *Virginia Magazine of History and Biography* 1 (July 1893–April 1894): 40. Jefferson is quoted in Jordan, *White over Black*, pp. 432–33; ibid., p. 82, covers the law that made killing a slave in the course of punishment not a felony. White women who owned slaves could be "despots" too: see Mary Beth Norton, " 'What an Alarming Crisis Is This': Southern Women and the American Revolution," in Jeffrey J. Crow and Larry E. Tise, eds., *The Southern Experience in the American Revolution* (Chapel Hill, N.C., 1978), pp. 207–8.

70. On the effect of slaveowning on whites, see Genovese, *Roll, Jordan, Roll*, pp. 93–97.

71. Mary Beth Norton, *Liberty's Daughters: The Revolutionary Experience of American Women, 1750–1800* (Boston, 1980), pp. 45–50; Linda K. Kerber, *Women of the Republic: Intellect and Ideology in Revolutionary America* (Chapel Hill, N.Y., 1980), chaps. 5 and 6; Smith, *Inside the Great House*, chap. 4; Suzanne Lebsock, *The Free Women of Petersburg* (New York, 1984).

72. Mill Swamp Baptist Church Records, p. 3; other church interventions into private family life appear on pp. 2–3, chastising an excessive drinker, and pp. 4–5, setting policy for disciplining members who fail to conduct daily family prayers. The destruction of the Bay Church is in Isaac, *Transformation of Virginia*, p. 313.

73. Henry's loss of his mortgaged land is in Deed Book 21, p. 91, cited in Upton, "The Virginia Parlor," p. 9. In 1809, the Isle of Wight county court appointed four men trustees of the estate of Henry Saunders, "who is now in the penetentiary." The court also ordered three men to appraise the Saunders estate, but I have located no record of the appraisal. Order Book 1806–1809, p. 457.

THE LIMITS OF LIBERTY:
RICHARD ALLEN,
FREEDMAN OF PHILADELPHIA

1. Gary B. Nash, *Red, White, and Black: The Peoples of Early America* (Englewood Cliffs, N.J., 1974), pp. 310, 313–14; Winthrop Jordan, *White over Black: American Attitudes Toward the Negro, 1550–1812* (Baltimore, 1969), pp. 102–4. On legal definitions of chattel slavery, see Leon Higginbotham, Jr., *In the Matter of Color; Race and the American Legal Process: The Colonial Period* (New York, 1978).

2. Edmund S. Morgan, "Slavery and Freedom: The American Paradox," *The Challenge of the American Revolution* (New York, 1976), p. 141; Benjamin Quarles, *The Negro in the American Revolution* (New York, 1973), pp. vii–x, chaps. 5–6; Douglas C. North, *The Economic Growth of the United States, 1790–1860* (New York, 1966), pp. 75–76. The quotation is from Morgan, "Slavery and Freedom," pp. 141–42.

3. On the strains of thought that contributed to changing white attitudes toward slavery, see Jordan, *White over Black*, chap. 7; David Brion Davis, *The Problem of Slavery in Western Culture* (Ithaca, N.Y., 1966), chaps. 10–14; Bernard Bailyn, *Ideological Origins of the American Revolution* (Cambridge, Mass., 1967), pp. 232–46. Jupiter Hammon is quoted in Quarles, *Negro in the American Revolution*, p. 182.

4. Leon F. Litwack, *North of Slavery: The Negro in the Free States, 1790–1860* (Chicago, 1961), chap. 1; James Horton, "Race and Class in Colonial America," ms. chapter of a forthcoming study of northern slavery, pp. 25–26; Quarles, *Negro in the American Revolution*, pp. 38–40, 43–50, chaps. 5 and 8.

5. Horton, "Race and Class," pp. 3, 9–11, 21–22; Jordan, *White over Black*, pp. 187–90, 304–8.

6. Mark Miles Fisher, "Richard Allen, An Interpretation," *The Crisis* 44 (July 1937): 208. Gary B. Nash raises some of these questions of "identity" that faced freed people in the Revolutionary era in " 'To Arise Out of the Dust': Absalom Jones and the African Church of Philadelphia," *Race, Class, and Politics: Essays on Colonial and Revolutionary America* (Champaign: University of Illinois Press, forthcoming), p. 3.

7. Sydney E. Ahlstrom, *A Religious History of the American People* (New Haven, Conn., 1972), pp. 209–10; Richard Hofstadter, *America at 1750: A Social Portrait* (New York, 1973), pp. 17–30. 197–200. Estimates of Philadelphia's 1760 population vary widely owing to the lack of pre-Revolutionary censuses and to different authors' decisions to include or exclude suburbs in the count. I am following Gary B. Nash, *The Urban Crucible: Social Change, Political Consciousness, and the Origins of the American Revolution* (Cambridge, Mass., 1979), p. 409. Cf. Carl Bridenbaugh, *Cities in Revolt: Urban Life in America, 1743–1776* (New York, 1955), p. 5; Arthur M. Schlesinger, *The Birth of the Nation: A Portrait of the American People on the Eve of Independence* (Boston, 1968), p. 27.

8. Bridenbaugh, *Cities in Revolt*, pp. 15, 39, 13–14; Schlesinger, *Birth of the Nation*, pp. 44, 51.

9. Bridenbaugh, *Cities in Revolt*, pp. 33, 34–35, 81, 106, 27. The quotations on street lamps and noise are from Schlesinger, *Birth of the Nation*, pp. 104, 100.

10. Bridenbaugh, *Cities in Revolt*, pp. 49–50; David E. Dauer, "Colonial Philadelphia's Intraregional Transportation System: An Overview," *Working Papers from the Regional Economic History Research Center*, 2, no. 3 (1979): 1–16; Bridenbaugh, *Cities in Revolt*, pp. 57, 50–52, 44.

11. Eric Foner, *Tom Paine and Revolutionary America* (New York, 1976), pp. 20–56; John K. Alexander, *Render Them Submissive: Responses to Poverty in Philadelphia, 1760–1780* (Amherst, Mass., 1980), pp. 7–10; Nash, *Urban Crucible*, pp. 13–18.

12. Nash, "Slaves and Slaveholders in Colonial Philadelphia," *William and Mary Quarterly*, 3rd ser., 30 (1973): 243, 244, 247–51, 242–43.

13. Jordan, *White over Black*, p. 194; Ahlstrom, *Religious History*, pp. 176–78.

14. Fox and Woolman are quoted in Jordan, *White over Black*, pp. 194, 273. On the sources of Quaker antislavery thought, see ibid., pp. 271–76, 282–83, and David Brion Davis, *The Problem of Slavery in the Age of Revolution, 1770–1823* (Ithaca, N.Y., 1975), chap 5. On John Woolman, see also Davis, *Slavery in Western Culture*, pp. 483–93. Nancy Slocum Hornich, "Anthony Benezet and the Africans' School: Toward a Theory of Full Equality," *Pennsylvania Magazine of History and Biography* p. 99 (1975): 404.

15. Ahlstrom, *Religious History,* pp. 211–12; Frederick Tolles, *Meeting House and Counting House: The Quaker Merchants of Colonial Philadelphia, 1682–1763* (Chapel Hill, N.C., 1948); Nash, "Slaves and Slaveholders," pp. 252–54; Jordan, *White over Black*, p. 271, notes the Philadelphia Yearly Meeting's condemnation of slavery.

16. Jordan, *White over Black*, pp. 274–75. The quotation is from Nash, *Urban Crucible*, p. 8. Nash examines Americans' acceptance of hierarchy in ibid., pp. 6–13.

17. Carol V. R. George, *Segregated Sabbaths: Richard Allen and the Rise of Independent Black Churches, 1760–1840* (New York, 1973), pp. 22, 19–20. On Cliveden, see Nash, *Urban Crucible*, p. 258.

18. No other historian has contributed so greatly to our understanding of slaves' active creation of cultural space and methods of resistance as Eugene D. Genovese, most particularly in *Roll, Jordan, Roll: The World the Slaves Made* (New York, 1974). George, *Segregated Sabbaths*, p. 20 mentions that Chew had become Anglican. Nash, "Slaves and Slaveholders," p. 240, notes the Anglican Church's willingness to baptize black children.

19. Horton, "Race and Class," pp. 9–13; Foner, *Tom Paine*, pp. 48–51; Nash, "Slaves and Slaveholders," p. 240.

20. Nash, *Urban Crucible*, pp. 247–56; George, *Segregated Sabbaths*, pp. 22–23. Gary B. Nash has identified Allen's new master, based on Richard Allen Freedom Papers, Pennsylvania Abolition Society Papers, box 29 (Manumission Papers), Historical Society of Pennsylvania, Philadelphia. I am indebted to Professor Nash for giving me a copy of Allen's freedom papers.

21. Richard Allen, *The Life Experience and Gospel Labors of the Right Reverend Richard Allen*, 2nd ed. (Nashville, Tenn., 1960), p. 6; John A. Munroe, *Colonial Delaware: A History* (Millwood, N.Y., 1978), pp. 197–99. On slavery in Delaware, see ibid., pp. 185–94.

22. Munroe, *Colonial Delaware*, pp. 197–200; Allen, *Life*

and *Gospel Labors*, p. 6; George, *Segregated Sabbaths*, pp. 23–24.

23. George, *Segregated Sabbaths*, pp. 24–25.

24. Ibid., p. 25.

25. Ahlstrom, *Religious History*, pp. 324–28; William Henry Williams, *The Garden of American Methodism: The Delmarva Peninsula* (Wilmington, Del., 1984), pp. 1–21.

26. Williams, *Garden of Methodism*, pp. 22–27, 121–23. The quotation is in Rhys Isaac, *The Transformation of Virginia, 1740–1790* (Chapel Hill, N.C., 1982), p. 286.

27. Rhys Isaac, "Preachers and Patriots: Popular Culture and the Revolution in Virginia," in Alfred F. Young, ed., *The American Revolution: Explorations in the History of American Radicalism* (DeKalb, Ill., 1976), pp. 137–40. The phrase "spiritual egalitarianism" is from E. P. Thompson, *The Making of the English Working Class* (New York, 1966), p. 363.

28. Williams, *Garden of Methodism*, pp. 74, 98–103. The Anglican minister is quoted in ibid., p. 147. The account of the Methodist meeting is from Thomas Rankin to John Wesley, June 24, 1776, quoted in Isaac, "Preachers and Patriots," p. 137. Some Americans' fearful response to their first contact with the emotionalism of Methodist conversion is described by Freeborn Garrettson in Nathan Bangs, *Life of the Reverend Freeborn Garrettson: Compiled from His Printed Manuscript Journals, and Other Authentic Documents* (New York, 1838), pp. 52–53. See also preacher Jesse Lee's account of the "trembling and shaking" and other behavior that sometimes attended conversions, in Charles H. Wesley, *Richard Allen, Apostle of Freedom* (Washington, D.C., 1935), p. 29.

29. Allen, *Life and Gospel Labors*, p. 5; George, *Segregated Sabbaths*, pp. 25–27.

30. Ahlstrom, *Religious History*, pp. 362–28, 373; Isaac, *Transformation of Virginia*, pp. 262–64; Isaac, "Preachers and Patriots," pp. 137–40.

31. Ahlstrom, *Religious History*, pp. 326–28, 373–74; Isaac, *Transformation of Virginia*, pp. 263–64; Isaac, "Preachers and Patriots," pp. 127–37. The quotation is in Williams, *Garden of Methodism*, p. 89.

32. George, *Segregated Sabbaths*, pp. 27–28; Allen, *Life and Gospel Labors*, p. 7. The quotation is in Albert J. Raboteau, *Slave Religion: The "Invisible Institution" in the Antebellum South* (New York, 1978), p. 102.

33. On white preachers' message to slaves (and slaves' own interpretations of them), see Genovese, *Roll, Jordan, Roll*, pp. 202–55. Jordan, *White over Black*, chap. 5, and Davis, *Slavery in Western Culture*, pp. 203–22, discuss the ambiguities of whites' efforts to "Christianize" black slaves in the New World.

34. Genovese, *Roll, Jordan, Roll*, pp. 3–7, 306, 620–25, 649–57, and passim; Allan Kulikoff, "Tobacco and Slaves: Population, Economy and Society in Eighteenth-Century Prince George's County, Maryland," Ph.D. dissertation, Brandeis University, 1976, pp. 216–18, 207; Raboteau, *Slave Religion*, pp. 98–99, 102–3, 122, 127–28, and passim. Preacher Freeborn Garrettson's encounter with a slaveholder fearful that religion would "spoil his slaves" is described in Robert Drew Simpson, ed., *American Methodist Pioneer: The Life and Journals of the Reverend Freeborn Garrettson, 1752–1827* (Rutland, Vt., 1984), p. 389.

35. George, *Segregated Sabbaths*, pp. 27–28.

36. Williams, *Garden of Methodism*, pp. 157–59. Thompson, *Making of the English Working Class*, pp. 354–57, 368–69, 381–89, stresses the role of Methodism in disciplining a new working class and deflecting believers from social action to spiritual concerns.

37. Isaac, *Transformation of Virginia*, pp. 262–64; Isaac, "Preachers and Patriots," pp. 137–40. On the community of Methodism, see also Thompson, *Making of the English Working Class*, pp. 379–80.

38. Allen, *Life and Gospel Labors*, pp. 5–6.

39. The quotation is in Wesley, *Richard Allen*, p. 36. On early Methodism's antislavery attitudes, see Williams, *Garden of Methodism*, pp. 161–66; Donald G. Mathews, *Slavery and Methodism: A Chapter in American Morality, 1780–1845* (Princeton, N.J., 1965), pp. 3–7.

40. Foner, *Tom Paine*, p. 76. Adams is quoted in Litwack, *North of Slavery*, p. 9.

41. Quarles, *Negro in the American Revolution*, chap. 1. The quotation is on p. 15. See also Ira Berlin, "The Revolution in Black Life," in Young, *American Revolution*, pp. 349–82.

42. Williams, *Garden of Methodism*, pp. 40–44. For the

harassment of one Methodist preacher in Delaware, see Ezra S. Tipple, *Freeborn Garrettson* (New York, 1910), pp. 46–48. Examples of different Methodists' feelings about serving in the patriot army are "Jesse Lee on Military Service" and "Thomas Ware on Military Service," in Frederick A. Norwood, ed., *Sourcebook of American Methodism* (Nashville, Tenn., 1982), pp. 61–66.

43. Allen, *Life and Gospel Labors*, pp. 6–7; George, *Segregated Sabbaths*, p. 28. On Freeborn Garrettson, see Simpson, *American Methodist Pioneer*.

44. Richard Allen Freedom Papers.

45. Allen, *Life and Gospel Labors*, p. 8; Richard Allen Freedom Papers. On the importance of the freedman's act of taking a surname, see Nash, " 'To Arise Out of the Dust,' " pp. 9, 11.

46. Allen, *Life and Gospel Labors*, pp. 8–12; George, *Segregated Sabbaths*, pp. 28–31.

47. Mathews, *Methodism and Slavery*, pp. 8–9; Allen, *Life and Gospel Labors*, pp. 10–11; George, *Segregated Sabbaths*, pp. 30–31.

48. Allen, *Gospel Life and Labors*, p. 13. Among white Methodists, the security of having "brothers and sisters" on whom to rely for economic support in times of trouble was similarly important; see Williams, *Garden of Methodism*, pp. 159–61.

49. Alexander, *Render Them Submissive*, p. 26.

50. Ibid., pp. 27–28; Sharon V. Salinger, "Artisans, Journeymen, and the Transformation of Labor in Late Eighteenth-Century Philadelphia," *William and Mary Quarterly*, 3rd ser., 40 (1983): 62–84.

51. Litwack, *North of Slavery*, pp. 7, 12–13; Jordan, *White over Black*, pp. 271–76, 343–44. On Quakers' changing attitudes, see David Brion Davis, *The Problem of Slavery in the Age of Revolution, 1770–1823* (Ithaca, N.Y., 1975), chap. 5. On the emancipation law, Gary B. Nash, "The Black Revolution in Philadelphia," paper presented to the Philadelphia Center for Early American Studies, February 28, 1985, p. 30.

52. Foner, *Tom Paine*, pp. 56–69 and passim.

53. Ibid., pp. 107–44.

54. *Heads of Families at the First Census of the United States Taken in the Year 1790: Pennsylvania* (Baltimore, Md., 1970), p. 10. Richard Allen is listed as living on the north side of Dock Street in 1790 (p. 236). Interestingly, his former master, Benjamin Chew, owned three slaves at the time (p. 238). Litwack, *North of Slavery*, pp. 154–55.

55. Allen, *Life and Gospel Labors*, p. 13; George, *Segregated Sabbaths*, pp. 37, 30. Williams, *Garden of Methodism*, pp. 105–6, discusses the appeal of Methodist discipline to people in poverty or on its edge.

56. William Douglass, *Annals of the First African Church in the United States of America* (Philadelphia, 1862), pp. 119–21; Nash, " 'To Arise Out of the Dust,' " pp. 9–12; George, *Segregated Sabbaths*, p. 52. See also Ann C. Lammers, "The Reverend Absalom Jones and the Episcopal Church: Christian Theology and Black Consciousness in a New Alliance," *Historical Magazine of the Protestant Episcopal Church* 51 (1982): 159–83.

57. Allen, *Life and Gospel Labors*, pp. 18, 14.

58. Ibid., p. 14. Will B. Gravely discusses the desire for a separate church as a response to white prejudice and as positive outgrowth of black community in "The Rise of African Churches in America (1786–1822): Re-examining the Contexts," *Journal of Religious Thought* 41 (1984): 58–73. On free blacks' need for community and identity, see also Gary Nash, " 'To Arise Out of the Dust,' " pp. 2–3.

59. "Preamble of the Free African Society," September 12, 1787, in Douglass, *Annals of the First African Church*, pp. 15–18, 20–21; Wesley, *Richard Allen*, pp. 56–65; Nash, " 'To Arise Out of the Dust,' " pp. 12–14.

60. Douglass, *Annals of the First African Church*, pp. 21–24; Allen, *Life and Gospel Labor*, p. 18; Litwack, *North of Slavery*, pp. 193–94; George, *Segregated Sabbaths*, p. 59.

61. Nash, " 'To Arise Out of the Dust,' " pp. 14–21; Litwack, *North of Slavery*, pp. 192–94.

62. Allen, *Life and Gospel Labors*, pp. 14–15; Nash, " 'To Arise Out of the Dust,' " pp. 21–23. Douglass, *Annals of the First African Church*, p. 10, suggests that blacks may have anticipated the confrontation and planned the walkout in advance.

63. Nash, " 'To Arise Out of the Dust,' " pp. 23–25; Douglass, *Annals of the Free African Society*, pp. 85–92.

64. George, *Segregated Sabbaths*, pp. 57–62. Douglass, *Annals of the Free African Society*, p. 110, says that Allen's

renovated blacksmith shop could scarcely hold 150 people in 1795, when Jones's congregation numbered 427.

65. An excellent analysis of the general development of separate black worship is Gravely, "Rise of African Churches," pp. 58–73. On mutual-aid societies in other northern cities, see Arnett G. Lindsay, "The Economic Condition of the Negro in New York, Prior to 1861," *Journal of Negro History* 6 (1921): 190–92; Leonard P. Curry, *The Free Black in Urban America, 1800–1850: The Shadow of the Dream* (Chicago, 1981), pp. 197–204; John J Zuille, comp., *Historical Sketch of the New York African Society for Mutual Relief, Organized in the City of New York 1808, Charted by the Legislature of the State of New York 1810* (New York, 1892). Benjamin Rush is quoted in Litwack, *North of Slavery*, p. 193.

66. Jordan, *White over Black*, pp. 375–401, 322–23, 330. On the changes in southern attitudes to slavery, see also Davis, *Slavery in the Age of Revolution*, pp. 196–212.

67. Robert L. Brunhouse, *The Counter-Revolution in Pennsylvania, 1776–1790* (Harrisburg, Pa., 1942); Foner, *Tom Paine*, pp. 136–38.

68. Alexander, *Render Them Submissive*, pp. 51, 61, 82–85; Morgan, "Slavery and Freedom," pp. 143–52.

69. Jordan, *White over Black*, pp. 435–40; Davis, *Slavery in the Age of Revolution*, pp. 164–95. On the development of racism in response to Revolutionary egalitarianism, see also Duncan J. MacLeod, *Slavery, Race, and the American Revolution* (Cambridge, 1974).

70. John Harvey Powell, *Bring Out Your Dead: The Great Plague of Yellow Fever in Philadelphia in 1793* (Philadelphia, 1949); Nash, " 'To Arise Out of the Dust,' " pp. 25–30.

71. Absalom Jones and Richard Allen, *A Narrative of the Proceedings of the Black People During the Late Awful Calamity in Philadelphia in the Year 1793* (London, 1794), pp. 4–19.

72. Jordan, *White over Black*, pp. 364–65; Mathews, *Methodism and Slavery*, pp. 18–29.

73. Mathews, *Methodism and Slavery*, chaps. 2 and 3.

74. George, *Segregated Sabbaths*, pp. 62–71; Allen, *Life and Gospel Labors*, pp. 20–24; Gravely, "Rise of African Churches," esp. pp. 67–72.

75. On colonization, see Litwack, *North of Slavery*, pp. 20–25. George, *Segregated Sabbaths*, chap. 6; Mark Miles Fisher, "Richard Allen, An Interpretation," *The Crisis* 44 (July 1937): 198–99, 208. George, *Segregated Sabbaths*, p. 139, notes reports that 3,000 gathered at Bethel against colonization. For the broad range of Allen's other antislavery activities in the nineteenth century, see ibid., chaps. 3–5.

76. Richard Allen, "An Address to Those who Keep Slaves and Approve the Practice" and "To the People of Color," *Life and Gospel Labors*, pp. 51–56. The quotations are from pp. 55 and 56.

77. Litwack, *North of Slavery*, pp. 64, 74–80, 84–86.

78. George, *Segregated Sabbaths*, p. 158. On nineteenth-century hardships of the Philadelphia black community, see Curry, *Free Black in Urban America*, pp. 18–20, 49, 150, 163–64, and passim. On the importance of black churches to black community, see ibid., p. 195; Gravely, "Rise of African Churches," pp. 58, 64–65, 72; George, *Segregated Sabbaths*, esp. chap. 5.

PICTURE CREDITS

Most artifacts and some pictures shown here come from and appear through the courtesy of the National Museum of American History, Smithsonian Institution; my gratitude to Smithsonian photographers Brenda Gilmore, Eric Long, Kim Nielsen, Dane Penland, Jeff Ploskonka, and Jeff Tinsley. I am also indebted to the following individuals and institutions:

Preface: p. xvii, "Job, Son of Solliman" from *Gentleman's Magazine* courtesy Library of Congress, Rare Book and Special Collections Division. **xxi,** "Joseph Brant" courtesy Independence National Historical Park Collection, Philadelphia. **1. The War at Home: p. 5,** Overmantel panel from Moses Marcy house, Southbridge, Mass., courtesy Old Sturbridge Village, Sturbridge, Mass. **9,** Map of New England courtesy Princeton University Library, Department of Rare Books and Special Collections. **10,** Map of home lots in Longmeadow from Henry Burt, *The First Century* (1889) courtesy Library of Congress. **12,** Doorways from Amelia F. Miller, *Connecticut River Valley Doorways* (1983), Allen sisters photograph from Pocumtuck Valley Memorial Association, Deerfield, Mass. **14, 19,** Samuel Colton doorway and house, photographs by Paisello Emerson (c. 1903) courtesy Longmeadow Historical Society, Longmeadow, Mass. **21,** "Keep Within Compass" courtesy Henry Francis du Pont Winterthur Museum, Winterthur, Del. **32,** Nathaniel Ames almanac courtesy Warshaw Collection of Business Americana, Smithsonian Institution. **34, 35,** Coins and paper money courtesy L. W. Vosloh. **37, 38, 42,** "A Hint" and "To the Public" from *Boston Gazette* (April 26, 1779; April 21, 1777); "Boston Cannonaded" and "Prospective View of the Town of Boston" courtesy American Antiquarian Society, Worcester, Mass. **2. The Farm and the Marketplace: p. 46,** Ship woodcut courtesy Massachusetts Historical Society, Boston. **47,** Map of New Sweden from Jeannette Eckman, *Crane Hook on the Delaware* (1958) courtesy Delaware Swedish Colonial Society, Wilmington. **48,** "Plan of an American New Cleared Farm" by McIntire (1793) courtesy Houghton Library, Harvard University. **49,** Wheelwright's traveler courtesy Daniel M. Semel. **49,** "The Wheelwright" courtesy Historical Society of Pennsylvania, Philadelphia. **52,** "Wethersfield Girls Weeding Onions" courtesy Wethersfield Historical Society, Wethersfield, Conn. **55,** "View from Bushongo Tavern" courtesy New-York Historical Society, New York City. **56,** Hay knife courtesy Philip Briscoe, Jr. **59,** "Venerate the Plow" courtesy Library of Congress. **61,**

"Straining and Skimming" courtesy Princeton University Library, Department of Rare Books and Special Collections. **63,** "The Weaver" courtesy Historical Society of Pennsylvania, Philadelphia. **66–67,** *The Frugal Housewife* courtesy Dibner Library, Smithsonian Institution. **68,** "Man–Mid-wife" courtesy Wellcome Institute Library, London. **69,** "Treatise on the Management of Pregnant and Lying-In Women" courtesy Library Company of Philadelphia. **70,** Redrawn map, from Shallus Map of Delaware and Maryland, 1799, Ridgeway Library, from Grenville and Dorothy Bathe, *Oliver Evans* (1935) courtesy Historical Society of Pennsylvania, Philadelphia. **73,** "Miss Ann Proctor" courtesy Hammond-Harwood House Association, Annapolis, Md. **79,** Banan and Burke ad courtesy New-York Historical Society, New York City. **80,** "Wilmington and New-Castle Mail" courtesy Landauer Collection, New-York Historical Society, New York City. **82,** Oliver Evans automated mill courtesy Library Company of Philadelphia. **3. The Ambitions of a Tidewater Planter: p. 90,** "Overseer Doing His Duty" courtesy Imperial Tobacco Co. Ltd., Bristol, U.K. Maryland Historical Society, Baltimore. **92, 93,** "Life Is a Smoke!" and "Hiatts Fine Mild" courtesy. **93,** "Surby's Best" courtesy George Arents Collections, New York Public Library, Astor, Lenox, and Tilden Foundations. **94, 95,** Slave ship diagrams courtesy Schomburg Center for Research in Black Culture, New York Public Library, Astor, Lenox, and Tilden Foundations. **96, 97,** "Group of Negros, as imported to be sold for Slaves" from J. G. Stedman, *Narrative of a five-year's expedition against the revolted Negros of Surinam . . . from the year 1772, to 1777* (1796) and "To be Sold . . . a Cargo of Guinea Slaves" courtesy Library of Congress. **105, 106,** Tobacco warehouse and transport from William Tatham, *An Historical and Practical Essay on the Culture and Commerce of Tobacco* (1800), courtesy Library of Congress. **107,** Detail of "A Map of the Most Inhabited Part of Virginia . . ." by Joshua Frye and Peter Jefferson (1775) courtesy Maryland Historical Society, Baltimore. **108,** Tobacco note courtesy Swem Library, College of William and Mary, Williamsburg, Va. **110,** "Peter Manigault and Guests" courtesy Henry Francis du Pont Winterthur Museum, Winterthur, Del. **113,** "Billiards in Hanover Town, Virginia" courtesy Maryland Historical Society, Baltimore. **117,** Pulpit of Christ's Church courtesy Foundation for Historic Christ's Church, Inc., Irvington, Va. **124,** "Mill Creek (Mauck's) Meeting House" photograph by Harold Wickliffe Rose courtesy Beinecke Rare Books and Manuscripts Library, Yale University. **127, 128,** "To Be Sold"

and "Toussaint Louverture" courtesy New-York Historical Society, New York City. **134,** Face masks from "Injured Humanity" courtesy Schomburg Center for Research in Black Culture, New York Public Library, Astor, Lenox, and Tilden Foundations. **135,** "Run-away from the Subscriber" courtesy New-York Historical Society, New York City. **137,** Saunders house photograph by Dell Upton courtesy National Museum of American History. **4. The Limits of Liberty: p. 142,** "Yarrow Mamout" courtesy Historical Society of Pennsylvania, Philadelphia. **143,** "Elizabeth Freeman" courtesy Massachusetts Historical Society, Boston. **144,** Philadelphia tavern scene courtesy Library Company of Philadelphia. **145, 147,** "South East Corner of Third & Market Streets" and "Arch Street Ferry" courtesy Free Library of Philadelphia. **147,** "The Ship-Wright" courtesy Historical Society of Pennsylvania, Philadelphia. **148,** Trade card of Joseph Lownes courtesy American Antiquarian Society, Worcester, Mass. **149,** "The Shoe-maker" courtesy Historical Society of Pennsylvania, Philadelphia. **150,** "Negroes for Sale" courtesy Schomburg Center for Research in Black Culture, New York Public Library, Astor, Lenox, and Tilden Foundations. **151,** "Cliveden" from Marion Harland, *Some Colonial Homesteads and Their Stories* (1897) courtesy Library of Congress. **152,** "The Accident in Lombard-Street" courtesy Henry Francis du Pont Winterthur Museum, Winterthur, Del. **154,** "Thirty Seasoned Negroes" courtesy Schomburg Center for Research in Black Culture, New York Public Library, Astor, Lenox, and Tilden Foundations. **156,** "Bunn, the Blacksmith" courtesy Maryland Historical Society, Baltimore. **158,** "Lemuel Haynes" courtesy Museum of Art, Rhode Island School of Design, Providence. **163,** Engraving of James Armistead Lafayette courtesy Virginia Historical Society, Richmond. **165,** Wedgwood medallion courtesy Dr. Lloyd E. Hawes. **166,** Clergyman woodcut courtesy American Antiquarian Society, Worcester, Mass. **168,** Freedom suit courtesy Mahwenawasigh Chapter, Daughters of the American Revolution. **169,** "Liberty Displaying the Arts and Sciences" courtesy Library Company of Philadelphia. **172,** "Cooper" from *The Encyclopedia of Early American Trades* (1837) courtesy Library of Congress. **172, 173,** "Ladies Dressmaker" and "The Cabinet-maker" courtesy Historical Society of Pennsylvania, Philadelphia. **174,** Portrait of Benjamin Banneker courtesy Maryland Historical Society, Baltimore. **177,** "Gaol in Walnut Street" courtesy Free Library of Philadelphia. **179,** "A View of the House of Employment . . ." photograph by Will Brown courtesy Dietrich American Foundation, Chester Springs, Pa. **184,** Portrait of Richard Allen courtesy Moorland-Springarn Research Center, Howard University, Washington, D.C.

Color Plates

Register of the Samuel Colton family courtesy Longmeadow Historical Society, Longmeadow, Mass.

"Residence and Slave Quarters of Mulberry Plantation" courtesy Carolina Art Association/Gibbes Art Gallery, Charleston, S.C.

"The Old Plantation" courtesy Abby Aldrich Rockefeller Folk Art Center, Williamsburg, Va.

"Market Folks" courtesy Maryland Historical Society, Baltimore.

"Carte de La Partie de La Virginie" courtesy New-York Historical Society, New York City.

African instruments, palm-oil jar, and Akan drum courtesy National Museum of Natural History.

"Old Lutheran Church, in Fifth Street" courtesy Free Library of Philadelphia.

"High Street, from the Country Market-place" courtesy Free Library of Philadelphia.

"Map To the Citizens of Philadelphia" by Peter C. Varle (c. 1796) courtesy Historical Society of Pennsylvania, Philadelphia.

Index

Page numbers in *italics* refer to illustrations.